Sushi Das is an award-winning British-Australian journalist of Indian origin who has worked at *The Age* newspaper for seventeen years. She currently holds the position of opinion editor. Educated and raised in London, she migrated to Australia in 1991 and began her career as a news reporter at Australian Associated Press. Her work has been recognised with two Melbourne Press Club Quill awards, including Best Columnist (2006).

T0150582

DERANGED MARRIAGE

a memoir

SUSHI DAS

BANTAM
SYDNEY AUCKLAND TORONTO NEW YORK LONDON

A Bantam book
Published by Random House Australia Pty Ltd
Level 3, 100 Pacific Highway, North Sydney NSW 2060
www.randomhouse.com.au

First published by Bantam in 2012

Copyright © Sushi Das 2012

The moral right of the author has been asserted.

Text from *Erotic Art of the East* by Philip Rawson © Piers Rawson/Estate of Philip S. Rawson reproduced with permission of Piers Rawson

Lyrics from 'Lookin' After No. 1' by Bob Geldof reproduced with permission of Mushroom Music on behalf of Mute Song

Lyrics from 'Free Bird': words and music by Ronnie Van Zant / Allen Collins © Universal Duchess Music Corp/EMI Longitude Music. All rights reserved. International copyright secured. Reprinted with permission

All rights reserved. No part of this book may be reproduced or transmitted by any person or entity, including internet search engines or retailers, in any form or by any means, electronic or mechanical, including photocopying (except under the statutory exceptions provisions of the *Australian Copyright Act 1968*), recording, scanning or by any information storage and retrieval system without the prior written permission of Random House Australia.

Addresses for companies within the Random House Group can be found at
www.randomhouse.com.au/offices

National Library of Australia
Cataloguing-in-Publication entry

Das, Sushi
Deranged marriage / Sushi Das

ISBN 9781742751566 (pbk)

Das, Sushi
Women, Anglo-Indian–Biography
Arranged marriage

305.48891411092

Cover art and design © Design by Committee
Internal typesetting and design by Midland Typesetters, Australia
Printed in Australia by Griffin Press, an accredited ISO AS/NZS 14001:2004
Environmental Management System printer

Random House Australia uses papers that are natural, renewable and recyclable products and made from wood grown in sustainable forests. The logging and manufacturing processes are expected to conform to the environmental regulations of the country of origin.

Contents

Author's Note

Some names and a few other details have been changed to protect people's privacy. The sources for this book include my diaries, interviews with family members, audio tapes, letters and, of course, fallible memory.

For Lotus

Prologue

'Do you know what your father's nickname was when he was a schoolboy?' asked Mum in Punjabi – the language she always used when maximum impact was required. 'They called him the Saint,' she said, putting down her knitting and leaning forward. 'And do you know why they called him the Saint? Mmm? Well, if you stop chewing that revolting bubblegum and sit down, I'll tell you.'

I did as I was told. 'Your father was about eight or nine years old when a boy in his class did something bad. Stole a few coins from another boy – something like that. The whole class knew who the rascal was. Anyway, when the teacher discovered there was a thief among his pupils, he was determined to catch him and punish him. He gathered the boys around and asked, "Who stole the money?" But nobody owned up. He asked again, but still nobody owned up. So then the teacher said, "I am going to ask you one more time. If the culprit admits his crime, he will be punished – as he knows he deserves to be. If he does not, I will punish the entire class. And it will be a caning the likes of which you have never seen before. You will remember it for the rest of your lives. And trust me, the punishment I give you will be nothing compared to the beating the culprit will get from his own classmates after my back is turned." '

Mum paused and resumed her knitting. She always knew when to pause.

'What happened?' I asked, chewing my gum with ferocious urgency.

'Well, the boys were trembling with fear, hoping the rascal would own up. But he didn't. So your father stepped forward and owned up to a crime he didn't do.' I stopped chewing suddenly, eyes fixed on Mum. 'He made a sacrifice for others,' she continued. '*That* is the kind of man your father is. He took the punishment to save the rest of the class, and from that day on they called him the Saint. Your father is a good man, a very good man.'

I sat still for a moment, thinking through the ramifications and implications of such gallantry. It didn't occur to me to ask how she came to know this story.

'So did he get caned?' I asked.

'No. The teacher made him do the chicken for an hour instead.'

Seeing the bewildered look on my face, she explained the punishment. 'The chicken was a punishment they used to give in Indian schools. You bring your arms around from behind, put them through your legs, squat down and hold your ear lobes. Not easy. They do it to humiliate you.'

I immediately stood up and assumed the pose that Mum had described, but the burning strain on my thigh and shoulder muscles was unbearable, not to mention the difficulty of keeping balance. I keeled over after just five seconds and lay sprawled on the floor, laughing and groaning.

'You may laugh, young girl,' said Mum, 'but remember, your father made a sacrifice, like so many sacrifices he makes for this family. He was just a boy and he held that pose for one hour in the blazing heat because, inside him, there is strength. Inside him, there is wisdom. He is a decent man, a man of good character, and I am very lucky that my parents found me such a fine man to marry.

'Now, go and spit out that disgusting bubblegum. All day long you're chomping and grinding that stuff – you look like a goat. You're twelve years old – it's about time you started behaving like a young lady. One day your father and I will have to find you a good man to marry. And, trust me, no man is going to accept a girl who chews gum like a goat.'

CHAPTER 1

Escape Plan

***'At sixteen, you still think you can escape your father. You aren't listening to his voice speaking through your mouth, you don't see how your gestures already mirror his; you don't see him in the way you hold your body, in the way you sign your name. You don't hear his whisper in your blood.' Salman Rushdie,* East, West**

I burgled my parents' house when I was fourteen. It was an inside job, by which I mean I didn't need to break in. It was wickedly late when I tiptoed out of my bedroom and down the stairs, holding my breath as I took each step, careful not to wake the household. Moonlight shone through the big arched window in the hall, lighting up the carpeted stairs that, obligingly, silenced my footfalls. I know there was a big round moon in the sky because earlier that evening Mum had performed her special husband-worship ceremony – the one she did every autumn on the night of a full moon.

I crept into the dining room with Pink Panther stealth, closed the door behind me and switched on a lamp. A handwritten cardboard sign on the dining table shouted: NO ENGLISH PLEASE! – a valiant but largely unsuccessful attempt by my dad to keep his three children in touch with *his* mother-tongue, Punjabi.

I knelt down and quietly opened the wooden cabinet where he kept his important things, and there they were – rows of neatly ordered photo albums. Photography was his hobby, and when he wasn't taking close-up shots of flower stamens in parks and gardens, he was taking photos of us kids. I took out the oldest album, the one with the black and green paisley cover and a soft, silky tassel on the spine, and opened it, carefully turning over the gossamer-thin lining paper between each page to reveal the black and white photos he had carefully mounted.

My pulse quickened. I knew which ones I was looking for: me as a baby sitting with my mum on the grass in a park; my handsome young dad lying on his back holding me aloft; me and my sister, aged five and three, standing with open umbrellas in the garden; me and my sister, slightly older, grinning proudly, sitting next to our baby brother. I removed the photos, dropped them into the breast pocket of my pyjamas, and crept back up the stairs to the darkness of my bedroom. Back in my still slightly warm bed I slid the photos under my pillow, the place where I usually kept a tight, anxious fist when I slept.

I could hear the soft, regular in-and-out breaths of my sister, Vin, asleep in the other bed. I took a few deep breaths to slow my heartbeat to the rhythm of her breathing. I liked sharing a bedroom with her. We grew up in each other's pockets: sneaking sugar sandwiches to bed, nattering endlessly into the night, sniggering behind our hands and harrumphing at the grown-ups.

She had a round, babyish face, slightly gappy teeth and two black, pliable plaits that made for excellent reins when she was the horse and I the cowgirl. She had this way of rolling her eyes that gave her an air of relaxed confidence, as if tomorrow didn't matter. I always called her Vin. Mum and Dad used her full name, Vanita. Though she was younger than me by a couple of years, she behaved as if she was older. Where my emotions were fierce, hers were restrained; where my tone of voice was shrill, hers was sage. Generally speaking, I felt I could influence her – that I simply had to say, 'I was born before you, so I know more than you,' and she would acquiesce. But sometimes I could tell by the way she pressed her lips together and drew in a long, slow breath that privately she didn't put much store in whatever it was I had said. Still, I could work out who I was because she was my yardstick. I grew up thinking of us, essentially, as one person. My opinion was her opinion. Her life was my life. My secrets were her secrets. Except one.

I never told her about the little suitcase. A dark brown case, just 40 by 10 inches, with two silvery clasps that snapped shut with a satisfactory click. It had been my dad's at some stage. I don't remember how it came to belong to me. Inside the lid I had painted in red letters the word SIOUX, because when you're a fourteen-year-old kid and you plan to run away from home, it's always a good idea to change your name to something daft.

I detested Sushila, my full name, because mumbled or spoken fast it sounded like Sheila, an even worse name. At school, half the teachers called me Sushilla (so that it rhymed with killer), presumably because they didn't know how to pronounce a 'foreign' name. It's a terrible name to say if you have a lisp: Thootheela. Even worse when you're drunk: Shoosheela. Loosely translated, it means 'good conduct' or 'good character', but at home everyone called me Neelum (blue sapphire). According to the story my mum tells, my maternal grandfather named me Sushila, even though my dad preferred Neelum. So Sushila became my official name and Neelum my unofficial 'home' name. At least *officially* I was a person of good character.

I considered changing my name to Sue, but that was obviously a Western name, and with my black hair and brown face, I looked nothing like a Westerner. I had been reading about Sioux Indians. Perfect. It still sounded like Sue, but I would spell it Sioux, and if anyone asked, I would just say I had a bit of Red Indian in me. I could be an Indian, just a different kind of Indian – the type that didn't have to have an arranged marriage.

The next day, I waited till Vin was out of the bedroom before I got down on my hands and knees and reached under my bed for the little brown suitcase. I'd been packing it for months. So far I had a toothbrush, a few spare clothes, a pen, sanitary pads and a ten pound note. Not much, but it was a start. I took the stolen photos from under my pillow and looked at them. Quickly, I slid them between the folds of a T-shirt in the case, clicked it shut and pushed it as far under my bed as I could.

From under a pile of books on my desk I pulled out my diary to make my daily entry, without mentioning the theft. The year was 1979. I was a fastidious chronicler of daily events, recording in minute and irrelevant detail the dull happenings of each day: *'Had to help Dad paint the skirting boards today. White gloss. Mum made aloo gobi for dinner again. YUK! God, my life is humdrum, can't wait to get back to school again, then I won't have to help Dad decorate the house. Stripping wallpaper from the back room tomorrow (using soapy water and scraper, not blow torch – that's only for painted wood).'*

I started keeping a diary in 1977 at the age of twelve and stuck with it for probably far too many years. Dad had mixed feelings. 'Never write anything in your diary that you wouldn't like to have read out in a court of law,' he warned. I have no idea what he thought I was writing, but clearly he had no faith in my judgment. I think he worried I would write something that might inadvertently bring shame upon the family. That's why I never wrote anything about running away. Sometimes I wrote in code. It was not unusual for Vin to see me furiously scribbling hieroglyphics late into the night as I recorded the latest development in my parents' single-minded goal to find me a suitable boy to marry.

I knew through gradual family osmosis that my parents expected me to have an arranged marriage. It didn't matter that they had migrated to Britain in the 1960s, or that I, as well as Vin and our brother Raja, had received an entirely Eurocentric education. Indeed, Western culture was the wallpaper for us, and not the type you can simply strip away, although my parents did try. As far as they were concerned, we were Indian and arranged marriages were the Indian way, regardless of where in the world we lived. Diaspora duty.

As long as an arranged marriage was either being planned or taking place, the world was as it should be. My parents had it all sorted: I would finish my school studies; a respectable Indian boy, educated to a level slightly above me, would be found, probably from Britain, but possibly from India; and I would marry in my early twenties. Their ideal suitable boy, like the ideal suitable boy sought by millions of Indian parents in Britain, America, Australia and anywhere else Indians lived, was, of course, a medical doctor.

There would be a splendid Indian wedding, probably in the local community hall, after which I would re-enact a scene from a

Bollywood movie – I would tearfully wave goodbye to my parents in my red wedding sari, laden with twenty-four-carat gold jewellery, and head for my husband's house, where I would live for the rest of my life, bearing healthy sons and dutifully looking after my husband and his ageing parents.

There was only one slight hitch: nobody asked me if this was what I wanted. I was simply expected to do as I was told. My destiny lay in my parents' hands and, naturally, that made me skittish. I bit my nails, sat on the edges of chairs, spoke fast, leapt up steps two at a time. I was perturbed not only by the robbery of my right to choose, but by the fact that I didn't share my parents' vision. How could I let someone else decide my future? An arranged marriage! The very idea was unhinged. What would it be like to have sex with a stranger? What if we didn't get along?

I wouldn't be forced into a marriage, they insisted. If I didn't feel comfortable, I was free to say no. I wondered how many times I could say no. I could say no to the first boy they introduced me to, maybe even the second one. But beyond that I had to start providing reasons. Could I say no forever? And if I did, would there be adverse consequences?

I had many other unanswered questions, mostly prompted by news reports about girls from Indian and Pakistani backgrounds – the daughters of first-generation migrants – running away from home to avoid an arranged marriage. There were stories of girls being locked up by their parents, even beaten if their behaviour harmed or threatened family honour. Sometimes they were taken to India or Pakistan to marry or to be de-Westernised.

Then there were the heart-stopping stories of honour killings – fathers, uncles, and brothers who killed, or played some part in murdering, daughters, nieces and sisters who brought shame on the family. I'm not talking about honour killings in India. I'm talking about honour killings in Britain in the 1980s. Indeed, they are still happening today.

I never feared that anything like that might happen to me. My parents were as horrified by honour killings as any right-thinking person would be. But I was never sure how far they would go to persuade me to follow Indian tradition. I feared my fate. What if I turned my back on the arranged-marriage system? What repercussions would I suffer? What repercussions might my parents suffer at the hands of the Indian community?

Brutal treatment of Indian and Pakistani girls who stepped out of line was the backdrop to my youth. It was a terrifying reality that seeped into our house through rumours in the Indian community and through the mainstream news. And there was no escaping those headlines because ours was a household bombarded by newspapers, radio news broadcasts and TV news bulletins.

The ease with which I was able to produce half-baked plans and harebrained schemes to get out of my bind were alarming, even to me. If running away didn't work out, perhaps I could, somehow, become famous. Nothing like the glare of the public spotlight to inoculate a person from parental pressure. Or maybe I could quietly but definitively repulse potential husbands so that they always rejected me, until Mum and Dad, in exasperation, would finally allow me to pick my own husband.

Unfortunately, such schemes lacked even a grain of realism, and I knew it. In search of a way out, I prowled the undergrowth of fantasy before turning to the wide-open plains of reality, where it was evident that a career might fulfill the dual function of income generation (and therefore financial independence) and an escape route. But which career?

Dad was a news junkie who didn't know when to stop. The BBC World Service was his friend. The Lilliburlero theme music, now seared onto an ancient part of my brain, never seemed to be more than fifty-nine minutes away. Then there was the day's newspaper, stuffed into the letterbox or brought home in Dad's briefcase at the end of the day. He was a man who took *The Times*, but later moved to the *Guardian*. Occasionally he'd buy other newspapers, but never the tabloids. He would clip articles he deemed important or particularly enlightening and file them in one of his many collections of cuttings.

Sometimes he clipped articles that he thought *I* ought to read for my intellectual nourishment. He would leave them on the dining table or by the phone, or any place he thought my eye might inadvertently fall upon them. There was no avoiding those headlines: '*Shocking Truth about Youth*'; '*Lazy Lifestyle of Teenage Girls Exposed*'; '*Teachers Warn against Late Nights*'; '*Broccoli: the New Super Food*'.

If Vin or I ever picked up the newspaper, it would be to check the TV listings on the back page. 'Why don't you read the front page?' Dad often said. 'That's the page most people read first. You might learn something.' He wanted us to be intelligent girls, not dithering ninnies, which he feared we might become without his constant guidance.

Every evening he watched the BBC News at nine o'clock. Chattering, giggling and smirking were prohibited during the broadcast. Anyone who wanted to talk or laugh was sent out of the room. Even Mum was ordered out once. Things got unbearable if the newscaster ever mentioned the 'bloody war in Northern Ireland', which he did virtually every night. Without fail, the word 'bloody' would induce uncontrollable laughter from me and Vin, and we would be marched out of the room immediately. Dad was never more angry than when his nightly news was ruined by our frivolous twittering.

The BBC's foreign correspondents Kate Adie and John Simpson seemed to be on the news every night. I would dream of wearing a khaki flak jacket, standing in front of a tank delivering news reports from strife-torn regions with an urgent, authoritative yet compassionate tone of voice. Reporters with scruffy hair wearing a safari suit or hunter's jacket with epaulettes excited me. I thought the BBC must have an endless supply of those jackets, and I wanted one.

It was the romance of journalism that attracted me. After all, I was unaware of what the job actually entailed – a bit like girls who wanted to become glamorous air hostesses, unaware that the job actually meant being a dehydrated servant in the sky to irritable travellers. In truth, I didn't read the front page of newspapers – not because I was uninterested in the news, but because the world was complicated and I didn't always understand the news. Nonetheless, I wanted to be part of the adventure of gathering it. I was in love with the idea of being a journalist, not in love with the news itself.

Dad took journalists seriously but it was not a role he wanted for his own daughters. 'It's a man's job. Look at him,' he said pointing to John Simpson on the TV. 'He used to be a young man. How quickly he has aged. It is a hard job, unsuited to women. You will never be settled in one place, it will be difficult to have a family life, and I don't think they get much money.'

I suppose I will never know whether my desire to be a journalist was a result of my early exposure to newspaper clippings, or whether a growing feeling of being an outsider to my parents' culture drew me to a vocation built on scepticism and inquiry. I was inflamed by injustice, and there was so much injustice that people didn't know about. Indian girls in Britain couldn't even choose who they could marry. Did anyone out there know about that? There was a veneer of choice, but when you lifted the veil, there was, I thought, repression underneath. By the time my teenage confusion ripened into indignation, I was sure I wanted to be a journalist because I felt an urgent desire to tell people things they didn't know.

But Dad had other plans. I wouldn't be allowed to choose my own husband and I shouldn't pursue the career I wanted. What injustice. I felt a profound uneasiness, a creeping anxiety that all my problems stemmed from being a brown girl in a white world.

Everywhere there were currents pushing me this way and that and I was muddled. I heard the untroubled laughter of my friends, their free and easy manner; I saw people kiss with open lips on TV; I heard the Sex Pistols tell the Queen she ain't no human being; and I watched Kate Adie make it in a man's world. I was lifted by 'Jerusalem' at the end of term, the way my teachers sang full-throated; I saw the gleam on my prefect's badge, the placards on the streets, and the world at Heathrow. I wanted to tell people everything was not okay. I wanted everyone to be as indignant as I was and for women to have everything men did. I wanted to speak freely, to question the world, to mock the prevailing orthodoxy. I hankered for it all.

Nearly four years later my suitcase was still under the bed. When I packed it, and for a long time afterwards, I believed I might one day get the hell out. But when the time came it was always raining, or there was homework to be handed in. Once, I had everything sorted: coat on, money for the bus, suitcase out from under the bed. Heart galloping, I was about to go down the stairs when Mum and Dad came back early from Tesco after doing the week's shopping. I heard the key in the lock and had to rush into the bedroom and put the suitcase back in its hiding place. Vin wanted to know why I had my coat on, but I told her to mind her own business.

I never told her about my plan for two reasons. First, she would almost certainly have thought it an irrational idea and tried to dissuade me; and second, her knowledge of it would have made her an unwitting accomplice. Mum and Dad would have questioned her after I was found missing. She would be scolded for failing to stop me, or for not telling them of my plan, and I couldn't let that happen.

I was eighteen years old now, well past the age my departure would be classified as running away. At eighteen I could legally walk out of the house and never return. But in fact I couldn't leave, not only because there was nowhere to go, but because I lacked the courage. Besides, an unmarried Indian girl leaving her parents' house without permission would have brought great shame on my family. Still, I kept that suitcase packed, hidden and at the ready because it was possible that one day I might do *something* that would force Mum and Dad to disown me – and if they threw me out of the house, at least I'd have my things ready. I just didn't know what that *something* might be.

I was living in a state of low-level panic by now. Mum and Dad had stepped up their search for a suitable boy. They were making phone calls and asking friends and family if they knew any boys of marriageable age. The hunt for marriage material was on and I had no say in the matter.

Girls. They are an economic liability for Indian parents. They cost money to raise. They can trash a family's reputation with the power of immodesty. They need a dowry when you marry them off, and what do you get in return? Nothing but worry and misery. Boys, on the other hand, are productive economic units. As men, they earn a salary, bring home a wife, scoop up a dowry and act as the welfare state for elderly parents. Who wouldn't crave sons?

Luckily, we had a son in our family. My brother's birth brought not only joy, but relief. Mum had carried and brought safely into the world that most precious of cargos. She was no longer just a mother of daughters, she was the mother of a son. The only thing better would have been to be the mother of several sons, but Mum was grateful for just one.

Vin and I were pleased to have someone else to play with. We remained, in our youth, totally ignorant of the meaning of a brother. In manhood, he would be the carer of his parents and the protector of his sisters – a notion that satisfied my parents profoundly. Mum in particular felt she had been rewarded by a higher authority and she was able to extend her deepest sympathy to any woman god neglected.

Mum had a friend – an Indian woman with seven daughters. Yes, seven. People were always kind to her. An epic tragedy had befallen her house. A misfortune for every day of the week. What was the poor woman to do? You couldn't accuse her of not trying to have a son. Look where that had got her. But the woman was remarkably sanguine. Always smiling and confident that things would turn out well in the end. The kind of person who would start a crossword puzzle with a pen. Her beautiful girls graced our house when they visited. Seven sylphs with intelligent, mouse eyes, swan necks and confident smiles. All seven together could turn a room into an oil painting.

But it's hard for Indians to see seven girls and not also see the shadows of seven dowries, seven opportunities for the family's honour to be sullied, seven burdens.

When Mum's friend fell pregnant for the eighth time, everyone prayed for her, including my mum. A son, please bestow her with a son. When she gave birth to twin boys, it was as if the heavens had opened up, sending forth great rivers of rain after seven hundred years of drought. There were tears of joy, elated hearts and sweet, sweet relief. Not one, but two boys. Sons at last, sons at last, thank god almighty, we have sons at last.

Life for Indian boys is different. Right from the day of their birth, which, by the way, is celebrated with a great deal more gusto than a girl's, things are easier. Parents are much more reverential towards their sons – after all, they are the ones who look after them in their old age (or, more accurately, it is daughters-in-law who will look after a boy's parents in their old age).

More importantly, boys' sexuality is nothing to fear (unless they're gay – that would no doubt be considered a calamity). They can't fall pregnant out of wedlock and bring shame on their families as a daughter can. Yes, they can bring shame through acts of criminality or gambling or drinking, but shame through sexual immorality, the really serious kind of shame, is a disgrace that only women can bring crashing down on their family. All things considered, boys are best.

But sometimes even my brother Raja was no consolation for my mum's deep frustrations with my failings. 'You're too tall,' she often complained, as if I was deliberately growing beyond the stipulated height for an obedient Indian girl. 'We have to find a boy taller than you.'

Her concern with my height was dwarfed by her alarm over the size of my bust, the correct size presumably being a pair of plump mangoes. I didn't make the grade. When a marriage is being arranged by an Indian mother, a defective daughter can be a big problem, or, in this case, two small problems. A girl with no breasts. Two aspirins on an ironing board. Damaged goods.

I was ordered to visit the doctor to find out what was wrong with me. Dr Hall, who was shorter than the average man, told me I was not alone – lots of girls wished they had bigger boobs. 'I wish I was a couple of inches taller,' he added pointlessly. When I told him I was quite comfortable with my lighter than average load and that it was Mum who felt burdened with my deficiency, he kindly offered to talk to her.

That evening he called her. I listened from the top of the stairs. 'Yes, doctor, yes, doctor. Yes, thank you, doctor,' I heard her say before she hung up and made her way slowly up the stairs.

'That was the Dr Hall calling on the phone,' she said in her wonky English, sitting heavily on my bed with a disappointed sigh.

I waited for the verdict.

'He was drunk.'

'What!'

'Yes,' she replied. 'He say you are healthy, attractive girl. He say nothing wrong with you. Definitely drunk.'

Some months after the drunk-doctor incident, she was sitting on the edge of my bed again, crying: 'It's my fault, it's all my fault,' she sobbed, nodding in the direction of my chest. 'In India, when I discovered I was pregnant with you, I went to see a special doctor,' she continued in Punjabi. 'I asked him to make you a boy. So he gave me some herbs.'

'What! You went to see a witch doctor?'

'I took the herbs,' she continued. 'But when you were born, you were a girl and I just assumed the herbs hadn't worked. But now that you're older and things haven't grown properly, I see that the herbs only *half* worked.'

She burst into a fresh round of sobbing. I was at a loss to know how to console her, a task made harder by the anger ballooning in my flat chest. Not anger with her naïve and superstitious belief that when she was pregnant, the child she was carrying could be turned into a boy with a magical potion. Not anger with her instinctive maternal drive to blame herself for something she should have known was clearly beyond her control. But anger with myself for having the misfortune to be born into an Indian family coming to grips with raising daughters in Britain. In such moments, I could see before me a chasm of communication between me and my parents. Their Eastern expectations. My Western desires. Any thoughts beyond that were rendered shapeless by immaturity and simply fell off the cliff into a sea of self-loathing.

CHAPTER 2

A Passage to England

'Sing the Lover's Litany;
"Love like ours can never die!"' Rudyard Kipling

Dad migrated to London from New Delhi in February 1964 at the age of twenty-six. He was carrying a Zeiss Ikon camera and little more than bare essentials when he arrived, but his suitcase was heavy with hundreds, if not thousands of years of cultural baggage. He had no family in Britain to greet him, but several friends, who had migrated earlier, were at the airport to pick him up. It was going to be the adventure of a lifetime.

They found him a rented room in Twickenham, in south-west London, which he shared with two other young Indian men. Within a week he had a job at a local bakery. Just as well, because when he stepped off the plane at Heathrow he had only £3 in his pocket.

Two years earlier, in 1962, Prime Minister Harold Macmillan's government had introduced employment vouchers for skilled and unskilled Commonwealth citizens to come to Britain and work in areas where there was a shortfall of local workers. Britain, which more than a hundred years before had looked to Ireland to plug acute labour shortages caused by industrial expansion, now turned to recruiting from the Commonwealth to fill skills gaps created by the post-war boom.

Dad had left his home state of Punjab in northern India and had been working as an auditor for a government department in New Delhi for five years when he applied for an employment voucher. His university degrees, youth and fluent English ensured his passage to Britain was mere paperwork. 'At that time there was a sort of craze among people to go abroad and make a life,' he says. 'There was an attraction for better living.'

He wasn't a refugee escaping from brutality; he was looking for excitement and a chance to improve his life. And where better to find such things than in London in the swinging sixties? However, I doubt he was expecting to find a city in the throes of a historic cultural revolution that even the British found confronting. Sex, drugs and rock 'n' roll pervaded the cultural landscape. Just days before Dad arrived in London, The Beatles had landed in New York to an absurdly tumultuous reception at JFK Airport from a throng of manic, screeching fans. The newspapers reported Beatlemania had spread to the land of the free.

It was all happening at a cracking pace. Doc Martens were on sale for the first time, women could buy the Pill, the Great Train robbers were in the dock and the Queen was about to give birth to her fourth child. The steel, coal and motor car industries were booming. The whole country was richer. The average weekly wage was £16. Macmillan's oft-quoted words must have been ringing in the ears of people up and down the land: 'Let us be frank about it – most of our people have never had it so good,' he had told a Tory rally just six years earlier. 'Go around the country, go to the industrial towns, go to the farms and you will see a state of prosperity such as we have never had in my lifetime – nor indeed in the history of this country.' In this environment the need for labour from the Commonwealth was essential for future growth. Britain needed men like my dad.

Just as well he arrived when he did. There was mounting unease over the influx of 'coloured' people, so the following year Harold Wilson's Labour government modified the Immigration Act, getting rid of vouchers for unskilled workers and dramatically cutting the number for skilled workers. But that wasn't the most dramatic feature of 1965. A far more startling development was about to take place, one that would shock not only new arrivals such as my dad, but the whole of British society: the launch of the miniskirt.

Suddenly, pointy-boobed girls in short skirts and tall boots were everywhere, along with long-haired men and newspaper reports about marijuana use and free love. Hedonism for all, sex aplenty. And there was Dad with his side-parting and Errol Flynn moustache fresh off the plane from a third-world country where grinding poverty carpeted the land, female modesty held up the sky and family duty marked the boundary between economic success and moral decline.

In Punjab it would have been highly immodest for a woman to wear anything that exposed expanses of flesh or brazenly showed off the contours of her body. The traditional Punjabi dress is the *salwar kamiz* – the *salwar* being a loose-fitting pant that gathers into a cuff at the ankle, and the *kamiz* a tunic, generally knee-length but sometimes shorter. The ensemble also includes a shawl or long scarf known as a *dupatta*, a versatile symbol of modesty and an integral part of Indian women's clothing. It can be used to cover the head to show respect and piety, slung over both shoulders and tied in a knot at the back to keep it out of the way when performing domestic duties, or worn across both shoulders but pulled down to cover the breasts when modesty is required.

I recall Mum talking to her father-in-law 'through' her *dupatta*. She was covering her head to show respect. But she also pulled it forward on one side of her face, and held it there while she spoke to him, using it as a veil of modesty – extreme respect, when head-covering is not enough. I never once saw my maternal or paternal grandmothers with their heads uncovered.

For Britain's growing Indian community in the 1960s, immodestly dressed white girls were bemusing, but they also represented a somewhat distasteful aspect of Western society. Wild and wanton women equalled wicked Western ways. Dad never passed judgment on the way British women dressed – his was a 'live and let live' Hindu attitude. But he was acutely aware of the views of others in the Indian community, particularly those who, unlike him, had migrated from rural areas. As a collective force their point of view mattered to him because, in the bigger picture, he was *of* the Indian community. He was not *of* the English community, no matter how much he admired their courteous niceties, their efficient bureaucracy and their exemplary educational institutions.

As a father, Dad was very strict. Vin and I had an exceptionally disciplined upbringing: we were instructed to speak respectfully to elders, discouraged from pursuing careers that involved music or dance and ordered to dress modestly in Indian clothes at home, particularly at the dining table. Tight jeans, leggings and short skirts were unacceptable. Whistling was frowned upon, as was wearing our hair down. While Dad may not have minded how British women conducted themselves, he certainly did not want his own daughters dressing like them and he was prepared to take whatever action he thought necessary to protect them from such influences.

Sons, on the other hand, were a different matter. Indian boys were encouraged to be brave, even experimental – within boundaries, of course – as these are the qualities that could be the harbingers of wealth and fortune. My brother was by no means mollycoddled, but the restrictions imposed on him were looser. There were expectations that he should do well at school, pursue a career and look out for his sisters, but he was never reprimanded for whistling, or ordered to wear traditional dress, or discouraged from having English friends, including girls.

But when Dad was working in the bakery, before Raja, Vin and I were even born, how he might raise his children in Britain was the last thing on his mind. He was busy sorting loaves of bread and packing currant buns from daybreak to nightfall. With his Bachelor of Commerce and Master's degrees in Business Studies, he was absurdly over-qualified to be a bakery boy, but it paid the rent and it taught him, strangely, a thing or two about lack of want.

One evening as he was packing up to leave at the end of his shift, he saw two young men, fellow workers, playfully kicking a bread roll around in the flour on the bakery floor. '*Arré!* What is this?' he thought. 'Kicking the staff of life?' In India, malnourishment for millions of people was, and still is, a daily peril.

But in Britain, where people had never had it so good, bread was a football. It was a deeply shocking sight, and one that Dad recalled, unprompted, nearly fifty years later, sitting in his house in London one afternoon idly reminiscing about his youth.

But ask him specifically about his first impressions of England and he won't mention miniskirts or bread rolls. 'The British were disciplined and well dressed. They had good manners and I was impressed,' he says. 'I never regretted coming. I had moments when I felt I had left my family back at home and I had no people to talk to. But because I was working full-time and overtime, I didn't have time to reflect. I didn't have time to plan. The first priority was to build a financial base. Everyone was working wholeheartedly, and also we had to send money back home. But I wasn't disappointed at all.'

I always think of Dad's admiration for the British as a reflection of Jawaharlal Nehru's pro-British attitude before he abandoned Western attire and turned to wearing the Indian *sherwani* and leading his country to independence from British rule. Dad was ten years old when India gained independence and Nehru became the first prime minister. Indeed, Nehru was still the prime minister when Dad left for England.

Just three months after Dad's arrival, on 28 May 1964, he bought a copy of *The Times*, as he did daily, to discover that the only Indian prime minister he had ever known, and the man who had shaped his thinking about the importance of education, had suffered a heart attack and died. He was deeply affected and kept that copy of *The Times* for years, not only because he is a compulsive archivist but because it was a modest memento of an era of his own life that had passed.

The future was all about Britain now and the next thing on

Dad's to-do list was to bring to England the beautiful, bashful eighteen-year-old girl he had left behind in India. They had been brought together in an arranged marriage just two and a half months before he migrated – enough time for his new wife to knit him a woolly jumper – the one he was wearing when the winter air greeted him at Heathrow.

Mum was fifteen years old when the sound of a rickshaw pulling up outside the house woke her one Sunday morning. She was staying at her aunt's house in Hissar, Haryana, about 160 kilometres north-west of Delhi. There was much fluster over the visitors as her aunt ran about making tea, shouting orders and finding a colourful outfit for Mum to wear. Nobody had said anything about visitors coming to the house that day, certainly not about a handsome young man with a thick head of glossy raven-black hair and a moustache so thin it could have been drawn on his upper lip with a fine-tipped pen. She was given a yellow *salwar kameez* and a black *dupatta*. 'A suitable boy has been found,' said her aunt, smiling, 'and he's here to see you.'

Struck by something akin to stage fright, Mum lost her tongue. My dad, twenty-two at the time, had arrived with some relatives. He asked for a glass of water, providing an opportunity for Mum to enter the room to serve him, but she turned away shyly when he tried to look at her face. Had he had the chance to see her face properly, he might have noticed the mole on her chin, her unique mark. Later, he came into the kitchen and commented favourably on the *dal* that she was stirring on the stove but she stayed silent.

He can't have drawn an accurate picture of who she was, or any picture at all. It would surely have taken a considerable period of time before he discovered that she was in fact a jolly, sometimes childlike and very superstitious young lady. And perhaps even longer to discover that she was bolder than him, more outspoken and less daunted by life.

It rained heavily that evening and the visitors were invited to stay the night. The next day, Dad again attempted to speak to Mum, asking her for a towel. Without a word, and with her head covered, Mum dutifully fetched one and handed it to the handsome boy, who had by now completely stolen her heart, even though she had not spoken a word to him. Dad, too, was interested.

'So, do you like her?' asked the matchmaking aunt.

'Yes, I like her,' he replied.

Mum's aunt, pink-cheeked with excitement, set about putting in train preparations for the forthcoming *Roka* ceremony. Hindu arranged-marriage traditions are elaborate and ritualistic. They begin long before the wedding day. The *Roka* is the first pre-wedding ceremony and marks the beginning of a formal relationship between both families. *Roka* comes from the word halt or arrest. The ceremony signifies that the couple is formally engaged and so stops either party seeking a match elsewhere. Dad was arrested with confectionery and a symbolic single rupee. His side of the family sent my mum five kilos of cardamons, dates, bangles and bindis.

That was the only time my parents set eyes on each other until their wedding day – four years later. In that time they courted by writing love letters. My parents have been married nearly half a century and Dad still has the letters Mum sent him. When I recently asked Mum to reflect on the day that Dad first came to see her, she said in her crooked English, 'He was good-looking. I was excited. I didn't look him in his eyes. He try to talk to me but I am shy. We don't refuse whatever our parents chooses for us. He was educated, he was working, he had civil service job in Delhi.'

On their wedding day Mum was eighteen years old and Dad was twenty-five. He arrived wearing white and in a horse-drawn carriage. 'He look like Elvis Presley,' said Mum, giggling. 'He had a lot of big hair on his head.'

Arranged marriages have been a part of Indian culture for centuries. Practices vary from region to region, but essentially parents choose who their son or daughter will marry. Such marriages hold an enduring fascination for Westerners, whose romantic trajectory starts with meeting someone, dating and falling in love. This continues until one of three things happens: separation, cohabitation or marriage. When this type of courtship leads to marriage, Indians call it a 'love marriage' – a strange description perhaps, since it implies that all other types of marriage do not involve love.

When Mum said, 'We don't refuse whatever our parents chooses for us,' she was conveying several tenets of the arranged marriage system. First, that choosing a life partner is a huge undertaking and parents are better equipped to do this as they have more life experience and therefore wisdom. Second, accepting someone your parents have picked shows respect that ultimately maintains order in a community. And third, that the coming together of two individuals is important but not necessarily the sole aim of marriage. The future economic stability, prosperity and longevity of both families are the real aims.

So, an arranged marriage is not a contract between two individuals, it is an economic joining of two families into one big community. Not a negotiated individual transaction, more a company merger.

This doesn't mean there is no tradition of love in Indian society. Indeed love as an ideal is everywhere you look. Whether it's in Urdu poetry, Bollywood movies, Punjabi folk songs, or stories from Indian mythology, love plays a central role. Indian women from my mum's generation dreamt of romantic love and hoped to find it within the walls of their arranged marriages, but the undeniable reality is that married life for many represented the end of their carefree girlhood and the start of life as a child-bearer and husband-server. Romantic love did not always get a look-in.

Such expectations of women have faded or are fading fast among urbane, educated Indians and among diaspora Indians too. But to know where these ideas originated we only have to look at how the perfect woman, whether as a wife or a lover, is described in the Sanskrit epics of ancient India, the *Mahabharata* and *Ramayana*. Through the centuries these epics set the ideal patterns of behaviour and presented women as the indispensable half of man. A passage from *Erotic Art of the East*, by art expert Philip Rawson, describes the ideal wife as depicted in Indian art and poetry:

> 'Her whole aim in life should be to efface herself completely, and minister with total dedication to her husband. She should look upon him as a god, treating his lightest whims as divine commands; she must eat only what he leaves uneaten and bear him as many sons as possible. She must observe total obedience to her mother-in-law, fear her father-in-law; she must never speak to her husband unless he first addresses her. She must never speak to another man, never stand in the door

> gossiping, always walk a few paces behind her husband, and sit on a lower seat than him. She must not complain at, but rather glory in his amorous adventures. She may never display any public tokens of affection towards him or her children, nor may he to them or to her . . . When her husband dies the widow should if possible follow him to the next world as faithfully as she followed him in this, burning herself upon his funeral pyre as a *Sati* – a good wife. By this means she will stay close to him when they are both reborn. If she fails in this duty the only life to which the widow can look forward is miserable indeed, for only widows of the lower castes may remarry. A respectable widow will only be someone else's burden, and a prey to the sexual appetites of all and sundry. A woman whose husband leaves her has no hope of heaven.'

Such a frightening ancient ideal springs surely from the imaginations of men. Perpetuated by women, perhaps, but initially born of the male mind.

My mum would never wait for Dad to address her before she told him it was about time he cleared the garage of all the junk he'd accumulated over decades, but she has always walked a few paces behind him – a habit my dad finds intensely irritating. 'Why don't you walk alongside me?' he would ask. 'It can't be because I am walking faster than you. You are walking at the same pace as me, otherwise you would be getting further and further behind.'

Mum was always obedient to her mother-in-law and feared her father-in-law. And there was a time when she would refuse to eat dinner before Dad got home, no matter how long he had been delayed.

My parents' arranged marriage has lasted since 1963. It was the mode of marriage they were brought up with, accepted and wanted for themselves. No matter how hard things get, divorce is simply not an option. Ever. Their love developed *after* marriage and matured into respect. I suppose it is also enormously helpful that their relationship is equal too – sort of. Mum defers to Dad's superior knowledge of anything that falls within the purview of the 'big picture' and Dad defers to Mum's superior knowledge of all things within the purview of the 'small picture', by which I mean the domestic sphere.

Naturally, they consult each other, but this neat division of responsibility works for them because they know where they stand. That's equality within their arranged marriage. Of course, it also helps that no matter what purview we're in, or who has or has not been consulted, ultimately, at the end of the day, when all is said and done, Dad is the head of the household and he has the last word. Enough said.

So from the day Elvis Presley with his big hair arrived to sweep Mum off her feet, her life changed. Her status became upgraded from unmarried virgin living under her father's roof to married woman living under her husband's roof. With this elevation came the understanding that a husband is to be revered because his happiness is the route to a wife's own happiness.

Three months after their wedding Dad packed his bag and migrated to Britain. As is often the case with Asian migrants, men travel alone first to prepare a base before they call their womenfolk. Dad had only been in London a few months and was still absorbing the news of Nehru's death when he received a letter from Mum telling him she was expecting a baby. He asked her to join him in London immediately so that the baby could be born there (always thinking ahead, he wanted the baby to have British nationality), but Mum was just a child herself and frightened of the changes that were taking place within her body. Traditionally, Indian women go to their parents' house when a baby is due and that's what Mum wanted. She was a new bride, a mother-to-be and a terrified teenager. She chose to stay in India to have her first baby and that's how I came to be born in Punjab in the town of Moga, delivered by my grandmother at ten o'clock in the morning on 9 October 1964.

My mum: engaged at fifteen, married at eighteen, mother at nineteen.

It was not an easy birth. It took Mum months to recuperate. I was the baby who never stopped crying and Dad wasn't there to comfort Mum. 'I should have known you were going to be a difficult child,' she once said. 'You were screaming from the minute you were born.' Actually, I haven't stopped screaming. I was about six months old before Mum was ready to travel to Britain. Alone, with a babe in arms, she boarded a plane for the first time in her life and jetted off to a new country to live among people whose language she couldn't even speak.

There are three stages of culture shock and anyone who has migrated recognises them instantly. The first stage is the romance of arrival: you are excited, everything is different, you love your new life and you're high on traveller's delight. The second stage is filled with resentment and longing: things are not going to plan, you hate your new life, all these terrible things wouldn't be happening if only you were back in your own country – oh, how you miss your old friends. The third stage is reconciliation: you've been a migrant for so long you've got used to things. It's not the same as home – some things are better, some things are worse – but you've stopped comparing your old home with your new home. Romance, resentment, reconciliation – a migrant can always be found walking somewhere along that path.

Unlike Dad, who progressed through each stage methodically, Mum skipped the first – the romance of arrival – and went straight to stage two: resentment. She was isolated and lonely. Her days consisted of feeding a baby, washing nappies in cold water and drying them next to a paraffin heater so they were ready for the next day's drudgery. Homesickness became her best friend as memories of India danced in her head, only to be locked away by day's end.

Mum and Dad's landlord, who worked night shifts, slept through the day. Not wanting to disturb him with her child's constant crying, Mum went to the local park and pushed me around in a pram. No sunshine, no friends, no laughter. Only misery, she thought. 'I don't like it here. I don't want to stay,' she told Dad. But there was no turning back now. Returning to India without giving it a go in Britain would have been failure for him.

So Mum carried on trudging through the park daily until one day she stopped to chat to a withered old Indian woman who was on her way home from her shift at a local factory. Mum thought, 'If this old woman can work, so can I.' Within a week she had found herself a job packing boxes of fruit and nuts. Dad was pleased. He didn't mind her going out to work because they needed the money. I was nine months old and grown-up enough to be left with a carer called Mary. When Vin was born two years later, Mum stopped work briefly and then returned, leaving Vin with a carer called Jane. Work and saving money became more important than ever before, for not only were there now two little mouths to feed, but two big dowries looming on the horizon too.

Even with employment to occupy her mind, Mum found no comfort in an isolated existence. The extended, intergenerational joint family was the norm in India and she missed the company of other women, in particular her mother and younger sister. So it wasn't long before my parents embarked on a plan to bring members of their family to join them in Britain. My dad sent for his younger brother (who was in his twenties and of marriageable age) and my mum sent for her younger sister (also of marriageable age) as well as her parents. And before you could say chicken tikka masala, it was obvious that a marriage would have to be arranged soon.

For two and half years Mum and Dad lived in rented accommodation, until they had saved enough money to buy their first house: a three-bedroom terrace for £5000 in Twickenham. Mum shopped by pointing at things and smiling, and Dad, having found better paid work at an engineering company that made parts for the shipping industry, upgraded his Zeiss Ikon camera to a Pentax.

When my dad's brother and my mum's sister arrived in the late 1960s, they lived with my parents. We kids simply referred to them as uncle and aunt. After all, we knew of no other uncles and aunts so there was no need to suffix their titles with names. Mum's parents, who we called *nanna* and *nanni*, also migrated and came to live with us. All eight of us, three generations, in a three-bedroom house in a particularly white part of Twickenham.

Only Indians know the oriental secret of cramming an army of people into the tightest of spaces.

My uncle was a skinny, bespectacled, unnecessarily humble, mathematically inclined young man and my aunt was a chortling, thigh-slapping, rotund young lady with an ear for a joke and an eye for fashion. They didn't have anything in common, but at least marrying them off would help organise the household's sleeping arrangements better.

So with as little fuss and chaos as an Indian family can muster, my uncle and aunt were married in the back garden of our house. Somehow, with deft use of those karmic powers, my mum and dad managed to squeeze what seemed to be half the population of Delhi into a garden the size of a postage stamp. We saw our polite English neighbours peeking out from behind their net curtains to catch a glimpse of the bride dressed in her wedding finery of red and gold silk, bangles jangling, hair bedecked with flowers.

Luckily, the bride and groom didn't need a car painted with 'just married' to drive into the sunset because both of them were already at home. Presumably, after all the wedding guests had left, Mum and Dad just moved the furniture around so that my uncle and aunt could share the same room. It had all turned out conveniently neat. Two brothers married to two sisters, living in the same house. There isn't anything that Indians can't arrange.

It wasn't long before my aunt and uncle had earned enough money to buy a house of their own, and then my grandparents did the same. Those were the days when able-bodied people in ordinary jobs could realistically save enough money in a reasonable period of time to put a deposit on a house.

Soon after, there was great joy in our house when my brother was born in 1972. At last my parents had a son. There were big smiles and much hearty slapping of backs. As is the custom, Indian sweets were distributed to friends, family, colleagues and neighbours. Indeed, such was the delight, he was named Rajesh, meaning 'king of kings', and my mum's status in Indian society automatically became upgraded from mother to mother of son. I was eight years old when he was born and Vin was six. His arrival was clearly a big moment in our household, and with the nonchalance of kids, we took it in our stride. But it was a turning point in my parents' lives. Bearing a son gives an Indian woman confidence and Mum was emboldened. Dad was a proud man and now ready to show his children off to his own father and mother in India.

Within a year my family made our first trip to India. My grandparents lived in a newly built cream-coloured house with a spiral staircase and two kitchens (a Western kitchen for cooking standing up and an Indian kitchen for squatting and cooking). This house was built with remittances sent back from England by my dad and uncle.

There is method in migration. Young male migrants don't move overseas just for fun and adventure. They send money back to their home country so the wealth can be spread among members of their family. For Indian migrants, the object of the game is survival, everything else – holidays, entertainment, fashionable clothing, the very apparatus of what is commonly known as 'lifestyle' – takes a back seat. Earning money and sharing it among your people becomes the priority.

During our three months in India, Vin and I discovered a magical world full of peculiar and wonderful things. Each day, we pumped water from a hand pump just outside the house. There were no taps. We saw women make patties from cow dung and leave them in huge, finely balanced piles to bake in the sun to use for fuel the next day. We plucked huge swollen purple jamun fruit off trees and gorged ourselves till we looked like little sated vampires with bloodstained mouths. Geckos lost their tails on the verandah and goats bleated like babies. We celebrated the spring colour festival of *Holi* with local children who ran amok, laughing and throwing handfuls of coloured powder till every street and laneway looked like god had spilled a palate of paint.

Vin and I were timid little girls in my grandfather's presence. He walked with the help of a stick and spoke to us gently. He had a full head of polar-white hair but his thick moustache still carried a faint reminder of the colour his hair had once been. It was on this trip that I saw Mum speak to him through her georgette *dupatta*, pulling it across one side of her face and holding it there with feminine fingers, her profile slightly visible through the sheer fabric.

Afternoons were yellowy warm and languid, and life was lived on the verandah. My then one-year-old brother, who was now walking, was often the centre of adult attention, while Vin and I found our own little corner where the two of us, like chattering chimps, could sit giggling and teasing one another.

Amid the chitchat and banter sat a very old man, cross-legged and silent, on a rope bed in the sun, usually with his eyes closed. He wore a loose white turban wrapped around his head and a pair of round metal-rimmed glasses perched on the end of his nose. Bare-chested, with only a white *dhoti* wrapped around him, he looked like Gandhi, except he was much, much older. He was as thin as a man could be and his golden brown skin hung loosely from his armpits, groin and knees. 'This man,' said my dad in a hushed tone, 'is your great-grandfather.'

My dad had built a house for my grandfather, and my grandfather in turn was looking after my great-grandfather in it. The power of duty can produce a remarkably efficient system of care. My great-grandfather, my grandfather, my dad and my baby brother – all on the verandah together. Those three months in India were the only time I saw four generations of males in our family gathered in the same geographical spot.

Throughout our school years and with only a short break when my brother was born, Mum worked non-stop. Indeed, if she was not working, the earth was off its axis for her. She was incapable of relaxing, even at home, because there was always something to do: soak the *dal*, make the lunches, knit mittens, sew duvet covers, yell at Dad for reading the newspaper, sweep the kitchen, pound the dry chillies, whack the kids with a wooden spoon. Mum's work was never done. Over the past forty or so years, apart from rearing three children, serving her husband and boxing fruit and nuts, she has also made nameplates for motor cars, laundered other people's clothes, checked rubber washers for defects, assembled car wipers, soldered components onto printed circuit boards, massaged heads at a hair salon and fed old people.

And did she do all this without a single word of complaint? Of course not. She will readily spill her woes, even if only the doorpost is listening. And does anyone contest the depth of her sacrifice? Of course not.

When Vin and I started school, Mum was working virtually every available hour. It was usually our *nanni* who met us at the school gates when it was home time. On the odd occasion, when Mum had a day off work or had left work early for a dental appointment, she'd pick us up from school. At home time, we'd leave our classroom and look for *nanni* with her green coat and 'emerald' buttons among the knot of parents near the school gate. On the surprise occasions that we spotted Mum, smiling and waving at us, we'd break into a sprint, cut across the grass and arrive panting, circling her like excited terriers.

But the regular pattern of our lives usually meant Mum was forever getting ready to go to work, her face anxious, her bag at the ready. She'd comb her long black hair and plait it quickly, flicking it over her shoulder when she had finished so it hung like a rope down her spine. Then she'd stand in front of the mirror, examine the mole on her chin, and smile a false smile to flatten her lips so she could apply her red lipstick in a couple of swift strokes. It made me happy to watch her getting ready for work, not because I was pleased she was leaving the house, but because I liked the way her face looked when she put on her lipstick. I thought she was smiling because she was happy.

But happiness was a thing of the past. She was no longer a girl. Her courtship had been conducted by mail. The romance of marriage had lasted just three short months till Dad had left for London, and by the time she saw him again nearly a year and a half later, she carried with her all the burdens of motherhood. And now there was nothing but work ahead. But at least she was no longer alone. She was no longer sitting next to a heater drying the nappies. She had her sister to talk to and her parents weren't far away. Dad had his brother near him and the bonds forged within a small extended family provided comfort in a strange and sometimes peculiar land.

While Mum moved from one job to the next, full-time to part-time and back again, accommodating the various stages and needs of her children, Dad stayed relatively stable in his work. After a few years he left the engineering company and trained to become a tax officer – a good 'government job' as Indians like to call such work. He was posted to a tax office in Twickenham and there he remained for the rest of his working life, devoted to robbing people of their hard-earned cash on behalf of Her Majesty's government.

'I'm looking after the tax affairs of Hot Chocolate,' he announced one evening.

'What, Hot Chocolate, the pop group?'

'Yes.'

'How much money do they make?'

'I can't tell you that. It's confidential.'

'But we're your kids. We won't tell anyone.'

'Sorry. Tax is a private business. I can't tell you their private business.'

My dad: honest, ethical, upright citizen of Britain.

Whatever he turned his hand to, he achieved successfully. Except one thing: teaching Mum to speak English properly. Admittedly, he was up against forces beyond his control. No matter how hard he worked at helping her with her pronunciation and spelling, the Cockney influence of the people Mum worked with in factories rapidly undid all Dad's efforts. As far as she was concerned, she was fluent in Hindi and Punjabi and competent in English, so why all the fuss over pronunciation and getting every single word right? What she developed over time was a unique way of speaking English without an Indian accent, but with an unmistakable Indian style overlaid with a slight Cockney lilt. We three kids tried to help her, but she resisted our attempts too.

'Gimme help with irrrening, may.'

'Mum, it's help me with the ironing – *iyuning.* And you shouldn't call me "mate". I'm your daughter.'

'This is wor I say: gimme help with irrrening.'

'It's *what!* Not wor! It's *what*, you say. T, T, T where's the T?'

'Iss in the cupboard.'

Most of her issues related to pronunciation, but her biggest problem was with the word 'the'. She simply never worked out where to put it in a sentence: 'Chapatis is made. Call the dad. Dinner is ready.' Even her swearing was back to front and upside down. 'He charge me three pound for tomaterr. Bastard bloody. I say him you charge me extra. He just look me. Three pound! Bloody.'

Talking to Mum in English was mostly successful, sometimes frustrating and occasionally embarrassing. Dad was always patient, but in public her word-mangling skills could leave him red-faced – especially if she spoke too loudly.

'Why don't you take some photos?' she yelled to him during a family picnic at Kew Gardens. 'Where your Tampax? Check that bag. I think your Tampax in there.'

'Pentax, it's Pentax,' said Dad through gritted teeth. 'You see why I don't take you to the office Christmas party.'

And things have never got much better.

'So, what does your daughter do, Mrs Das?'

'She is a generalist.'

'A generalist?'

'Yes, she write the story in the newspaper.'

'Oh, a *journalist.*'

Eventually we gave up trying, although I still throw corrections into the conversation sometimes. Dad is mostly philosophical: 'If she had only just tried a little harder, she might not have been stuck working in factories all her life. She could have got a good job in the post office like Mrs Singh.'

CHAPTER 3

Starving in a Sari

'Where a Western woman misses a meal in the interests of her figure, her Indian sister dedicates her starvation to a cause, usually a male one.'
Shashi Tharoor, The Elephant, the Tiger and the Cell Phone

It was four in the morning and the click of my parents' bedroom door opening woke me. I heard my mother's footsteps on the carpet as she crept downstairs to the kitchen. I turned over in my warm bed. It was still dark outside. I knew what she was doing.

At the kitchen sink, the spot where she could most often be found, she was filling a small silver jug with water – the one she used every year – and placing it on a round tray. Then she would place on the tray a small heap of uncooked rice grains, a few pieces of fresh coconut, a stick of incense and a knob of sweet, fudge-like confection. Standing in her nightdress and slippers, with the cold night air circling her exposed ankles, she would put her hands together and close her eyes to say a solitary prayer before the morning gloom seeped through the curtains. Soon daylight would come tumbling into the house but she would eat breakfast before it did, because afterwards she would not eat or drink again until she saw the moon in the evening.

It was the day of the *Kurwa Chauth* ceremony, when Hindu married women fast from sunrise to moonrise to pray that their husbands live a long life. Millions of Indian women have performed this ritual for centuries. And my mum would, as she had done ever since her status was elevated from unmarried girl to married woman, sacrifice nourishment without complaint to demonstrate her utter devotion to my dad.

Traditionally, her small meal before daybreak, or *sergi*, would be prepared by her mother-in-law, but my mum was in London and her mother-in-law was in India so she always made her own *sergi* – some fruit, maybe some chapati and a cup of tea. And so it went, every year on the fourth day of a waxing moon in the Hindu lunisolar calendar month of Kartik (usually September, October or November), Mum celebrated a custom that was the very essence of what she lived for: her husband, her protector.

Every morning she made the tea and Dad washed the breakfast dishes. When they left for work they never kissed each other goodbye – physical affection in front of the children would be unseemly. *Kurwa Chauth* this year was much like any other. By the time I hauled myself out of bed, they had already gone to work. I lurched downstairs for breakfast and saw Mum's tray on the kitchen bench. On a chair in the living room she had left all the things she would need in the evening: one of her finest saris, bangles, some make-up, a bindi and a small amount of *sindoor*, vermilion powder to daub in the parting of her hair

– the distinctive mark of an Indian woman whose husband is alive.

When we were younger schoolgirls, Vin and I would be home by four and Mum would be waiting with a scarf covering her head. She didn't normally cover her head at home, but on the day of the *Kurwa Chauth*, when it was time to tell the *Kurwa Chauth* story, she would pull her *dupatta* over her head as a gesture of piety and Vin and I would be handed scarves to cover our heads. If my aunt had the day off work, she would join us, but often there was only the three of us: Mum, Vin and me. We would sit in a circle on the floor with Mum's tray in the middle. She'd drop a few silver coins into her jug of water and then give me and Vin a pinch of rice each from the tray, and take some for herself.

There would be a strange sense of excitement and trepidation as the three of us sat cross-legged with our heads covered – as if Mum was about to start a séance. Eagerly, we would search her face for a sign that she was about to begin. She would look down, start massaging the rice in her cupped palm with the fingers of her other hand and then slowly and deliberately start narrating in Punjabi the story she told every year at exactly four o'clock in the afternoon on the day of *Kurwa Chauth*:

> A long time ago, there lived a girl who had seven brothers. After she married and it was time to perform her first *Kurwa Chauth* ritual, she happened to be visiting her parents. She took *sergi* before sunrise and kept a fast all day. No food, no water. By the time the evening came, she felt weak with hunger. But she could not eat because the moon had not risen yet. Her brothers became worried for her; after all, she was their only sister and the youngest. So they hatched a plan to

dupe their sister into thinking the moon had risen. A couple of them went into the forest and lit a fire behind a hill. Then they called for their sister. Her brothers said, 'Come, sister, come into the forest – there is a glow behind the hill. The moon has finally risen.' Seeing the glow and mistaking it for the light of the moon, she returned to the house to break her fast.

In her first mouthful, she bit into a stick. In her second mouthful, she found a hair. When she took her third mouthful there was a knock at the door. She opened it to find a messenger, who had come to deliver bad news: her new husband was fatally ill and on his deathbed. The girl's mother told her to immediately return to her husband's house and if she met anyone en route to touch their feet as a mark of respect so that they might bestow on her a blessing that her husband should survive so that she would remain a married woman.

So, grief-stricken, she ran and ran until she met a woman walking the other way. The girl touched the woman's feet and the woman blessed her, but the blessing was not the one she desired. She continued on her journey until she met a second woman. The girl touched her feet and the woman blessed her, but again it was not the precise blessing that she required. The girl continued like this until she met a seventh woman. The girl bent down and in desperation clung onto her feet. The woman blessed her, saying, 'Bless you, my child – may you always remain a married woman.'

The girl thanked her and asked, 'But how can I remain a married woman? I am on my way to my husband's house and he is on his deathbed.' Unbeknown to the girl, the woman who blessed her was the mother goddess, and she said to the girl, 'Your husband lies on his deathbed because you did not maintain your fast until the moon rose. I was on my way to bring death to him, but you took hold of my feet looking for a blessing and now I must keep your husband alive. Here, take this holy water. When you get home, sprinkle it over your husband's body and he will remain alive. May you always stay a married woman.' The girl ran home, sprinkled the water on her husband and to her joy he awoke, and she remained a married woman.

God willing, may all husbands live long lives, so that we may remain married women.

With these words, my mum would bring the story to a close, drop her grains of rice into the silver jug and gesture for me and Vin to do the same. Following a short prayer, which sounded as if she was chanting, we would be allowed to go about our business and Mum, no doubt very hungry by then, would start preparing the evening's feast.

When Dad returned from work, we would have to wait until moonrise before we could eat dinner. From about eight o'clock Mum would go into the garden at regular intervals and look up at the sky, searching for the moon. We would all become increasingly worried if there was cloud cover and the moon was not visible. Frequently around autumn time in London there were heavy clouds and there were many occasions when the whole family would be in the garden looking up at the sky. Mum, Dad, Vin, Raja and I, by now all hungry, turning circles looking skyward in the hope that someone might catch a glimpse of the moon as it slid out from behind a cloud.

Eventually, there would be moans of 'I'm starving' from me, Vin or Raja and Dad would turn to Mum and say, 'Come, the children are hungry, perform your prayers and let's go in and eat.' But Mum, pious, faithful, devoted Mum, would say, 'No, how can I? I have not seen the moon yet.'

So Dad would fetch the newspaper and check the time of that day's moonrise. 'The moon rose several hours ago,' he'd say reassuringly. 'It has definitely risen, it's just hiding behind a cloud. Come, it is time to pray and eat.' And finally Mum would succumb and start her *Kurwa Chauth* prayer.

This evening the sky was not cloudy. It was cool in the garden and there was a smell of winter in the air. A crescent moon was visible as it moved through its phase from new moon to full moon. It was bright enough to see and everyone was excited because tonight we would not be eating late. We stood in the garden waiting for Mum, arms crossed tight to stay warm, including Dad, because this part of the ritual couldn't be performed without him being nearby.

Mum stepped into the garden with her head covered, holding her tray. She had made a small diva lamp using half a coconut shell and a wick made of cotton wool dipped in oil, and it was burning with a bright flame on the tray. She muttered prayers as she held up the tray, offering it to the moon. Vin and I looked at each other, Dad looked at his feet. Then, placing the tray on the ground, Mum took the silver jug and poured a little water into her cupped hand before sprinkling it towards the moon and mumbling words that Vin, Raja and I didn't recognise, let alone understand. And because this water contained the silver coins and the grains of rice from the females of the house, we knew that what had been only tap water this morning was now holy water. I wondered if our English neighbours were peeping through their windows to see what our family was up to in the garden. Mum repeated the water-throwing ritual seven times. She was praying to the gods to guard her husband against an untimely demise and for him to be bestowed with a long life.

Eventually, she took a sieve that she had brought into the garden with her, held it up to the moon and closed her eyes. When she reopened them, she was looking at the moon through the sieve. It showed respect. It's inauspicious to view such a powerful symbol directly. Then she turned to face her husband and closed her eyes. When she reopened them, he was standing before her and she looked at him through the sieve. Placing the sieve on the ground, she reached to touch his feet, the tips of her fingers caressing the toes of his shoes. It was the most arresting gesture of respect – enough to take your breath away. One human bending down to touch another's feet. Somewhere in a garden in south-west London, a famished woman dressed in her loveliest sari had demonstrated her devotion through sacrifice and was bending down to afford the greatest respect in the world to the man with whom she had her most sacred bond.

My father placed his hand softly on my mother's head before taking her gently by the shoulders and bringing her level with him. They embraced each other for the tiniest of moments. Perhaps not even a moment, perhaps the smallest fraction of time in all the universe. And in that fleeting, ethereal slice of time, we saw between our parents a flicker of affection that burst our hearts. My father took the confectionery from the tray and placed it in my mother's mouth, and with that small intimate gesture, he, at last, broke her sacrificial fast.

That evening, after we had all feasted and everyone had retired to their rooms, I lay awake in bed wondering whether I would have to keep a fast for the man I married. My parents would probably want me married off by twenty-one – in only three years. I didn't have much time. I closed my eyes and tried to imagine myself starving in a sari, but the picture wouldn't materialise in my head. I had never even bent down and touched my parents' feet in respect – how could I touch some strange husband's feet? When Mum touched Dad's feet it was moving because, from an offspring's point of view, it's uplifting to see a gesture of sweetness between one's parents. But when I tried to imagine myself doing it to a man, I couldn't because a feeling of debasement got in the way. The *Kurwa Chauth* was an undeniably beautiful ritual motivated by the positive force of devotion, yet I felt it catapulted women into the past and tethered them to a mode of thinking that was out of step with the modern world. The ceremony poleaxed me: I was simultaneously moved and offended by it.

'Hey, Vin,' I whispered into the darkness.

'What?'

'When you get married, are you going to keep the *Kurwa Chauth* fast for your husband?'

'Dunno. Maybe.'

'You mean you might?' There was a note of alarm in my voice and Vin heard it.

'It's no big deal. You only have to stop eating for a day. You're not going to die.'

'That's not the point. I mean, would you actually starve for a guy? You know, to show him how devoted you are and all that?'

'Depends if he's good-looking or not,' she said. 'Don't tell me you're not going to do it because you're a bloody feminist or something. Anyway, you can't spend your whole life burning your bra, especially if you don't wear one!' I could hear her slapping the bed with her hand, laughing.

'You'll be laughing on the other side of your face when they marry you off to some nerd with oily hair and a side-parting,' I said, rolling my eyes in the dark.

'You're the oldest,' she shot back. '*You're* the one who's going to get married first. Let me know how it goes with the nerdy oil guy.'

She never took important things seriously. She didn't over-think, unlike me. I could think myself into madness. As little girls we had been one person, but now, as teenagers, I felt we were moving on different tracks. Still parallel, but different tracks. She had discovered Michael Jackson and Stevie Wonder, while I embraced David Bowie and Frank Zappa. She felt comfortable in the mainstream. I sought out the subversive. Long after she'd fallen asleep and I could hear her regular breathing, I was still awake, eyes wide open, lying on my back like a pharaoh, trying to imagine myself looking at a nerd through a sieve. But all I could picture was him pushing his tongue into my mouth as he tried to force himself on me.

My private annual panic following the *Kurwa Chauth* ceremony was as much a ritual as the ceremony itself. In fact, it was the *Kurwa Chauth* shortly after my fourteenth birthday that induced the wildest panic. I recall it well because that was the year I got out of bed in the middle of the night and went downstairs to steal the photos.

CHAPTER 4

Nignog

'I have become a queer mixture of the East and the West, out of place everywhere, at home nowhere.'
Jawaharlal Nehru

I misspent my youth trying to make myself white. It was a futile exercise but one that I pursued with great vigour from girlhood to mid-teens – the logic being that, as a white girl, I would become the new, improved version of myself.

In the bath, maybe around the age of twelve, I scrubbed my arms and legs with a pumice stone, convinced that if I rubbed hard enough, white skin would emerge from underneath. It was a failed experiment. I merely inflicted red sores on my limbs. Thank god I didn't scrub my face with it. After a day or so, the redness disappeared and a thin, brown patchy scab formed on my shins and forearms. Maybe I had simply scrubbed too hard – through the brownness, and right through the whiteness too. I tried scrubbing more gently next time. Nope. Still brown.

Talcum powder was another pointless venture. There's only so much of it you can put on your face without resembling someone who's just finished a shift in an asbestos factory. There were skin-bleaching creams in the chemist shops, but I didn't bother with them. They were for blemish removal, really. I needed something hardcore that could disguise racial heritage. I once asked a hairdresser to bleach my black hair blonde in the hope that it would make me look white. She refused on the grounds that it would 'fuck' my hair. Somehow, Dad knew what I was up to. 'You can be as English as you like,' he said. 'You can eat English food, you can wear English clothes. But every time you look in the mirror, you will be reminded that you are not English. You are Indian.'

If the skin-colour spectrum goes from Negroid black to Nordic white, then I suppose I'd have to say I'm at the paler end of the brown shades. But that's no consolation because when you're the only Indian kid in a class of white children, being more toffee than liquorice is no help at all. We're talking 1970s Britain here. Racial prejudice was all the rage and multiculturalism as a political idea was still taking shape. People's skin colour was very much a live topic – discussed, analysed and dissected in the mainstream media. TV sitcoms such as *It Ain't Half Hot Mum*, *Love Thy Neighbour* and *Mind Your Language* challenged ideas of racial prejudice but also reinforced stereotypes. We watched these programmes with Mum and Dad; we even laughed at the funny bits. But no one said, 'Hey, enough with this race thing.' We just accepted things as they were. It was as if the British didn't know any better.

Certainly, at primary school they didn't. A girl in my class asked me, 'In India, did you live in a mud hut?' I had no recollection of ever living in India, let alone in a mud hut. The playground was a dangerous place. White kids would corner you and chant, to the sound of an old English police car siren, 'Nig-nog, nig-nog.' So how do you handle that when you're six or seven or eight years old? You're outnumbered. Your back is literally up against a wall. The teachers are on playground duty. They see what's happening, but they don't intervene. You can't be a sissy about it and let half the class see you cry. You're brown, the only brown kid in the class and one of a handful in the whole school. It's beginning to dawn on you. You thought you were like all the other kids, except once in a while, when you were wearing short sleeves, you saw your brown arm next to their white arm. And that's when you saw it. *Really* saw it. That's when you felt like a nignog. And when you *feel* like a nignog, you *are* a nignog. So how are you going to deal with it?

'Nig-nog, nig-nog.'

Come on, deal with it.

'Nig-nog, nig-nog.'

What are you supposed to do? I'll tell you what you do: you close your eyes tight. You put your hands up and cover your face. Then you stay like that. 'Nig-nog, nig-nog'. Their voices are close up in your ears. It's like their mouths are in your head. Eventually it stops. Just trails off. It's over. It's time to go back into class now. You got through it. You got through morning playtime. You hope no one tells you off for being the centre of a commotion. Hope it rains after lunch. Hope afternoon playtime never comes. But it will. You know it will.

It was a time of skinheads and Paki-bashing. Shaved heads, tight jeans, cherry Docs and broken teeth. All of it scared me. Wogs were supposed to 'go home', like the graffiti said. But we weren't doing what the graffiti was telling us to do. And that made its authors angry. We were in their country and they didn't want us there. Once I was spat at by a boy racing past on his BMX bike. His gob landed on my shoulder. I was with my mum in a park. I'm not sure how old I was but I was definitely not taller than her. Or perhaps I was taller but remember myself as shorter because the humiliation shrank me. I shouted 'fuck off' and stuck two fingers up at his back as he rode off. My mum added her tuppence worth – 'Bastard bloody!' – and handed me a tissue from her handbag. He didn't turn to look over his shoulder, he just pedalled away with his bum lifted slightly off the saddle till he became a smaller and smaller dot in the distance. Then there was just me and my mum left standing in the park shouting swearwords into the air. A genuine bonding moment because it was the first time we'd ever sworn in front of each other.

Even in the 1960s when Dad migrated, there were rumblings about 'coloured people'. The rumblings built up a murderous momentum after 1968 – after 20 April 1968, to be precise, when Conservative MP Enoch Powell delivered his inflammatory 'rivers of blood' speech. Enoch Powell – now there's a name that petrified my parents. He wanted to stop immigration from the Commonwealth and send back all the 'coloured people' who had already arrived. He even spoke out against proposed anti-discrimination legislation. He warned that the 'black man will have the whip hand over the white man' in fifteen or twenty years, and he talked of immigrants as an 'alien element'. He told the story of a poor old white woman who was hounded because she didn't want to rent her house to black people, and how black kids, 'wide-grinning piccaninnies', abused her by calling her a 'racialist'.

If racists were shy about coming forward, the speech gave their voices confidence and volume. He lent legitimacy to poisonous racist thoughts, warning that unbridled immigration would lead to segregation and violence. He was every immigrant's nightmare because he represented the worst thing that could happen to them: forced repatriation. 'Study hard,' Dad said. 'They can send you back to India but they won't be able to take your education away from you.'

Kids at school openly told racist jokes. It gave racism validity in the playground.

'What do you call something transparent that lies in the gutter?'

'What?'

'A Paki with the shit kicked out of him.'

It didn't matter if you were from India or Pakistan. To these schoolyard comedians we were all brown. So we were all Pakis. Most of the jokes were brutal, but some were peculiarly funny.

'Why do Indian women have a dot on their forehead?'

'Why?'

(The answer was always delivered with the joke-teller viciously stabbing the air in front of him with his finger.) 'Because the immigration people at Heathrow are always saying, "No! You can't fucking come into our country."'

There was also a lot of talk about 'second-class citizens'. Where did I hear those words? On the TV news? From the Indian grown-ups who occasionally visited our house? At school? I don't know. Second-class citizens: the words ignited indignation which was at once extinguished by low self-esteem. I never asked Dad what they meant. I wasn't even across the basics of who we were, let alone anywhere near understanding what was happening around us, so I asked him different things instead.

'Dad.'

'Yes.'

'If we're Indian, why don't you wear a turban?'

'Because we're not Sikh.'

'What are we then?'

'We're Hindu.'

'What's the difference?'

'Sikhs and Hindus have different religions, but both are Indian.' His answer made as much sense as it needed to at the time. I never ran out of questions and he never ran out of answers. Right into my mid-teens I truly believed he knew everything there was to know in the world.

'Dad.'

'Yes.'

'Are we rich or poor?'

'We're neither rich nor poor.'

'Does that mean we're middle class?'

'No. I think we are probably working class.'

'How can we be working class when you said we're not poor?'

'In upper-class families, neither the mother nor the father need go to work. In middle-class families, only one of them has to go to work. In working-class families, both of them have to go to work. Your mother and I both have to work.'

'Dad.'

'Yes.'

'Are you a communist?'

'No.'

'Why do you hate America then?'

'I don't hate America.'

'Did you *used* to be a communist when you were a boy?'

'No. I was never a com*mune*-ist.' That's how he pronounced it. First the commune bit with an emphasis on the *mune*, then *ist* stuck on the end. Com*mune*-ist – as if to emphasis the communal part of communist.

'So, do you like America?'

'Yes. America is a country like any other country.'

'So, if you like America, does that mean we're capitalist?'

I didn't even know the difference between communism and capitalism. I just thought everyone had to be one or the other and I wanted to know which one we had chosen.

'Dad.'

'Yes.'

'What is the footsie?'

'You mean the FTSE. The Financial Times Stock Exchange Index?'

'No, the footsie they always talk about at the end of the news.'

'You're too young to understand. I'll explain it when you're older.'

I can't remember exactly how old I was when I asked that particular question. Perhaps around twelve. It's the only question I remember him not answering.

The thing I never asked him about was racism. I didn't need to. It was the default setting. I never told my parents what was happening at school either. When circumstances conspire to make you feel inferior, you believe you are. My teenager's instinctive drive to vehemently denounce social injustice had not kicked in yet. I just accepted things the way they were. Mum and Dad's generation accepted things because they were always aware of their migrant status and they didn't want to rock the boat.

Dad says the English only 'awakened' to the type of immigration that made them feel uncomfortable when Asians started arriving in large numbers. 'The English were used to black people [migrants from Jamaica, the West Indies and West Africa] because they came first. They were doing menial jobs such as street-cleaning so the English didn't have much contact with them. I think they saw them as doing jobs they were fit to do,' he says.

'When the Asians came, they went into manufacturing jobs and office work. This is where English people came into contact with them more frequently. Compared with other Indians, I was in a far better position. I came from New Delhi so I was used to living in a big city and I was familiar with dealing with Westerners. When I came to Britain, it never occurred to me that I was a foreigner. I never treated them differently.

'The biggest hurdle was the colour of your skin. Because either you yourself were feeling an inferiority complex in some sense, or they [the British] might have felt superior. Instead of getting to know each other, there was suspicion. And, therefore, the person who was in the weaker position was more . . .' He finished his answer there, but I understood what he meant.

The experience of racism diminishes your confidence. It makes you smaller. I'd had my nignog moments; he'd had his own version. We didn't talk about it at the time because we were living our lives. We weren't doing a sociological analysis of our experiences. It wasn't until I was an adult that I asked him for his insights.

Dad's nignog moments were more subtle than mine. His were in the fine print of everyday interactions. He was never given a promotion to tax inspector even though his qualifications and experience were superior to those of the Englishman who snared the job. Then there was the time he had tried to buy a house in a part of Twickenham that was even whiter than the area in which we already lived, and the real estate agent had been obstructive. These were just incidents: privately painful, ruefully remembered.

Racism, in all its overt and insidious ways, has the capacity to sear its mark on a person. It doesn't always hurt so much when it's actually happening to you as a child – like pulling a plaster off your knee really fast. The pain comes in adulthood, when you look back at the wound and realise it's bigger and uglier than you thought. Delayed trauma seeps into your heart and hardens it ever so slightly. The feeling doesn't turn into pity. That's what other people feel. It doesn't even become despair. It's just a big solid lump that you carry around in your rucksack for the rest of your life. Your strength and stamina will determine how far you travel with it, how crooked your back becomes, how quirky your gait.

I hated being Indian, and for good reason. I couldn't go anywhere or do anything without it getting in the way. Walking home from school one day, Vin and I passed a couple of bikers who were standing chatting outside a motorbike shop. They were cool, with their leatherjackets and big biker boots. Their faces were kinder and softer than those of skinheads. They were like rockstars. Maybe they *were* rockstars. As we walked past, one of them looked at me and smiled. I returned a flirty smile just as he sniffed the air and said, 'Phwoar, what's that smell? Curry, isn't it?'

I was gutted. They'd smelt curry on our clothes. How many times had we pleaded with Mum not to cook curry, *again?* How many times had Dad told her to at least open the kitchen window if she was going to cook curry? The smell got in his suits. He couldn't go into the office smelling of fenugreek. How many times had we asked her for fishfingers for a change? What about sausages? Chips, maybe. Now it had come to this. We were offending people on the streets. I couldn't take it. I was embarrassed by my curry clothes, ashamed of my parents speaking their own language in public, horrified by the gaudy colours of Indian women's *salwar kamiz*. Couldn't they wear navy blue or grey? Couldn't we stop being so loud and un-English? Couldn't we just blend in? Teenage anger coursed through me. I didn't want to have anything to do with my culture, my family, my entire racial lineage. Everything I hated about my life stemmed from being Indian. If only I wasn't brown. If only I could be white.

But the pumice stone experiment hadn't worked and nor had the talc. All I could do was stay out of the sun to stop the situation getting any worse. All Asians like to stay out of the sun, because dark skin is the mark of a poor man who works in the fields and, presumably by extension, a person of low-class status. Even Indian people accept that being too dark is not ideal, particularly for a woman who is to be married off. Who would ever marry a blackie? (At least I wasn't damaged in that department.) Highly desired light brown skin is frequently celebrated as a 'wheatish complexion' in matrimonial advertising columns in Indian magazines and newspapers, which parents scour for suitable matches for their sons and daughters. It's not uncommon to see an ad selling 'Slim girl from respectable family. Wheatish complexion, university education, Green card. Caste no barrier.' (It's the 'Green card' bit that always gets me. So ruthlessly pragmatic.)

Even Indian weddings include a gesture towards fairer skin. A pre-wedding ritual performed the day before the wedding ceremony involves the prospective bride being prepared for the big day by having her face and arms smeared with a creamy yellow paste usually made from gram flour (ground chickpeas) and ghee. It gets its yellow colour from turmeric and is designed to stain the skin. When it's washed off, the bride supposedly looks fair and radiant for her wedding day.

In India a new skin-whitening cream for men called Fair and Handsome is now on the market. Bollywood's biggest star, the already fair and handsome Shah Rukh Khan, promoted it. Enami, the company behind it, claims it can make men fairer in just four weeks. It's interesting that the cream's presumably scientifically proven success period coincides perfectly with one month of the Gregorian calendar. Enami claims men need a fairness cream because their skin is more often exposed to sun, pollution and stress factors than women's. The implicit message here is that women in India already have plenty of creams aimed at making them fairer, and now it's time for men to whiten up too.

Disturbingly, in 2012 a vagina 'brightening wash' was also launched, targeting women in India. It promises to make genitals 'many shades fairer'. Needless to say, there was a huge outcry after the TV advert went to air, showing a wistful woman having a coffee with an uninterested date. Presumably she was fretting because her private parts were the wrong damn colour. But after a shower using the new product, her date is swinging her around in the air and the music changes from morose to chirpy. Now, before we go any further, try to imagine the meeting when the marketing team, which almost certainly would have included some women, met to pitch the idea: 'As we all know, vaginas are way too brown these days . . .' Whoever came up with the idea should be stabbed in the head.

Across Asia, a growing number of women, and men, are willing to change their ethnic features. From double eyelid surgery for people from the Far East to skin-lightening for those from the subcontinent, it's all available because there's a demand. Many deny they are trying to achieve a 'Western look', arguing instead that their radical move to make their eyes bigger or their skin fairer is in fact about looking more beautiful – a Western definition of beauty, maybe. Trust me, my ham-fisted attempts with chickpea flour and talc had nothing to do with beauty and everything to do with wanting to be Caucasian. As my sister kept telling me at the time (and still often does), 'You're fucked in the head.'

But skin colour is only, well, skin deep. To be fair, pardon the pun, deep down it wasn't my brownness I objected to, but everything it stood for. It was the Indianness that annoyed me. It made me different at a time when I wanted to be like everyone else. But it was impossible to live my life without my ethnicity constantly being a reference point.

Even that most significant of female milestones, starting one's periods, did not take place without my ethnicity entering the room and taking centrestage. I was fourteen years old. My mum hadn't told me anything. No, nothing. Maybe her mum didn't tell her anything either. Maybe the whole topic was too icky for her. Maybe she always meant to tell me but never got round to it. Maybe that was the Indian way. Who knows. To this day, I don't even know the word for period in Punjabi. My knowledge of periods was the textbook version from sex education at school. I knew about menstruation because it was a sub-section of 'the reproductive cycle of mammals' in my science class.

So there I was, sitting in an English class at Twickenham Girls' School studying *The Tempest*, when my first period arrived like an unwanted visitor. I was reading the part of Shakespeare's Caliban and understanding very little, and the girl next to me was reading the part of Stephano and probably understanding everything. I felt a strong pain in my stomach and stopped reading. Stephano looked up, saw the pained expression on my face and asked, 'What's the matter? Have you started your period?'

'Shhh, no,' I said. 'I've just got a tummy ache.'

'I'll tell the teacher you've started,' she yelled.

'No, I'll tell her myself.'

When the pain became unbearable, I went to the teacher's table and asked to be excused. I must have been the fifteenth girl to start her period that week because I wasn't even asked what was wrong with me, I was just ordered to go straight to sick bay. I explained myself to the deputy headmistress, Mrs Gardner, a severe-looking woman who attended to me. 'You're lucky, the nit nurse is in the school today,' she said. 'Wait here.'

Great. I was bleeding to death and the nit nurse was going to check my head for lice. Mrs Gardner left the door open and I could hear her on the telephone in the adjoining room.

'Hello, nurse. There's an *Indian* girl in sick bay who thinks she's started her period. Would you mind seeing to her?'

An Indian girl? Why had she described me as an Indian girl? Were Indian girls' periods different from English girls'? Why did the nit nurse need to know I was Indian? It was as if Mrs Gardner was giving the nit nurse a veiled warning, an early alert: *There's an Indian girl in sick bay. Just watch out. You know what they're like. She's started her period. See if she's telling the truth. And check her head for lice while you're at it.*

I was the subject of a conversation that contained secret information: a nuance. Nuances are meant to be picked up by those listening. Mrs Gardner didn't know I had heard her on the phone. I'd picked up the nuance, but I didn't know what it meant. I felt instantly uncomfortable. But then, that was nothing new. My whole existence felt uncomfortable.

Happily, the nit nurse spoke to me just as she might have spoken to any other girl in the school. 'You're a woman now,' she announced.

'Do I have to go to hospital?'

'No, you're all right. This is going to happen to you every month.'

'Can I go home then?'

'No, there's nothing wrong with you. You need to go back to your classroom.'

So that was that. I became a woman, an Indian woman, in the midst of *The Tempest*.

I thought I managed the period incident rather well. I didn't get emotional about it like an Indian, for whom every action has an equal and opposite over-reaction. Indeed, I handled it with the stiff upper lip of a true Brit. I stayed calm and carried on. I learnt such skills at my junior school: Archdeacon Cambridge's Church of England Primary School in Twickenham. I was a pupil of that fine institution from the age of five to eleven – the nignog years. I made great personal discoveries there. First and foremost, I discovered that god truly moves in mysterious ways. At school he was a bearded man suffering on a cross; at home he had an elephant's head, sat on a pink lotus flower and was always accompanied by a small mouse.

Every Wednesday, our teacher would lead the class to the Holy Trinity Church across the road. The church was built in 1841.

You could lose yourself in the stained-glass windows, and the organ was magnificent (made by Henry Willis, one of England's most famous organ-builders). But I disliked going to the church because it was always dark and cold, and it made me feel like an intruder.

The vicar, in his black dress, would stand at the front and speak in an unnatural manner. We always brought our red hymn books with us, but before we could get to the singing stage we had to say prayers. As children we were taught to copy the vicar. Slowly and precisely he would join his hands in front of his chest and we would follow. He would take one hand and point to himself, saying, '*I* am a Christian,' the emphasis always on the 'I'. Then we would point to ourselves and repeat the words. This was the part that made me feel uncomfortable. I knew that I wasn't a Christian and nor should I pretend to be. It felt wrong to point to myself and say, '*I* am a Christian.' I feared someone might accuse me of being a fraud. Perhaps a teacher would pull me out of the pew and speak to me in the way that teachers did: 'How dare you call yourself a Christian, young lady.' I didn't know brown people could be Christians too. I thought only white people were Christians. So every Wednesday when the crucial moment came, I would point to myself with the smallest, barely noticeable hand movement and mumble under my breath, 'I am a Christian,' as fast as possible in the hope that nobody would see me performing my fraudulent gesture.

Despite my misgivings, my yawning in the pews and my general fidgeting, I owe much to that church. Where else would I have learnt the Lord's Prayer? I watched the teachers walk solemnly to the front of the church in single file, whereupon they would kneel and the vicar would put in their mouths something that looked like a small disc of white paper and then give them a drink from his big metal cup, always careful to clean the lip of the cup with a crisp white napkin before moving on to the next teacher. Apart from singing hymns, watching the teachers being fed paper was the best bit. Back at school, if you stood near the teacher's desk as she explained something, there was an unusual smell on her breath. It was the smell of whatever she had drunk from the big metal cup. My parents' breath never had that smell.

My mum and dad never asked about what I did at school. I'm not sure they even knew I went to church. They were aware we were learning about Jesus, though, and were, as far as could tell, untroubled by it. Mum said, 'Tell me about Jesus. What is his story?'

I gave her an outrageously truncated version that went something like this: 'He was born in a manger because there was a census and there wasn't any room at the inn. Mary and Joseph were his mum and dad and three wise men followed a star and came with gifts. Then he got crucified on a cross, but somebody moved the rock back and he went to heaven. That's called Ascension. Christmas isn't really his birthday, and Father Christmas is not Jesus when he's old.' I didn't mention anything about suffering. I suspect she might have related to it.

There were many times when I asked her about Hinduism, but her answers always involved characters with complicated names and scenarios with far too many twists and turns for me to keep track. Somewhere along the line Lord Krishna would be mentioned and I knew he was the god who was depicted in pictures – sometimes as an adult playing a flute and sometimes as a small child, but always with blue skin. Ganesh, the elephant god, was always mentioned with cheer in her voice, but I didn't understand where he fitted in.

A paper calendar with pictures of a different god for every month of the year hung in Mum and Dad's bedroom. Vishnu, the preserver; Parvati, the divine mother; Ganesh, the remover of obstacles; Lakshmi, the goddess of wealth; and so on. Many of the deities had four or more arms. I was fascinated by these pictures because they were intricate, colourful and intriguing. They meant something to my parents, but I didn't know what. I understood the gods were to be revered. Mum, in particular, believed her destiny was very much in their hands – their *many* hands, as it happens.

I was surrounded by far too many gods. That's probably why I was never able to commit myself to any one of them. I had a seminal god moment in my teens, when I developed an obsession with The Boomtown Rats – Bob Geldof in particular. The headboard on my bed was made of white plastic – like a blank white page waiting for words. For some inexplicable reason I used a permanent black marker to write three words in an arch of huge block capitals across it: GELDOF IS GOD. Dad was horrified by the blasphemy. 'Why did you do that?' he kept asking. I had no idea, except that I rather liked the alliteration.

'What kind of person writes such a thing?' he said, fuming. 'Can't you see how wrong it is?' He told me to scrub it off with soap and a nailbrush. I managed to remove much of it, but there was nothing I could do about the faint outline of GELDOF IS GOD that refused to come off, offending my dad every time he walked into my room. One day, he came home with a new headboard and attached it to my bed. Then he ordered me to take down all my Boomtown Rats posters, even the one inside my wardrobe – the one that had a greasy splodge on Bob Geldof's lips.

'Why can't you like a pop group with female members?' he demanded.

'What, you want me to put up posters of ABBA?'

'Certainly not, that group has two men in it.'

On his way out of the room, he issued one last instruction: 'You are not to write to The Boomtown Rats fan club ever again.' Having joined the fan club, I regularly received newsletters with pages of interviews with 'The Rats', dates for their forthcoming gigs (not that I was ever allowed to go to any) and coupons for Rats merchandise. Now I was robbed of even that small pleasure.

Wednesday 21 November 1979: *'Dad has forbidden me to write any letters to The Boomtown Rats fan club. Why doesn't Dad understand? He really is not reasonable. It is only a sport and something I like doing. How can it ever get me into trouble? It's not like I'm going to get pregnant just writing to the Rats. Why doesn't he understand? Why?'*

Well, he could stop me writing to The Boomtown Rats and he could make me take my posters down, but he couldn't stop me listening to their records with the volume turned up (when he and Mum were out of the house, of course). Just as an individual needs only one good teacher to change their world, I only needed one good band. The cover of their first album is a picture of Bob Geldof trying to get out of a plastic bag. It resonated with me. But, more than that, it was the lyrics to *Lookin' After No. 1* that pulled at something within me:

I am an island
Entire of myself

And when I get old, older than today
I'll never need anybody's help in any way.

I loved my parents, but I had no desire to be like them:

Don't wanna be like you.
Don't wanna live like you.
Don't wanna talk like you, at all.

It was the first time I had thought about being something other than an appendage of my parents. And it seemed to me that Bob Geldof, with his angry voice roaring out of the speakers, was trying to tell me, and a million other teenagers like me, something we all needed to hear:

I'm gonna be like
I'm gonna be like
I'm gonna be like ME!

Had it not been for the uproar that Geldof caused in our house, I might never have thought about god seriously. Vin would lie in bed every night saying prayers in her head for what seemed like a lifetime. I would lie in the darkness wondering who she was silently talking to, and waiting for her to finish. Eventually, I would become impatient and start the conversation with a whisper. 'Hey, Vin.'

'What?'

'Have you finished praying?'

'No, I've only got up to the "Bless *nanna* and *nanni*" bit.'

Minutes later: 'Hey, Vin.'

'Shut up. I haven't finished. How come your prayers finish so quickly? Are you actually saying any prayers?'

I did not pray, not only because I wasn't sure which god I was supposed to be praying to, but because I didn't know *how* to pray. I thought praying was a list of things you wanted to get done. 'Dear god, please let me pass my maths exam. Please let Mum be in a good mood tomorrow. Please let me somehow meet Bob Geldof. Thanks, amen.'

Once, I did the thing you're never supposed to do, ever. I tested god. 'Dear god, I'm praying because Vin told me to. If you're really there, could you please leave £10 under my pillow? Thanks, amen.'

He never listened to any of my prayers, so I didn't bother with them. But I didn't let Vin know.

'I've said mine,' I told her. 'I just say them quickly. I don't go on and on, boring god like you do.'

'Liar.'

We decided to put in place a system to officially stop prayer interruption. Once a person had finished, they would give a signal, which in our case was the word 'ding-dong', sung softly like a doorbell. Needless to say, I was the one ringing the doorbell all night. Most nights Vin fell asleep mid-prayer and I'd lie awake wondering how to make myself white or whether I should starve for a husband.

I figured I didn't have the constitution required to be a believer. If god was really there, why did he make me an Indian living in Britain? I could have handled being an Indian in India or a Brit living in Britain, but an Indian living in Britain? Hadn't he heard of culture clash?

Vin joined Archdeacon Cambridge's school a year after me,

along with a handful of other Indian enrolments. Twickenham had a relatively small Indian community, unlike Southall in west London, where it was becoming increasingly difficult to spot a white face. I didn't play with the other Indian kids. I didn't think they were very cool. There was a Sikh boy called Balka. Too young to wear a turban, his mum would twist his long hair into a tidy knot on the top of his head and wrap a white hanky around it, using a rubber band to hold it in place, the way grannies put a rubber band around a piece of material on the lid of homemade jam. Poor kid. Some of the English children said he kept his lunch under the hanky, but he didn't. He used to have school dinners like the rest of us.

I was an observer rather than a participant at school, always peering out of my face. I spoke English and Punjabi fluently, but had no historical perspective on England or India. Somewhere in the cultural moshpit, I was scrambling around on the floor looking for the basic building blocks of myself while everyone else, confident in their skin, was getting on with their lives and having a great time to the music.

God provided no anchor. I didn't buy the spin. That left me with no hook on which to hang my coat. I was adrift, unable to find, define or refine whatever I was searching for. I had two heads – one for my Western friends and one for my family, yet both joined together on one body. I was a human Y, constantly popping into one or other head. A girl at school asked me, 'When you think in your head, do you think in English or Indian?'

Good question, but I did not know how to tell her about my two heads, my East and my West, my twin unbelongings, and, in between, the great gulf into which I was always falling, falling, falling.

CHAPTER 5

Fraternising with Undesirable Elements

'Ek jhooth chipaanay kay liye, dus jhooth bolnay padatay hain.'
(Translation: You have to tell ten lies to cover the first lie.) Indian proverb

It was a regular Sunday night. Dad was ironing on the floor again, using several folded sheets to protect the carpet. I have no idea why we didn't have an ironing board like normal people. Mum was in the kitchen making cheese and mango-pickle sandwiches for his lunch the following day. If she added a few slivers of onion to his sandwich, she would slip a couple of mints into his lunchbox too. Best to have fresh breath, even though your suit smells of curry.

Vin and Raja were watching TV when they were meant to be doing their homework. It wasn't a picture of domestic bliss, but there was at least a semblance of familial harmony, with everyone occupied with matters of either comforting routine or relaxation. Except me. I was in my bedroom, frantically filling in my diary and fuming at all the injustice in the world. But, more importantly, I was hatching a cunning plan to get out of the house that Friday evening so I could go to the pub with my friends from college.

I had finished secondary school at the age of sixteen with a clutch of respectable grades in my exams, and was continuing my studies at Richmond upon Thames College, a sixth-form college around the corner from our house. This seemed a natural progression, as I intended to keep studying until I had a degree. The longer I studied, the further away the dreaded arranged marriage seemed. I was eighteen years old and considered myself mature enough to go to the pub, as did the law. But I was a daughter whose status had not yet been upgraded from unmarried girl to married woman, which meant I was still subject to the rules of my father's house. And according to his rules, a young girl drinking alcohol in a pub in the company of men was totally unacceptable and strictly prohibited. That's why I needed a plan. I put away my diary and went to speak to my dad.

'Dad.'

'Yes.'

'Some of my friends from college are going to see a play next Friday. It's at the theatre in Richmond. I'd be back before eleven o'clock . . .'

'Why do you need to go to the theatre *again*?'

'Just for entertainment.'

'What is the purpose of entertainment?'

'To enjoy yourself?'

'Finish your studies first. You have the rest of your life for entertainment after that.'

'But Daa-aad,' I whined. 'What's wrong with entertainment? Everyone needs to go out from time to time.'

'That is all you ever want to do: get out of this house. Who else is going?'

'A group of my friends from college.'

'Will there be any undesirable element?' This was my dad's reference to boys.

'No, it's just girls.'

He was pushing the nose of the iron into the awkward corners of the shirt with unnecessary force. There was an excruciating silence before he spoke.

'What are their names?

'It's just going to be me, Clare, Kathy and Fiona.' I didn't mention Dan and Paul and John.

The plan was going well, I thought. The interrogation suggested there was a possibility he might give me permission to go. Better than an outright refusal.

'Why do you insist on making these unreasonable demands?' he said, putting down the iron. 'Why do you have to go out all the time? It's too much for your mother. She can't bear it. We are sick of your lying.'

'But I'm not lying,' I lied, raising my voice.

'Watch your tone. I am your father, show some respect. Your non-stop demands to go out are hurting your mother. She is not strong. Why are you killing her like this?'

'I am not killing anyone,' I cried. 'I just want to go to the theatre with my girlfriends. Why is that too much to ask? You never let me go out. You never let me go anywhere.'

'Have you finish the irrening?' yelled Mum from the kitchen, making her presence felt without entering the room. She received no reply.

'Enough,' snapped Dad.

'So, can I go?'

'No.'

'But Dad . . .'

'I said no.'

I had lied one too many times in the past – and been caught out. I was as convincing as a used-car salesman. My lies weren't always watertight. I was rarely home by the time I said I would be. If I phoned home mid-evening, Madonna at top volume or the sound of clanking pint glasses suggested I wasn't where I'd said I would be, and I could never truly hide the smell of cigarettes in my clothes or the watery look in my eyes as I staggered through the front door. It was a relief to come home when Mum and Dad had already gone to bed. But there were nights when the lights would still be on and they would be waiting for me, armed with the dreaded question: 'Where have you been?'

I would repeat the lie I had told them before I went out. They would demand answers: 'What time did the play start? What time did it end? How did you get from the theatre to the station?' Sometimes the questions were too tricky for me to handle. 'If the play finished at nine forty-five and the train left at ten o'clock, as you say, you should have been home by eleven o'clock at the latest. It is now half-past midnight. Where have you been all this time?'

After too many vodka and tonics, it can be exceedingly difficult to answer such questions with any degree of accuracy, especially when the questions are fired at you faster than your brain can think. Invariably, I would trip up and someone would start crying. Usually me. Exasperated, I would sometimes admit the truth – that I'd been to the pub and there had been boys present, and my parents' rage would boil over. There would be a horrible, dry lecture, and their voices would bury me like gravel being poured on my head from a tip truck.

Mum would start crying until she became stricken with hypertension or a migraine. Sometimes it would be palpitations and nausea. I once dared to suggest her sudden maladies were the tools of emotional blackmail to keep me in check, and was severely reprimanded for my cold-hearted insolence.

I was the cause of much unhappiness for my parents. Everything I wanted was anathema to them. Ours was a house of slamming doors, shouting people and wretched tears. So much time lost fighting.

I wasn't the only one who lied. Vin told lies too, just not as often as I did. On one occasion she said she was going to a friend's engagement party, where only girls would be present. She managed to get permission without a row. She had not been caught lying as often as I had, so she still had good behaviour credits in the bank. *And* she was Mum's favourite daughter. I know because Mum would put her arm around Vin's shoulders and say, '*This* is my favourite daughter.' Irrefutable evidence. I attributed Vin's favoured status to the fact that she had not been a constantly crying baby and her nappies hadn't needed drying in front of a paraffin heater because Mum had access to a washing line by the time she was born.

As requested by Dad, Vin wrote on a piece of paper the name of her betrothed friend, her telephone number and the address where the party was being held. Who knows where she was really going, but there were bound to be undesirable elements there.

About an hour after Vin had left, Dad picked up the piece of paper, put it in his pocket and said to me, 'Put your coat on.' Raja put his coat on too, but Dad insisted he stay home. Presumably wherever Dad and I were about to go was no place for a ten-year-old. The age gap between him and his older sisters meant he remained largely outside the day-to-day dramas in which Vin and I often became entangled.

Dad and I drove to the address in the neighbouring town of Teddington that Vin had given as her destination. I felt giddying unease and my adrenal glands started working overtime. I was a spy's accomplice.

When we arrived, Dad parked the car on the other side of the road and we both stared at the house in horror. The windows were boarded up and there was a cracked glass panel in the front door. Weeds were trying to climb out of the garden and one hinge held the gate in place. Looking past the skip of old bricks and rubble that stood outside, we could see there were no lights on in the house.

Dad turned the key in the ignition and we drove home in frightening silence. Of all the addresses in Teddington, Vin had picked a half-dilapidated house in which to pretend she was attending a respectable, all-girl engagement party. I quickly tried to think of a plan that might help her explain her lie, but I couldn't get past my first thought: 'Shit, shit, shit.'

When Vin returned, Dad led her into the living room. I followed, chewing my nails.

'How was the engagement party?' he inquired calmly.

'Great,' she replied.

'What was the house like?'

'It was a normal two-up, two-down.'

'Was there anything unusual about it?' Dad persisted. Vin darted a look at me. I tried to indicate with my frozen face that she was in big trouble – big, you-totally-fucked-this-one-up, trouble.

'No,' she said.

'You didn't see a skip outside? Windows and doors boarded up?' asked Dad with a tone that suggested he was on the cusp of nailing her.

'A skip?' she said without hesitation. 'Oh yeah, there was a skip outside the house next door.'

'But this piece of paper,' said Dad, pulling it out of his pocket and unfolding it. Vin grabbed it out of his hands and looked at it briefly.

'Oops, sorry, I wrote 28 Manor Road. I meant 26,' she said, smiling apologetically. 'Anyway, how do *you* know there was a skip outside the neighbour's house?'

Checkmate. Later that evening, as we climbed into our beds, I asked Vin, 'So where did you really go?'

'None of your business,' she snapped and turned off the lamp.

Leaving the house for any form of teenage fun necessitated military planning: documentation recording our whereabouts and carefully crafted timetables giving arrival and departure times had to be submitted to Dad. For our own benefit, a contingency plan was always a good idea, or at least the mental agility to effect an adroit move at short notice if circumstances required.

Dad had an in-built radar that was constantly scanning for the presence of undesirable elements. So Vin and I frequently operated under the radar, using covert means and secret rendezvous. But even then Dad was able to outfox us by introducing bizarre bans, outlawing activities that our peers took for granted – like going to the local pool.

> Wednesday 5 August, 1981: *'Dad said that Mum was not to take us swimming. He thinks it's indecent for grown girls like Vin and I to parade around in swimsuits. He thinks Indian men might be there. BIG DEAL.'*

Even within the house there were rules to obey and standards to maintain. Take off that make-up, you are still a child. Don't loll in the doorway with your arms akimbo. Do you know what kind of women stand in doorways like that? Don't stomp around the house in shoes, wear slippers. Your jeans are too tight. Go to your bedroom and put on your Indian clothes. Don't wear your hair loose, it is a sign of mourning in our culture. Tie it up. Why are all your clothes black? That skirt is too short. It's cold outside, put on a longer one. Don't bite your nails. Who was that on the phone?

Despite our parents' strictness, we managed to satisfy our desires for a social life by lying, thatching over our lies when the rain came in and covering for each other when necessary. When a person is unjustly imprisoned, I thought, any means to escape is acceptable, as long as one's means are not found out, which would explain why the first page of my 1983 diary states:

'There is no harm in deceiving society as long as she does not find you out, because it is only when she finds you out that you have harmed her; she is not like a friend or God, who are injured by the mere existence of unfaithfulness.'

E. M. Forster (A Passage to India)

There is a direct proportional relationship between the elaborateness of the lie and the desperation with which one wishes to achieve a particular outcome through deception. For me, the obstacles to achieving the simplest of outcomes were many and I developed a James Bond-like ingenuity to overcome them.

During term breaks I could not leave the house without having to account for my every move. Conveniently, my college was a one minute walk from our house. Inconveniently, Dad's office was not much further away. During his lunch hour he would sometimes come home, and if I wasn't there, I would have to explain where I was. On other days he would ring the house at random times, and if I didn't answer, I would have to explain where I had been when he returned from work.

In those days the telephone, an old-style ring-ring phone with a dial, sat on a highly polished wooden cabinet in the dining room. At the back of the phone was a small protruding shelf. Occasionally, while Mum and Dad were at work, I would leave the house for a couple of hours at a time to catch up with friends or go shopping or see a movie with a girlfriend. Had I told Dad where I was going, or what I was doing, it was sure to have necessitated a great deal of paperwork pertaining to my movements, and possibly a row, so I didn't bother.

Instead, I would place a small amount of talcum powder (very useful stuff, talcum powder) on the small shelf at the back of the phone. If the phone rang, the vibrations would knock some of the talc onto the surface of the polished cabinet. I would note the time I left the house and the time I returned. If there was talc on the cabinet when I came back, I'd know Dad had probably been ringing to check up on me. So when he came back from work at the end of the day, I would lend credibility to my lie by anticipating his questioning.

'Dad, did you call this afternoon? I think it was some time between two and four o'clock?'

'Yes.'

'Oh, sorry I didn't answer. I was in the garden hanging out the washing. When I came in, I heard the ringing, but it stopped.'

Being able to narrow the window of time to a mere two hours was the key. Remarkably successful though this tactic was, I could use it only sparingly.

On one occasion I tried a new tactic, with spectacularly unsuccessful results. It was a few days after one of my mum's malady incidents. My waywardness had prompted a ferocious row and the rapid onset of a migraine, the mischief being that I had lied about my whereabouts again and gone to the pub with my friends. Although commonsense suggested Mum would want to lie down in a dark room and stay quiet, her behaviour was inexplicably hysterical. She was crying and hollering, almost ululating at one stage. She appeared to have become completely unglued.

In my dad's *Reader's Digest Family Health Guide and Medical Encyclopedia*, I had read that hysteria could be quelled by a firm slap across the face, followed by a reassuring hug. So I grabbed her by the shoulders and brought my right hand down firmly across her face. I thought she'd thank me for it. Instead, she stared at me in shock as if I had killed an innocent child. I attempted to draw her close to me to deliver the 'reassuring hug', but she pushed me away as though I was the devil and wailed even more loudly.

I'm no medical expert but I suggest the administration of such treatment is more likely to leave the practitioner with a bad case of shock and hysteria, rather than cure the patient. I thought I was doing the right thing, but what I had in fact done was slap my mum, really hard. Nobody in the family believed me when I said I was trying to treat her hysteria. They thought it was the 'real me' taking revenge for not being allowed to go to the pub. Vin has dined out on that little incident for years. 'Remember that time when you slapped Mum? You idiot.'

For days, if not weeks, I felt ghastly about what I had done. I vowed never to lie about my whereabouts again – after all, that is what had started the migraine in the first place. I promised myself I would never say I was working late in the library when in fact I was at the pub; promised I would never say I was at Kathy's house when in fact I was at the pub.

A few days after the slap, I told Dad, with an invigorated boldness, that I was going to the pub with my friends on Friday evening. His answer was swift and wounding: 'No, you are not. You must remember to maintain the honour of an Indian girl. You are the eldest and therefore must set a good example to your brother and sister. You can go to the pub when you are married.'

Dad was a master of bringing things to a close with a brutally executed 'No.' He knew how to kill fun. He could flatten frivolity in one sweep. If decorum broke down at the dining table, the place we were meant to talk about serious things like politics, it was his job to restore equilibrium. If a bout of childish, unstoppable giggling broke out, he knew exactly how to handle it. First, he'd always allow a few minutes of laughter.

'Okay, that's enough,' he'd then say. Vin and I would continue giggling.

'I said enough.' If that didn't work, and sometimes it didn't, he'd get serious. Very serious. 'Laugh, go on laugh. Laugh to your heart's content while you are living under your father's roof. Because once you are gone from this place, you won't be laughing so much.' His words were enough to bring us hurtling back to reality.

If Dad was the disciplinarian, Mum was the keeper of the moral code. She would lecture me endlessly in Punjabi about the role of women, the duty of daughters, the responsibility of the eldest child and the biggest, heaviest, most profound topic of all, *izzat* – family honour. She always lectured me as she performed her domestic duties, often when she was chopping onions. That way the whole lecture could be delivered as part of her daily chores. To her, life lessons were meant to be passed on as a matter of routine, not a special event where you sat together, made eye contact and talked woman to woman. Perhaps her mother had once delivered the same lecture as she milked a buffalo somewhere in rural India.

English being my first language, there were times when I didn't understand the words she used or the poetry of her Punjabi proverbs. I absorbed the meaning of those parts of the lecture from her cadence. Once she started, it was almost impossible to find a natural break in her monologue, a suitable pause, where one might politely ask to be excused.

'You are my eldest daughter,' she would start, 'the product

of my first love, a fragment of myself. Your father and I have worked hard to feed all three of you children, clothe you, educate you. Look at your father – how hard he works. Without him this family would be nothing. I work my fingers to the bone. Feel how rough the skin is on my fingertips. We ask nothing from our children but to respect us and protect our family's *izzat*. Your father's father was a wise man with a very high standing in his community. Your father is also greatly respected. He is a learned man and many in our community come to him for advice and guidance. It's important to maintain our standing. Never take any action that will bring your father's good name into disrepute. Remember, no one ever gets lost following a straight path. A girl can bring ruin to a house. Ruin for herself and for her family. Look how some girls behave, how they have ruined everything. We don't want our family to be like that.

'When I was a young girl, out of sheer respect, I never looked directly into my own father's eyes. He was a strict man, but it was for my own good. Parents know best. Your father and I wish for nothing more than happiness for all our children. Live long. No matter where you end up in this world we hope you will always be happy. I hope god bestows all my children with good health, prosperity and happiness, and never lets any harm come to any of them.

'It won't be long before you and your sister leave this house to make your own homes elsewhere. There comes a time in every girl's life when she must marry and look after her own home. A holy man might perform your marriage ceremony, but he won't manage your house for you. That is your duty. Remember, if you love your husband with your whole heart and respect him, he will always return your love. Before you know it, the responsibilities of motherhood will be upon you, and then you will learn the true meaning of sacrifice. This is a woman's lot. Look at me – I sacrificed everything. I was only eighteen years old when I married your father. I was nineteen when you were born. I was just a girl. What has been my life? It has hardly been a life at all. This is my destiny. But what else is there? All you can do is work hard, live for your children, serve your husband. That is all.

'What I am saying may not mean much to you now, but one day you will remember your mother's words. Never forget: your family's *izzat* always comes first. Don't bring shame on this family. Your father would never be able to hold his head up high. People would taunt us, accuse us of losing control over our children. Please, I beg you, please remember there is nothing, nothing more important in life than maintaining your family's *izzat*.'

By now she would be weeping small fitful sobs of sadness, grieving over the loss of her own youth, her onion tears mixed with her real tears. I was helpless – unable to offer hope, comfort or cheer. Dispirited by her melancholy and discomfited by my own uselessness, I would inch backwards towards the kitchen door and simply acknowledge her misery: 'Okay, Mum.' And then I would take my leave.

Izzat is a multi-layered concept that can mean several different things: honour, self-respect, reputation, even virginity. The whole idea is laced with male pride. It is the pivot on which Punjabi family life spins, and women's behaviour can hurt or destroy *izzat* more than anything else. Ultimately, any unconventional behaviour by a woman can pose a very real danger to her family. A family without a good reputation is liable to be ostracised or cut off from the rest of the community. Indeed, *izzat* is not just a Punjabi or Indian concept. The broader idea of reputation is a powerful controlling force that can be found across Asia.

In Indian communities, particularly among Punjabis, a woman can bring shame on her family by doing things that are considered quite acceptable in Western societies today. She can do it by drinking alcohol, smoking, wearing make-up, fraternising with men, dressing immodestly, getting pregnant out of wedlock, marrying below her station or rejecting an arranged marriage for a love marriage to a man her parents consider unacceptable. If a woman has hurt her family's *izzat*, the family can redeem itself by making her an outcast. This can take the form of disowning a daughter – literally casting her out of the house or, in extreme cases, killing her.

At the time of writing the last honour killing recorded by British newspapers was that of Amrit Ubhi, a twenty-four-year-old Sikh girl who was murdered in 2010 by her father in Telford, Shropshire, because he could not accept her Western lifestyle. Her boyfriend was a British soldier. Her father, Gurmeet Singh Ubhi, was sentenced to fifteen years in jail. He claimed he had only applied 'minimal pressure' to her neck after they rowed about her playing music too loud.

The idea of *izzat* is entrenched in customs that some Indians have practised for hundreds of years. These days it may only be peasant communities (although not always) that follow these customs with unbending strictness, but the long shadow cast by centuries-old ideas falls unmistakably on Indians everywhere, including those living in Western countries.

These days India's economy is on speed. Its eye-popping growth rate has been accompanied by brisk modernisation that has allowed women into the workforce in ever larger numbers. They have greater representation in parliament and the business world, and many more attend universities now. But, still, the old-fashioned idea of female modesty runs deep in this patriarchal society. Even within the world of Bollywood, which is no stranger to liberal concepts, movies do not show a full kiss on the mouth. There may be erotic wet-sari scenes and bared midriffs, but there will always be some representation of female piety and modesty. Nor has the idea been diluted within the Indian diaspora. In London, Vancouver, Durban, Dubai, Melbourne, or any other part of the world where Indians have settled, female modesty remains paramount.

And it is worth noting that female modesty and the behaviour expected of women are not imposed and controlled entirely by men. They are also perpetuated, nurtured and policed by women themselves.

For Punjabis, where there is *izzat*, there are *dhanē* (taunts to insult and humiliate). Roger Ballard, a British anthropologist and expert in emigration from Punjab, argues that women, who do not have the brute force of men, have developed *dhanē* to a fine art and use them as verbal weapons. Punjabi women are often very skilled at delivering *dhanē* enclosed in *double entendres*, he says. Insulting taunts may seem harmless enough, but their power should not be underestimated. Taunts are not only directed at women in order to keep their behaviour in check, they are also fired at parents who fail to keep their daughters under control. The psychological impact on those subjected to taunts, especially in a close-knit community, can be devastating, and in some families it might become a matter of life and death. Ballard identifies *dhanē* as a distinctive feature in cases of honour killings.

My parents were deeply fearful of *dhanē* from the Indian community. I understood their wish – that the daughters of the house were seen to be doing the right thing to avoid a reputational calamity befalling our family. But, foolishly perhaps, I believed I could negotiate a path where I could please my parents by being a good Indian girl and simultaneously enjoy the freedoms that a Western lifestyle had to offer. It might have made sense to work out first how I was actually going to achieve such a balance. But immaturity, that great provider of optimism, led me to believe that while there was a big gap between the Indian and Western way of life, each was only one leap away from the other and one could conceivably spend one's life alternating between the two. The only problem was undesirable elements.

If Dad could have had his way, he would have banned boys from phoning the house or being within a one-kilometre radius of either of his daughters. In his mind's eye, any period of time Vin and I spent outside the house was time that we were vulnerable to the hordes of men who were presumably waiting to leap out from behind lampposts to lead us astray. Or was it we girls who might lead them astray?

Dad strongly objected to me wearing red clothes, which suggests he thought women had the power to ruin men. 'Red is the marriage colour. It attracts the eye,' he said. Somewhere, rattling around in his head, was the ancient idea that women were born of Eve. And taking his logic to its final end, a woman could, even without being aware of it herself, drive a man into a wild sexual frenzy beyond his control. We were all just animals – the females unconsciously sending out mating signals, as the males, to whose behaviour could be attached no moral or immoral value, simply responded instinctively. Why, on top of this precarious scenario built by nature, would a girl want to place herself in the path of danger by wearing that most lewd, eye-catching and lurid of all colours?

I was ordered to stay away from red clothes. But, being a teenager, it was my duty to engage in gross acts of defiance. In the heart of Twickenham was a school uniform shop called Len Smiths. There I found a bright-red blazer worn by the pupils of a school in the vicinity. It was far too small for me but it was the only red one they had, so I bought it and wore it around the house for several weeks.

Strangely, Dad didn't say anything, although Mum was keen to know why I was wearing an ill-fitting blazer belonging to a school I did not attend. Dad lost that battle. But my victories were short-lived. He generally won any fight relating to the telephone. Whenever the phone rang, it was usually one of my friends – a female friend, because male friends had been told not to call me in the evenings when my parents were likely to answer, as this could land me in a spot of bother. And there had been many spots of bother. If male friends ever dared to call, Dad immediately told them I was either out, asleep, too ill to come to the phone, in the bathroom or simply unavailable. I found out about their calls days later from them.

If a call from a boy was an offence of the most grievous kind, then a boy discovered *in* the house would take on the gravity of a major diplomatic incident.

Richmond upon Thames College had a reputation for being an 'arty' sixth-form college. Many of the students were the sons and daughters of parents who were politically active, socially aware and well educated. Many had connections that stretched into political, media or academic networks. The group of young people that I fell in with took great interest in art, music and literature. They were witty, sarcastic and cynical. They opened doors to other worlds for me and I longed to be like them.

The days of unchecked racism that had roamed my schoolyard had been buried and multiculturalism was all the rage, particularly among the kids of the metropolitan middle class who became my friends. I was entirely comfortable in their company but nonetheless felt myself to be an outsider in the group since I couldn't join them in activities such as film-making at weekends, seeing live bands or going to the theatre. Despite my dad's pressure to consider studying the sciences in the hope that I might become a doctor, I had veered firmly in the direction of the arts, much to his disappointment. 'Don't come home one day and tell me you want to be a poet,' he warned. 'There's no money in poetry.'

It didn't take long before I fell in love. Paul was the drummer in a band. He had long mousey hair that fell around his shoulders and a generous mouth that never smiled, only grinned. He rode a bike he called Ulysses, and wore paint-stained dungarees to college nearly every day. I thought he was the bee's knees.

Under no circumstances would Dad have approved of me dating a boy, let alone one who dressed like a hippie and played the drums. Paul would have been, in my dad's eyes, the antithesis of the very idea of a man. So when Paul and I started a relationship, it became my big secret. I didn't even tell Vin. I followed him to band practice, fawned over his poetry and generally behaved like a lovesick fool. He sang me songs, invited me to his house and borrowed my money without returning it. There are pages and pages in my diaries devoted to the celebration of anything and everything Paul-related.

Many of my college friends played musical instruments, even the economics students. Take John, an intelligent fellow with a dry mop of blond hair, who wore a pinstriped navy jacket with jeans – a look that was neither here nor there. He played the trumpet and had an obsession with Miró. Economics classes were the ones I missed most frequently, but living around the corner from the college was handy. John would pop round and leave me his notes if I missed a class.

After five months of college life I decided it would be an interesting experiment to see how Dad and Paul got along. I was certain that the last thing Paul wanted was to meet my scary dad, and Dad most certainly would not have been interested in meeting anyone called Paul. Paula maybe, but not Paul. Nonetheless, against my better judgment I decided to bring them together, and the only reason I can offer for such a monumentally stupid act is, of course, faithfully recorded:

> Thursday 3 February, 1983: *'I'm sure if they did meet and perhaps talk, some barriers would be broken. Perhaps Paul and my father would become more understanding. Well, I shall see how it goes tomorrow. I'm confident for a change! Bought some flowers for my mother, just to be nice, but she did not notice them.'*

I asked Paul to come to the house to hang out at one o'clock the following day. Dad would almost certainly leave the office and come home for lunch around that time and both would conveniently bump into each other. So that Dad didn't get an unexpected shock from an undesirable element in the house, I would ring him in the morning to warn him that a fellow student called Paul would be popping by around lunchtime to pick up some study notes.

As it happened, it was *I* who in fact needed some study notes because I'd missed a recent economics class. Good old John offered to pop by the house at eleven the next morning to drop them off. So I had it all planned: get the notes from John in the morning, Paul and Dad to meet at lunchtime.

Now, life is a slippery thing. Chance meetings can't be prearranged and prearranged meetings can turn into most unfortunate coincidences. Unpredictable things sometimes happen when East and West meet. Everything I had planned so carefully for that Friday went frighteningly wrong. It was as if Lucifer himself was in the house, intent on causing unforgettable mayhem.

John, who was supposed to drop by with the notes at eleven, was late. He didn't arrive till midday. He had time to kill before his next class and was angling for a cup of tea. It would have been rude not to accommodate him – he had after all been kind enough to give me his notes. So we made a cup of tea and chatted in the living room, where he pulled out a cigarette and asked if I minded him smoking. Not wanting to sound prudish or unworldly, I waved a dismissive hand and said, 'Of course you can. I'll get you an ashtray.'

Nobody in our family smoked, so all I could find was a saucer from Mum's 'special' tea set, which I brought into the living room and placed on the coffee table. I watched him light a cigarette and the smoke immediately invaded the homey air of my parent's living room. By the time the clock had clicked around to a quarter to one I was beginning to feel anxious about how to get rid of him so that Paul and Dad could have their chance meeting. But before I had time to think about a plan within a plan, I saw through the living room window Dad's car pulling up outside the house. He was fifteen minutes early! That's when I realised I had forgotten to call him that morning to warn him about Paul, who was allegedly popping round to pick up my notes.

I suddenly felt sick, and it wasn't just the smoke that was making me nauseous – the smoke that was seeping its way into Mum's curtains and carpet with the speed and vehemence that only cigarette fumes can. I looked at John and said urgently, 'John, you're about to meet my dad.'

Having heard some frightening stories about my dad's strictness and his hatred for alcohol, cigarettes and boys, John instantly reached for the saucer to hide it. 'Leave it,' I said abruptly, like a housewife issuing an order to her hen-pecked husband. As Dad approached the front door I saw him look at John through the bay window. His brow tightened and his face took on a fearsome expression. I opened the front door for him and he gave me an arctic stare, his nostrils flaring and the whites of his eyes suddenly more visible. Without a word he marched into the living room, threw open the windows and turned to face John.

'Good afternoon,' he said tersely.

'Good afternoon, Mr Das,' replied John, his cigarette quivering between his fingers as he reached forward to put it out on Mum's saucer.

Fresh air blew in through the window. John's face was so red I thought he was holding his breath. Dad sat down on the chair furthest from him and rustled noisily through the pages of the *Guardian* till he found the page he wanted. John watched him as I collected the teacups and made a cowardly escape into the kitchen. Dad started a conversation about university and I heard them talking in short, tight sentences. Holy mother of god, I thought, Dad is meeting the wrong guy!

When I returned, both men fell silent. I stood frozen, wondering what to do, when suddenly I saw a sight through the window that made my bones tremble. It was Paul walking up the garden path to the front door. I felt suddenly winded as if I had been slammed in the stomach with a hefty swing of a rounders' bat. There was a corresponding sharp pain in my chest and I wondered if I was having a cardiac arrest. It was going to be hard enough explaining to Dad what John was doing in the living room, let alone trying to explain why Paul had arrived too. Not to mention how I was going to explain to Paul why I was introducing John to my Dad.

I rushed to the front door to shoo Paul away before he rang the doorbell. Dad was disgusted enough with one undesirable element in his house. Two would be unconscionable, if not downright immoral. I flung open the front door and started waving my arms around like a fishwife.

'Go, just go,' I hissed. 'Quick, just go. Just . . .' I turned around to find Dad standing in the hallway staring at me. Momentarily the world fell away. I was looking at Dad through a tunnel and I felt rising within me a sense of impending universal doom. Dad glared at the long-haired lout in his front garden and said to me, 'He was coming into the house too, was he?'

'No, I was just passing,' said Paul limply. What, passing up the garden path? A likely story, lad, I thought, trying to mimic and thereby preempt Dad's thoughts.

Paul left, closing the gate behind him, and Dad followed me back into the living room, where John was sitting with an expression only an executioner could have seen on a man's face before. I picked up my bag and said, 'I've got to go – I've got a class.' John hastily reached for his bag too.

'He can go,' said Dad, nodding towards John. '*You*, Sushila, sit down. I want to talk to you.'

After John had gone, Dad delivered the mother of all lectures. What kind of girl was I? How indecent. How immoral. How disgusting to have one man in the house – smoking, if you please – while another knocked at the door. What did I think I was doing? The shame and ruin I was bringing on our household. What debauched and sinful things was I allowing to happen under my father's own roof? Had I no decency? No decency at all?

Had it not been for the fact that Dad had to go back to work, the lecture may never have ended. I felt crushed. There would be no reprieve. I had lost my father's trust, probably forever, and possibly even his love. What a disaster. My attempt to engineer a meeting between Dad and Paul in the hope that they might like each other had turned into a scene from the B-grade movie that was my pathetic life. *He* was an angry father on the brink. *They* were unsuspecting boys caught in the middle. *She* was a harlot on a mission. *Undesirable Elements* – coming to cinema near you.

CHAPTER 6

Searching for a Suitable Boy

'Remember, as far as anyone knows, we're a nice normal family.'
***Homer Simpson,* The Simpsons**

On Thursday 9 June, 1983, I voted in a parliamentary election for the first time. The Conservatives, under Margaret Thatcher, won by a landslide, while the Labour Party flopped around. Voting confirmed I was a grown-up now, but that triumph was at odds with my status in my parents' house, where I was still an unmarried girl and expected to 'eat with the kids' when relatives or other visitors came to our house.

I have no idea how anybody in my family voted. Dad, who I'm sure always *told* Mum who to vote for, kept his own intentions strictly confidential. Voting was a private business, he said. A bit like Hot Chocolate's tax affairs.

My uncle declared he would vote for the National Front.

'The National Front?' I screeched, shocked that anybody in my family would even consider voting for a far-right group of extremists. 'Why would you vote for a bunch of ugly racists?'

'Because I want to go home,' he grinned.

Then again, migrants do often drift right of centre, usually once they are firmly embedded within stage three of culture shock: reconciliation. That's around the time they stop being grateful for being given a chance to start a fresh life in a new country (I'm not suggesting they ought to be grateful) and start espousing incomprehensible views about the unsuitability of more migrants like themselves being allowed in. My mum can be like that.

'The government should stop any more Indians coming into this country,' she once said.

'Why?' I asked, incredulous. 'It's Britain's migration policy that allowed you to come here and build your life.'

'Yes, I know,' she replied. 'But too many Indians are moving into Twickenham now and they are bringing down the price of our house.'

Margaret Thatcher talked a lot about reducing the role of government, rolling back the state and increasing individual self-reliance. It sounded very much like the message Bob Geldof had been yelling about: 'I am an island/Entire of myself/And when I get old, older than today/I'll never need anybody's help in any way.' He might not have wanted to roll back the state, but he was fighting to get out of a plastic bag and he wanted to be himself. He didn't want to rely on anyone else and that's what I wanted too.

But I couldn't leave the house without interrogation, a social life involving the pub was strictly out of bounds, boys weren't allowed to phone me and I couldn't risk letting them into the house – ever again. Meanwhile, my oestrogen levels were blasting off the Richter scale.

Brian Eno and Ziggy Stardust kept me company while I filled in my diary each night, frantically and pompously recording '*the injustices of my life*'. I filled my time reading books – anything and everything that came my way (a childhood fascination with fairytales, which fed my hunger for escapism, had morphed into a penchant for science fiction). All the while, I continued to lie, unconvincingly, about my whereabouts, creating havoc at home when I was found out. *'Oh, will Mum and Dad ever learn that I know how to look after myself!!'* I ranted in the diary. I couldn't bear it.

Things weren't going well on the boyfriend front either. Paul and I didn't last longer than about a year. A secret relationship is at first a breathless adventure full of electric winks, nods and double meanings, but latterly it becomes a tedious hindrance to a properly functioning existence. Paul's band, predictably, broke up, and so did we. He said he didn't love me anymore. His so-called love for me was a hitherto undeclared feature of our relationship, but I was nonetheless heartbroken. It was my first lesson in the fickle nature of men's interest and their constant hunt for fresh flesh.

Mum never knew about Paul, but she had her views on English men: 'These English boys, these *Angrez* boys, they go when they finish with the girl. Indian boys get marry. English people is different to us. English parents want to kick the children out of the house when the child reach eighteen. If the children stay, they pay the rent to the parents. *Hai hai*, they take rent from their own children! Indian parents, we don't do that.'

But the source of my deepest angst came not from my lost boyfriend or my parents' strictness, but something much worse:

the idea of my impending arranged marriage. It had been a slow-burning worry that had taken years to reach the point of extreme anxiety. At first, I only wondered about it, like we wonder what we want to do when we grow up. Then I started worrying about when it would happen and who would be chosen for me. These were underlying nervous worries, similar to the apprehension induced by living in the midst of a nuclear arms race. They were followed by an intense anxiety that filled my sleep with nightmares.

> Thursday 13 August, 1981: *'Slept very badly last night. Firstly, it was extremely hot, and secondly, Vin and I didn't get to sleep until half past one – we were chatting. Then to bring the night to a treacherous climax, I had a bad dream. My marriage was arranged at the age of 16 to an English boy – looking like Lady Diana's brother. Mum arranged it in a terrible hurry, I wasn't dressed properly for the occasion, and the main thing was, that I didn't want to get married at the age of 16. I thought it to be too young, I told dad, he listened, but was unable to do anything about it, because mum over-powered him tremendously. She was very excited about my wedding and was running around arranging things IN A HURRY. It was a horrible dream and it's been nagging me all day.'*

Even if my parents had been contemplating an underage marriage into British aristocracy, they still wouldn't have asked for my views on the topic. By the age of eighteen my anxiety had morphed into open panic. It made me sick to think about arranged marriages.

There was constant talk among my parents and my uncle and aunt about keeping children 'under control'. I came to believe that I was actually in a sort of prison; that my bedroom was a cell and my parents the wardens. Yet I had committed no crime. Well, only thought-crimes against my parents.

I spent unfathomable amounts of time trying to engineer an escape. Like algebra, the more I thought about it, the harder it got.

The core issue remained that I had to manage the escape without it blackening my family's reputation. It was too late to run away from home, and besides, it would have induced maximum shame. So that option was dead.

There were only two other choices I could see. One, I could marry a man of my parents' choosing, make them happy and live in misery for the rest of my life because I certainly could not see myself being a good Indian wife, serving my husband, bringing up children and fasting for the *Kurva Chauth* ceremony every year. I had plans for a career.

Two, I could marry a man I chose who my parents did not approve of, ruin my family's *izzat*, be potentially disowned by Mum and Dad and live happily ever after – sort of.

Neither option appealed. It was a stark choice and a horrid bind. But I could not see a third way. It was them or me. Sacrifice or selfishness. The family as a whole was a bigger entity and a larger force than me alone, so I was sure to lose. But I could never abide the thought of being the loser in the fight against an arranged marriage. These thoughts loped about, troubling my daytime dreaming and haunting my night hours.

'*My civil liberty has been curtailed!*' I thundered in the diary. '*I am a human being. I have a right to have a right.*'

My college friends listened kindly and patiently to my problems and suggested simplistic solutions: 'Just tell your dad you don't want an arranged marriage and move out.' But move out to where? And live on what? They didn't understand. I wasn't just looking for a way to get out of an arranged marriage. I was looking for a way to get out of it without my family losing face. It was the losing face part they didn't grasp, because they were Westerners and losing face is a wholly Asian concept. My friends knew more about getting *off* their face than they did about *saving* face. I put their somewhat glib suggestions down to a lack of knowledge about Indian culture. But I had no right to expect them to have the answers to my problems, and I was grateful they listened to me. Where once I might have turned to Vin for solace, I now turned to them.

Vin was still at secondary school, wearing a uniform. We no longer saw each other in the playground or shared school tittle-tattle. I now hung out with people who dyed their hair and talked about what was wrong with the system. Against my nascent sixth-form-college cynicism, Vin appeared young, wholesome, naïve and ever so slightly further away.

I don't know how I came across the National Council for Civil Liberties (now called Liberty). Maybe I picked up a leaflet at the library or saw a documentary on TV, or maybe I heard my college friends talking. I rang and was told they promoted the values of individual human dignity, equal treatment and fairness as foundations of a democratic society. They protected civil liberties and promoted human rights. Sounded good to me, so I made a donation and joined.

Making a donation, like voting for the first time, meant I could help to effect change. I had a say in something. I also joined Amnesty International and diligently wrote letters and postcards to brutal dictators around the world to pressure them to release political prisoners (something Amnesty International encouraged in those days). But there was no authority to whom I could write to lodge a complaint against migrant Asian parents who wanted to control the lives of their sons and daughters by putting them through archaic marriage practices. I had no power to stop the juggernaut that was gathering momentum and hurtling towards me.

Dad had been alert to news of a suitable boy for some time, but after a visit from my grandmother in India, he set about looking for a match with renewed vigour. Mum, who felt she had been robbed of a life of glamour and romance, seemed determined to derive vicarious pleasure through the search for a husband for me and by arranging my wedding.

We were in the pre-internet age and a potential spouse was identified through family and friends using word-of-mouth and usually a matchmaker or a neutral go-between. Should negotiations between two families break down or a match prove unacceptable, using a go-between could avoid accidental disrespect and offence being caused. Nowadays, urban Indians living in nuclear families lack the social reach once enjoyed by the extended family, and the internet has proved to be an excellent modern matchmaker. The Indian matchmaking website shaadi.com claims to be the largest matrimonial service in the world.

The criteria for a good match vary. If my parents could have provided a full and frank list of their demands, it might have read something like this:

AGE: groom must be a few years older, but not too much older than our daughter.

RELIGION: Hindu, or at least a believer in some sort of god. No atheists.

HEIGHT: must be taller than our daughter (i.e. more than 5 foot, 8 inches).

EDUCATION: must be educated to around the same level as our daughter or slightly more, but definitely not less.

WEALTH: income or family assets must be sufficient to support a wife and family comfortably.

CAREER: must be in a respectable profession, e.g. doctor, lawyer or civil servant. Poet, drummer in a band or ballet dancer are unacceptable.

FAMILY STATUS: groom's family must have a good reputation, with *izzat* intact. Professional and marital status of his siblings should also be sound.

ASTROLOGICAL ATTRIBUTES: groom's characteristics and destiny must be compatible. [An astrological reading that indicated a man was destined for, say, an early death or poverty, would be considered unacceptable.]

ANCESTRAL LINEAGE: groom must not be a blood relative.

PERSONAL HABITS: a moderate social drinker and meat eater is acceptable. A smoker is unacceptable.

IN-LAWS: ideally groom's parents should live in another country so that our daughter does not have to be subjected to the demands of a nasty mother-in-law, but will readily accept groom who lives with his parents if all other criteria are satisfied.

VALUES: liberal thinker would suit our Western-raised daughter, but groom should maintain traditional Indian values – even if our own daughter has gone off the rails.

My parents often lamented that Indian boys brought up in Britain had lost their 'Indianness'. They became too Western, chasing after pleasures of the flesh and wasting time drinking. They ran away from the responsibilities of manhood and failed in their duties as sons. In effect, they lost their Indian values. Boys brought up in India, on the other hand, were considered better value. They were uncorrupted. No additives. They always put the family first and respected their parents – or so my parents thought.

In Indian families, particularly those from northern India, there is a hierarchical structure, and people's behaviour towards each other is shaped by the position they hold in this hierarchy. In my family two brothers are married to two sisters. (My dad is the eldest brother in his family and my mum is the eldest sister in her family, so my uncle and my aunt form the younger pairing.)

In the hierarchy, older men outrank younger men (so my dad outranks my uncle). Men, in general, outrank younger women and those of a similar age (my uncle outranks my aunt, but he does not outrank my mum). Younger siblings must show deference to older siblings. They are often encouraged to address them by respectful terms for brother and sister, rather than their names. (My mum would frequently remind my younger sister and brother to refer to me as *didi*, an affectionate term for sister. Although both of them ignored this instruction, neither would dispute the fact that I am more senior than them in ranking.) A new bride holds the lowest position in the family hierarchy and answers directly to her mother-in-law.

India, we are constantly told, is the largest democracy in the world where everyone is entitled to a vote. But within the traditional Indian family, everyone does not have an equal say. Children are raised with the expectation that their parents will fix their marriages and they grow up learning to accept the authority of those ranked higher than them. This is also true for many Indians who live in other countries.

Members of a traditional joint family depend on each other for support. Family bonds are extremely strong as Indians are generally raised with the knowledge that they are part of a larger extended family, whose needs overshadow those of each individual. When people interact with each other, they pay close attention to hierarchy and this guides them on the level of respect, honour and obligation they need to show towards each other. Etiquette facilitates this: touching someone's feet connotes great respect, as does addressing them by adding *ji* to the end of their name, for example, Gandhi-ji.

Within this quite complex hierarchy, the relationship between a new bride and her mother-in-law, or *suss*, is interesting. Traditionally, a man brings his new wife home to live with him and his parents. If there are several brothers, all the daughters-in-law of a household are likely to become friends, although they would remain mindful of their position within the hierarchy, with the wife of the youngest brother at the bottom of the pile, and likely to be bossed about not only by her mother-in-law but by her older sisters-in-law too.

Whichever way you look at it, the new bride gets the worst deal. Her acceptance in the new household – indeed whether she will thrive or even survive – depends on how quickly she learns to become part of her husband's family. If she falters in her household duties, or in showing respect, she will be quickly yanked into line by her mother-in-law. If her mother-in-law is cruel towards her or over-burdens her with housework, her husband may not necessarily protect her or fight her corner, as his first loyalty is to his mother, not his wife. Throughout the ages, men have set up a framework that allows women to be controlled, but it is frequently women themselves who police this system.

Given the way things work within old-style Indian joint families and the challenges faced by migrants in Western countries, it's understandable that my mum thought finding a suitable match from India was better than taking a risk with an Indian boy raised in Britain. The boy from India would have several advantages: he would not have lost his Indian values to Western mores. My parents would be in a strengthened negotiating position vis-à-vis a dowry as they offered not only a bride but a chance for the groom to start a life in an advanced country too. And, crucially, once married he would permanently migrate to Britain, most likely leaving his parents behind in India and thus providing me, the new bride, an opportunity to be married to a man who came without his mother-in-law, or sans *suss*.

The sans *suss* issue is important because it gives daughters of Indian migrants an opportunity to embark on married life as the female head honcho in her own home, rather than living under the potential tyranny of a mother-in-law.

'A boy from India is the best. A doctor, god-willing,' said Mum. 'You will have no *suss* and no sisters-in-law living in your house. It will be only you and your husband and then you will have all the freedom.' This was my mum's definition of freedom. For her, it was a matter of persuading me to accept her logic. But in my attempts to persuade *her* to see things from my point of view, I found myself arguing against a boy from India, rather than against the arranged marriage itself.

In true Indian style, the help of the entire family was enlisted to coax me into accepting a boy from India: my *nanna* and *nanni*, and my uncle and aunt. They all ganged up against me. Vin, who witnessed the pressure mounting, could offer little advice. In the privacy of our bedroom I would rant and rave about the injustice of it all and she would sit silently, simply listening. What else could she have done? What wisdom could a younger sister impart? I could hardly expect her to go in and fight for me. No, I was on my own, so I did what I usually did. I turned to my diary.

> Sunday 20 March, 1983: *'I talked to my mother today for a long while – we spoke about the usual thing: arranged marriages. I have protested now for a very long time, that I shall put up every resistance to marrying a man from India. I believe his upbringing would be too different from mine for a happy and true kind of relationship to develop. We will have very different sets of values. Political differences can be borne, but things like ethical differences are very difficult to bear. I cannot even find an equilibrium with my father who has lived here almost 20 years, how will I find a middle life with a husband from a country like India?'*

My protestations were pointless. Mum dismissed me as 'worried for no reason'. She appeared to misunderstand everything I said.

'Mum, I'm not worried because I'm scared of getting married. I'm just saying I don't want a boy from India.'

'You don't need to trouble yourself with these things. Your father and I will look very carefully and find the right boy to suit you. You are our daughter. Of course we will find the right boy,' she said in Punjabi.

'There would be no boy in the whole of India who would be acceptable to me because I don't want to marry anyone from *India*.'

'Now that's just being silly and unreasonable. There are many, many boys – it doesn't make sense to say there would not be a single one in the whole country who would not be right for you.'

'For god's sake, Mum, are you doing this deliberately? Are you not understanding me on purpose? You're not listening to what I'm saying.'

'I've been listening to you for a long time. I've heard it all,' she said, abandoning a kindly tone and adopting a harsher pitch. 'We are not forcing you to do anything. How could you even dare to suggest that your own parents would take any action that would bring you harm? You are the eldest, don't forget that. It is *your* actions that can harm *us* – your parents, your family. You have a responsibility to your sister and your brother to do what is right for you and for them. It's not as simple as marrying whoever you want. This is not how it works. We will all do this together. The whole family will look for the right person, and we will find him. And, trust me, trust your mother, you will be happy. Just wait till you are married. You will see things differently then.'

I did not yet fully understand the complexities of Indian family life. I did not understand my position in the hierarchy, my duty or the expectations placed upon me. Had I grown up in India with a large extended family around me, with my peers facing similar futures, it might have been different. But I was a British Indian. Neither British nor Indian, yet both, and I was seeking individuality in the world of the collective.

CHAPTER 7

Seeing the Doctor

'Like all the best families, we have our share of eccentricities, of impetuous and wayward youngsters and of family disagreements.' Queen Elizabeth II

Indians love functions: organising them, going to them, talking about them, arguing over them. Naturally, the greatest function of them all is a wedding. And if Indians are not celebrating at a wedding, they will be found celebrating at a pre-wedding ritual. Once, Mum took Vin and me to a pre-wedding ritual of a family friend. Following the *Roka* ceremony to mark a couple's formal engagement, there are a number of other pre-wedding rituals that allow for the prospective bride and groom to be blessed. One of the last ceremonies before the big day is the *mehndi* (henna) ceremony, and this is the one that Mum took us to.

The groom's family sends the *mehndi*, which is applied in intricate patterns to the girl's hands and feet by friends and family or a professional *mehndi* artist. The *mehndi*, which is not washed off until the following day, stains the hands and feet in detailed red patterns that last about six weeks. It is part of a girl's wedding decoration and the occasion provides the opportunity for women to engage in merriment, singing and feasting.

Vin and I did not know the girl who was soon to be married, but we knew she had come from India to marry a British-born Indian boy. Maybe his parents thought a girl from India would not be corrupted by Western ways. She was shy and spoke softly with her head lowered as the *mehndi* was applied to her hands. Women and girls gathered around, everyone smiling and happy.

> Saturday 14 May, 1983: *'They sang songs that I could not understand and chanted rhymes that were meaningless to the language and the kind of living I knew. Perhaps I felt a little uncomfortable or an outsider. I thought about my own marriage. They would paint my hands and feet with henna. They would rub the yellow flour and ghee into my skin too. They would sing songs that I wouldn't understand. Rites would be performed and prayers said in a language I could not really comprehend and then I would be married. Then they'd let me wear the red colour in the parting of my hair and a red dot on my forehead, to show I was married. Why do these things have to be done? I don't know, maybe they don't either. When customs and traditions have been passed down through the ages, people forget to question their origins and examine their relevance.'*

I wanted to grab the girl and shake her by the shoulders. I wanted to shout at her, 'No, don't do it. Don't place yourself permanently in the custody of men. You belong to your father right now. But soon you will belong to your husband and then, when you are old, you will belong to your sons. You will never belong to yourself. Break free. Break free before it's too late!'

I was a misanthrope among the party revellers. Women sang and ate samosas around me as I stood watching the *mehndi* being applied.

'How can she marry someone she hardly knows?' I whispered to Mum.

'Love grows,' she said. 'Love grows after you get married. You'll see.'

I watched the *mehndi* artist make deft swirling patterns on the girl's palms. Pausing with the nozzle of her applicator poised over her hand, she asked the girl for the groom's name so she could write it in tiny letters somewhere within the *mehndi* patterns. Later, when the wedding was over and they were alone at last, he would hold his new bride's hand and search for his name hidden in her palm. Maybe she would take the opportunity to look at his face, perhaps properly for the first time, and feel something that could be love. Maybe that feeling would grow and never go away and they would live happily ever after forever and ever and ever. Maybe Mum was right.

But then again, maybe not. I knew things had become preposterous when the introductions started. The first boy arrived at our house with two carloads of his family. His parents had probably forced him to wear that concrete-grey suit. A suitable boy in a suit. It had a sheen that I found instantly unattractive. He had a thick head of black hair and eyes like a squirrel: small, intelligent and furtive.

They all spilt out of the cars – short dumpy women with jingle-jangle gold bangles and long crepe scarves about their necks and sure-footed men in suits and with serious faces. There were children too – ten-year-old cousins in their Sunday best smirking on the inside of their mouths. They didn't all fit into Mum and Dad's living room, so the women and children were led into the dining room. Even if they could all have been comfortably accommodated in one room, the women and children would still have been separated from the men. The suitable boy with the shiny suit sat with the serious faces.

I had been ordered by Mum to wear 'something Indian'. I didn't always do as I was told but on this occasion I did. I didn't want to embarrass her and besides, what choice did I have? I can't remember the colour of the sari I wore, but I'm certain it matched my bindi and restrained my stride. 'Tie your hair back,' said Mum, fussing around me in my bedroom.

'Why?'

'So you look Indian.'

'But I *am* Indian. I've got a brown face. He's hardly going to think I'm English.'

She knew that, but she was operating on a subterranean level. Overt signals as well as nuances implying I had become Westernised had to be concealed. After all, we didn't want him to think I had been corrupted. Nobody likes a girl corrupted by the West.

In the kitchen I prepared the tea things and adjusted my sari for modesty, pulling it across my body to provide maximum breast coverage and minimum midriff exposure. It's astonishing how six yards of silk, with a slight tug here and there, can be transformed from a garment dripping with sexual allure to one that projects pure, incorruptible piety. When I entered the dining room and set the tea things on the table, the women from his side watched me with eager eyes. I pretended not to notice, keeping my eyes lowered so I didn't appear bold.

From my side of the family there were my mum, my aunt and Vin. I sat on the chair that Mum pointed to with a dart of her eyes, and the women continued to talk among themselves until the door opened and the suitable boy was ushered into the room. He was tall and I thought I saw the beginnings of a stoop. He looked uncomfortable, as men often do when they're outnumbered by women. With an artificial confidence born of attempted bravado, he immediately approached Vin and introduced himself. She didn't need to be ordered to wear Indian clothes. She was an obedient girl and knew what was expected of her.

Mum, noticing that he was talking to the wrong daughter, quickly interrupted their smiling banter and guided him to a dining chair she had placed directly in front of me, about a metre away.

'Hi,' he said, sitting down, looking at me for the first time.

'Hi.'

His chair was too close to mine but I couldn't push mine further back as I was up against a wall. My back was always up against a wall. Our knees were pointing at each other, like machine guns facing off.

'Nice weather,' he said smiling thinly. This is going to be hard, I thought, unless someone takes the reins. The women and children were seated around the walls like patients in a doctor's waiting room. I was aware of them in the corners of my eyes. Lipsticked mouths chatted. Cups and saucers clinked. Saris rustled. Samosas crunched.

'Have you got a degree?' I blurted.

'Yes,' he replied, snapping to attention.

'In what?'

'IT.'

'What did you get?'

'A third.'

I made a note on my mental clipboard: *Not a medical doctor, susceptible to hen-pecking, degree only third class, possible hunchback in old age.* He'd stumbled out of the corral.

We continued the interrogation, covering all the basics: education, age, place of abode, ages and marital status of siblings. It would have been quicker to exchange CVs. We were both friendly, courteous, accommodating – all the attributes we knew were expected of us, but I was bored.

'Do you have any hobbies?' I asked. It was a pointless question, but we were running out of things to talk about and we'd only been conversing for a few minutes. He shrugged.

'Not really.'

'Do you live with your parents?'

'Yes.'

'What's you star sign?' asked Vin barging into the conversation.

'Pisces,' he replied foolishly.

Things were beginning to disintegrate. So I looked at Mum, who put down her teacup and rose from her chair, smiling in the way she always did when visitors came to our house, the way I always wished she'd carry on smiling after they'd left. She started engaging the suitable boy in irrelevant chitchat as I turned to Vin and swallowed hard.

After the visitors left, Mum was excessively and unnaturally ebullient. 'Well, what you think him?' she asked eagerly, in a friendly attempt to be my equal, rather than my mother.

'No.' I replied.

'No? Why?'

'You know why. Because I want to get a degree and a job first. I want to be journalist.' I had a much longer list of reasons why I didn't want to marry anyone, let alone her suitable boy, but I didn't tell her. I wasn't in the mood for a row. Suddenly, she wasn't smiling anymore. She was sick of me. Her shoulders took on a familiar slouch as she padded out of the room.

A few days later we received news. 'The boy, he say yes,' said Mum, her eyes glinting with hope.

'I'm sure he's a very nice boy,' I said. 'But my answer is still no. Please stop looking for boys, Mum. There's no point.'

'But he is tall like you. And he study the computer degree.'

'Please. My answer is no.'

Mum and Dad would have to let his family know that I had turned him down. There was potential for embarrassment and humiliation for all parties concerned if the matter was not handled sensitively. But I didn't care, because when you're eighteen you don't care about anything. So that was the end of that. I never saw him again and he was never mentioned in our house again – it was as if the whole thing had never happened.

Within a few months I turned nineteen. My parents were permanently angry with me, probably because I disobeyed them most of the time. I went out when they told me to stay in; I argued with them over nearly everything; I never wore Indian clothes when they told me to and my exam results were rubbish. All I ever did was listen to music, brood and sulk. I was Holden Caulfield.

As winter drew in that year, so did my fears. It seemed as if Mum and Dad had contacted half the Asian population of Britain in a frenzied attempt to find a husband for me before I became completely derailed. Every time the phone rang I was sure it was one of my parents' scouts calling with a suggestion for a match. Mum once showed me a passport-sized photo of a fat Indian man with curly hair and a double chin. 'What you think him?' she asked, looking at me earnestly though her spectacles. 'He live in Germany.' I think I said no before she'd even finished the sentence. She and my aunt muttered in corners, and made phone calls to India.

By now, my uncle and aunt had had three kids of their own – two daughters, Surekha and Praveen, and a son, Ashwani. Of course, that's not what we called them because in any Indian family at least one child must have an absurd pet name. In our family, my cousins were known as Twinkle, Peen and Ash (my distant relatives also include a Happy and a Bubbly). They were old enough to know that my marriage was in the process of being arranged. My permanently knotted brow was an external indicator of the weight of responsibility I felt. As the eldest child, I was expected to set an example for Vin, Raja, Twinkle, Peen and Ash. Any unconventional action by me was likely to ripple into their lives. Friends would tell me to 'lighten up'. A workman on a building site once yelled, 'Cheer up, love! Can't be that bad!' Other girls got wolf-whistles from builders. I got counselling.

Going to university was my only hope. I could leave home for three years. It would at least delay things. I sent applications to numerous far-flung universities and polytechnics in the

British Isles, in the hope I might be accepted somewhere. While I searched for educational institutions far enough from London to warrant leaving home, my parents continued the search for a suitable boy. It was nearly Christmas and, like Colombo, they had a few more leads.

One evening some months later, as the family sat around the dining table for dinner, Mum looked at Dad and said, 'Shall we talk to Sushila about it, then?'

I froze. It was the way she called me Sushila, my official name, and not Neelum. I wanted to skip the row and go straight to the crying. I wanted to throw open the front door and run down the street screaming. I wanted to be anywhere but my parent's dining room about to hear their plans for my destiny.

'Someone in our family has recommended a boy for you,' she said in Punjabi. 'We saw him at a party last Saturday. He's all right, tall and thin and everything, but his hair's a bit funny. Sort of thinning. His parents want to marry him soon.' She was trying to sell me a half-rotting pumpkin.

'He's practically bald,' laughed Raja.

'I suppose he's got a hairy chest and wears medallions too,' I sneered. Everyone laughed.

'His hair isn't thinning,' said Dad. 'It was merely combed back.' No, of course the pumpkin's not rotting.

'Apparently he has a degree from London University,' said Mum, going in for the hard sell.

'In what?'

'Electronics, or something like that.' So, they couldn't find a doctor, after all, huh? I had to have something from the next shelf down. 'He's quite nice to look at,' Mum continued. 'He was wearing a gold chain and he was smartly dressed.'

'So he *was* wearing a medallion,' I cried. Everyone laughed again, except Dad. When they stopped, I noticed they were all looking at me expectantly.

'Er, you're not serious about this, are you?' I said.

'Yes, of course we are,' replied Dad.

'Look, I have no inclination to get married before at least twenty-three or twenty-four.'

'*Hai, hai!*' cried Mum. 'You'll be an old woman by then. Nobody wants to marry an old woman.'

'I will not be an old woman at twenty-three, and it doesn't matter what people say.'

'It does matter to a certain extent,' interrupted Dad. 'It's important to stay within the boundaries set by society.'

'You take society's conventions as god-given truths! You allow society to dictate the course of action you should take in your life,' I yelled.

'No, we just do what is good for us and also keeps us within society's decent limits.'

'Don't get heated up,' interrupted Mum. I was spoiling her fun. I'd been spoiling her fun since I was born.

'Look, you know I want to go to university and I don't want to marry as soon as I get out. I want to get a job.'

'These are ideals,' said Dad, affecting patience. 'They sound nice when you talk about them, but in reality they don't exist.' He had expounded the benefits of educational attainment so often, yet now he seemed to be at pains to discourage me from going to university. It was as if, as a man he understood the importance of a university education in securing a good job, but as an Indian father he felt compelled to stop me from leaving home, so I could marry instead.

'But I'm too young,' I pleaded, looking from Mum to Dad. Mum breathed out a disappointed sigh and I left the room before anyone could say anything more.

'I'm sick and tired of this,' I thought, leaping up the stairs two steps at a time to get to the safety of my bedroom. 'I'm not marrying a fucking balding half-rotting engineer pumpkin.'

The next day, I had some questions.

'Dad.'

'Yes.'

'Why do we have arranged marriages?'

'Because it's our culture.'

'But we're not in India now.'

'It's still our culture.'

'But I can't marry someone I don't know anything about and I don't love.'

'A husband is not like a commodity in a shop,' he said. 'You can't inspect him and sample him and then pay your price. You can only judge him as he is and if you say yes, then accept him as he is. He will not be perfect, because he is human. You must expect some kind of defect and accept it. Love simply grows from this acceptance.'

'How can you put your kids through a British education system, expose them to British culture, let them have British friends, and then expect them to abandon all that for an arranged marriage?'

'You can do anything you like once you are married and gone, but while you are still in my house, you live under my rules.' By this he meant I was free to abandon the arranged marriage system once I was married, by not imposing it on my own children.

'So you accept that change will have to come some day?'

'Yes.'

'Then why not let change happen now rather than wait for the next generation? Why don't you break free from the tradition and let me marry someone I choose?'

'Because the Indian way is what I know. It is who I am. It is too difficult for me to change.'

Friday 14 October, 1983: *'It's not really my father's strictness and moral rigidness that upsets me, because I can understand that that is all due to his background. He believes that by being a conformist one succeeds in anything. [He believes] rules set out by society may not always be correct, but adhering to them and becoming one of the herd is better than sticking out like a sore thumb and being noticed, because it is that kind of thing that gets one into trouble.*

[I think] if one believes that society's rules are wrong, one must change them by becoming one of the first of the non-conformist group, instead of leaving that job to the next generation.

Unfortunately, my father refuses to become one of the first Indian non-conformists of his generation. He believes that the job of changing Indian society in England can only be handled by people like Vin and myself; but that is where he is wrong. It is he who must change radically. One of two things may then result. Either he will be ejected from Indian society, or Indian society will begin to change too, as one domino will have started a chain reaction.'

Saturday 15 October: *'Musing over what I wrote yesterday – it is more likely that a radical change from someone like my father would cause the whole [Indian] community to reject him rather than follow his example. This, my father believes, is an extremely unstable position, as he is then neither a part of the 'English' nor the 'Indians'. Instability leads to breakdown. Furthermore, my father has been brought up an Indian. Why should he change in any way? Why should he forsake everything? It's people like Vin and I who wish for change. We ask our father to help us and increase the rate of that change. He refuses, and he has every right to.'*

Within a few weeks, the arranged marriage circus was back in town with a new act. 'There's a doctor,' said Mum bluntly in Punjabi. I looked at her and sighed. 'We haven't seen him, but we've heard he's tall and slim. They say he's sharp.'

'Oh god,' I muttered under my breath.

'He lives in India,' Mum added quickly.

'I've told you, no boys from India,' I yelled. 'It won't work, I know it won't.'

'A friend of the family has been to visit him,' she said. Negotiations had been taking place without my knowledge and were clearly quite advanced.

'We've received a letter telling us he's a pleasant and modern man. Apparently his ideas are like yours. His name is Dinesh.'

'What do you mean his ideas are like mine?'

'Well, you know – he's your kind of person.'

As far as I could tell, my parents had thus far understood my ideas to be abnormal, extreme, rebellious, English and wild. Now, all of a sudden, Mum was claiming a suitable boy had been identified with similar 'ideas'. A suitable boy for an unsuitable girl.

'Mum, I'm a feminist,' I blurted childishly. 'And I want to be a journalist. *Those* are *my* kind of ideas.'

'Yes, I know. These fads will pass.'

I was livid. She still wasn't listening to me. She was my mother and she hardly knew who I was. My head felt like a pressure cooker and I could barely speak for the fury.

Then, one night, Vin, Raja and I were playing Monopoly when there was a knock at the front door. It was the family friend who had been to India to check out Dr Dinesh. We continued our game of Monopoly as the friend talked about his trip to India. He had a small, neat round face like a cartoon character, and he sat with his legs together as if he was trying to take up as little room as possible on the sofa. Reaching into his jacket pocket he pulled out a reel of photographic film. 'Neelum, go make some tea,' said Mum. Her tone was urgent, indicating I was being ordered to leave the room rather than actually being asked to make tea. I left immediately.

Some minutes later I returned with a tray of mugs and a pot of tea, but stood outside the living room door listening to the conversation. 'I'm sorry the film got spoilt,' I heard the cartoon say. 'That's why I only have the transparencies.' I thought I felt a moth in my rib cage.

I entered the room and set the tea things on the table, on which a box of transparencies had been opened. Vin and Mum had taken a handful each and were holding them up to the overhead light. I took a few too and joined the rest of the family, squinting at the tiny photos.

All I could see were Indian people I didn't recognise standing in a 'we're-having-our-photo-taken' pose, with a yellowy Indian sun glinting off their oiled black hair. I flicked through them quickly and chanced upon one of a man in a white shirt and grey suit. His arms hung loosely with both hands in his trouser pockets. His face, although hard to see clearly, looked as if he wanted the photographer to hurry up. 'That's him,' I thought, and quickly pushed the slide back into the rest of the pack. Mum complained that the images were too small for her to see properly, so Dad set up his projector and screen and somebody turned off the lights as the device whirred into action. Mum sat on the edge of her chair, and there was an air of excitement in the darkened room, as if we were about to see the opening scene of a new blockbuster movie.

Dad clicked methodically through the slides. The images, which moments ago had been minute when illuminated through the tungsten light, now appeared in gigantic form on the screen in front of us. He stopped clicking when he reached the man with his hands in his pockets. 'Oh, isn't that him?' cried Mum, almost catapulting herself out of the chair. Everyone leant forward to study the photo of Dr Dinesh, as if their being a few centimetres closer might reveal the kind of husband he would be.

It's not uncommon for families involved in arranged marriage negotiations to exchange photos. Mum and Dad would have supplied Dinesh's parents with a photo of me, but I didn't know which one they had picked. Vin looked at me, her eyebrows raised, inviting me to react. I remained silent.

Mum was beaming. She could have leapt into the air and given Dad a high five and it would not have seemed out of place under the circumstances. 'He look nice,' she said, turning to me. 'Neshy look nice.' She already had a nickname for him! I felt faint.

All around me there was excited chatter as the family conducted a forensic examination of the photo of Dinesh. I zoned out, withdrawing into my thoughts, ruminating over the pros and cons, as I had done many times already.

Strange, really – love marriages and arranged marriages begin so differently, yet the goal for both is that two people should stay together forever. So which one achieves its goal most often? Let's deconstruct for a minute. In Western marriages, love can die. People can pack their bags and walk out. In the postmodern age we manage these relationship breakdowns in many different ways. There is long-term separation, on-again-off-again, bitter recriminations with children in between, and, of course, marriage's fatal bullet – divorce. It's not ideal. And the numbers never seem to drop – in fact, year on year divorce rates keep rising.

Now let's take a ride around the mystical East. Arranged marriages mean parents know best, so why not let them choose? No waiting for the phone to ring; no wondering whether the relationship's serious now. Parents make it practical. There are no pretensions about love: it 'grows' *after* you marry. But isn't that just a euphemism for familiarity? If you stay together for long enough, don't you simply get used to each other?

How many times have we heard that arranged marriages are more successful than love marriages? Disillusioned Westerners love that line, as do Easterners who want to assert the supremacy of their ways. But there are no reliable figures. Put this 'growing' love within a community that frowns on divorce and what have you got? True love or bondage? If your husband is a drunk who beats you every night and divorce is unacceptable in your extended family-cum-community, where do you go to build a new life? If your husband is a cheat or neglects you, who can you turn to? What structures has Indian society or the worldwide community of expatriate Indians created to cater for these women? When divorce is taboo and the gauge of a successful marriage is a low divorce rate, then of course arranged marriages appear to be successful. A better measure might be one that gauges happiness. But no one has invented a happy arranged marriage index yet, so the divorce rate is the only measure we have to work with.

But it's not all that bad. Look at the bright side – at least you'll never be alone in an arranged marriage. They consolidate wealth and community; they provide a massive network, like a club; they preserve and continue the ancestral lineage. They've got a lot going for them, haven't they? Remember, it's not an individual contract, it's a company merger. Your future is with the firm. The firm's success is your success.

Suddenly I heard Vin yelling my name.

'Sushila, Sushila! Are you listening?'

'What?' I said, snapping out of my thoughts.

'I said, what do you think of Dinesh?' Vin was leaning into me, her face contorted with impatience. Raja was packing up the Monopoly board and the cartoon character had left the room. I looked at her like a patient in a hospital ward unable to understand what the nurse was asking, before opening my mouth and letting the words fall out.

'Look, he's okay,' I said. 'But fucking hell, Vin, what's going on here? Mum called him Neshy, like we're already married or something. I don't know. I really don't know. I'm sure he's a nice guy, but it's the idea, the idea of letting them choose. I mean, I wouldn't let them choose a dress for me, so why would I let them choose a husband?'

'It might be okay in the end,' she offered.

'In the end? What about the sodding beginning?'

CHAPTER 8

Men, Women and Wombs

'It is probably true to say that the largest scope for change still lies in men's attitude to women, and in women's attitude to themselves.'
Vera Brittain, **Lady into Woman**

My dad never left me in any doubt about what he expected of me. When I came home with a grade A in geography once, happily skipping into the house in the knowledge that I was about to make my parents proud of me, Dad studied my report card and said, 'Good. Now make sure you get an A next year as well.' There was no time for whoop-whooping, no moment to luxuriate in pride, just an immediate mental leap to next year so I had as much time as possible to fret about how to stay on top of the mountain I had climbed.

Dad never let up on his demand for high academic standards, but he had made it clear many times that there was a point in a woman's life where study stopped and marriage began. It was as if the purpose of study, other than to 'improve oneself' on a personal level, was to be able to present the best academic credentials on paper in order to command a high price in the marriage market. An educated girl can secure an educated husband and therefore she has greater potential for wealth and comfort in the future for her and her children. With an education, a girl is no longer a simpleton from a village whose parents can only secure for her a poor, ignorant weakling. (I am certain Dad would have had no problem if I had studied to become a nuclear physicist or brain surgeon, as long as it didn't obstruct his marriage plans for me.)

The remarkable irony of viewing a girl's education in this way is its failure to realise that while an education may improve a girl's chances of snaring a better husband, it is also the doorway to her free thinking. An educated mind has the potential to scrutinise tradition, question it, even destroy it. Perhaps Dad never thought this far ahead. He saw no contradiction in encouraging me to excel academically, but then drop my studies for marriage. What would have been unacceptable to him was studying for the purposes of delaying marriage. Parental expectations can be so exacting.

When Dad told me he was planning a trip to India for the whole family to meet Dinesh the doctor, it was obvious there would be expectations. 'You're not going to be unreasonable when we get there, are you?' he asked. I sensed I didn't have what people like to call 'wriggle room'.

'No, I won't be unreasonable,' I said. What else could I say?

Fortunately, the trip never eventuated. In June 1984 the Indian government imposed a curfew in Punjab shortly before troops stormed the Golden Temple in Amritsar, where Sikh militants had amassed heavy weapons in protest at what they believed to be discrimination against them by the Hindu majority. More than a thousand people were killed in the battle and it ultimately led to the then prime minister, Indira Ghandi, being assassinated by two of her Sikh bodyguards, in October that year. Dad was shaken up by what was happening in his home state. Unwilling to take his family into a danger zone, he abandoned his travel plans.

Around that time I came across an article in my college magazine titled *Tug of War*. It was written by Faraza, a Muslim student with whom I had a loose friendship. She was finger-thin with sharp, pointy elbows and exceptionally fine features, except for a podgy nose that didn't seem to belong on her face. We used to share our anxiety over arranged marriages. Being a Muslim, her parents were much stricter than mine. I was moved by her article. 'Everyone feels sorry for the Muslim girl,' she wrote. 'They pity her because she misses out on so much enjoyment; because she has no freedom of choice and because she has to have an arranged marriage.'

I admired her for her clarity of thought and for trying to explain her relationship with her parents: 'It is not like the relationship between a prisoner and her captors, as some tend to think. There is love and filial loyalty as in any normal Western family. The young Muslim will eventually have to make a choice, because society makes it impossible to stay on the cusp forever. What many do not realise is that it is not really a choice between two cultures. It is more a choice between risking it all in order to find one's true identity and happiness, and taking the easy way out by compromising and following the kind of life one is expected or born to lead. The final decision has to be made alone, and it is alone that one bears the responsibility for the consequences. Too few have the courage and strength to take that responsibility in order to lead a life that is real and true to themselves.'

Once I had read her words, I could not unread them. Once you know an idea, how can you unknow it? One day I'd have to stop standing on the cusp and make a decision, and I'd have to make it alone. Either I must go through with an arranged marriage, as I was expected to, or I must break out of the system, face the consequences and bear the responsibility. I resolved to find Faraza the next day and talk to her. Without knowing exactly how, I thought we might be able to help each other. I looked for her everywhere at the college, but nobody had seen her around. I asked one of my lecturers about her whereabouts and she told me Faraza had returned to Yemen. Apparently she had left without saying goodbye to anyone. I felt sudden fear and rushed to seek out a mutual friend at the college, who was also a Muslim. I figured she'd know the details.

'Where is Faraza?' I asked.

'She's gone back to Yemen.'

'With her parents? But why?'

'They took her back,' said the girl. 'They're keeping her there under heavy restrictions.'

'Oh my god.'

'Faraza was a sad case,' she said blankly. Her use of the past tense unnerved me. Faraza's article had appeared in that week's edition of the college magazine: her last shout before they took her away. The last time I had seen her was in the library, sitting at a desk taking notes from a text book, her long hair hiding her face. Were they going to force her to marry someone in Yemen? Maybe she had agreed to marry him. But why the heavy restrictions? What had she done? Perhaps they'd taken her back to be de-Westernised? How does that work? How do you de-Westernise someone? Do you make them wear traditional clothing? Do you forbid them from speaking in English? Do you stop them from reading Western books, watching Western movies, listening to Western music? Do you isolate them in a religious environment? Do you slap their face? Do you beat the living daylights out of them?

There's a difference between forced marriages and arranged marriages. A forced marriage involves duress and a lack of consent from one or both parties. In an arranged marriage, the families organise the marriage but the choice of whether to accept the arrangement is up to the couple. That's the theory. If only it was that clear.

Most people deplore the idea of forced marriage, not only because the individuals concerned are allowed no choice, but because the arrangement of such marriages can involve physical violence, usually to get the woman to submit.

But people are less resistant to the idea of arranged marriages because they see them as a cultural phenomenon, and, as I've said, often justify them by the spurious argument that they have a high success rate. There's no denying that many arranged marriages are happy and successful. But there's also no denying that arranged marriages can involve mental manipulation or emotional coercion. We cannot conflate the emotional coercion behind some arranged marriages with the brutality of forced marriages or honour killings.

But nor should we blindly accept arranged marriages, because what lies behind them is not just occasional emotional coercion but an entire social system that has its roots in the subjugation of women.

My parents would never have turned to using physical force, and they were open-minded compared to some, but coercion has many faces: your mother will suffer a heart attack if you ruin our *izzat.* How can you be so selfish and do this to your parents? If you destroy this family's name no one will marry your sister, so you'll be ruining her life too.

Mum and Dad feared what might happen to them if either of their daughters brought shame on the family. Nobody in our family had broken ranks and refused an arranged marriage before; no one had had a love marriage. There was no shortage of rumours to fuel my parents' fears, particularly rumours of girls raised in Britain who had become 'too Westernised' and had run off to marry an Englishman. They were 'bad girls' – selfish, wild-eyed maniacs who had dived into the ditch of ill-repute and pulled their families down with them. I didn't actually know any girls like that, but I heard a lot about them at social gatherings where middle-aged Indian women would gossip, their gasps and tut-tuts bouncing off the walls like ping-pong balls.

One can only imagine the kinds of taunts these girls might have been subjected to, not to mention the taunts their parents would have faced. In the crevices of my memory, where the thinnest chink of light barely illuminates, I have a recollection of an Indian man, his shirtsleeves rolled up, waving his hands about wildly, standing at the top of the stone steps that led to his front door. He was shouting at another man who was leaving his house: 'Just you wait, just you wait till *your* daughters grow up.'

He must have been at the receiving end of taunts about whatever it was his daughters had done. I don't know how far back that memory goes, but I remember his pitiful attempt to fight taunt with taunt, as he wiped away tears with the palm of his hand.

The disconcerting feeling that other Indian families were always watching and passing judgment was a poison that laced social interaction as I grew up. While I agonised about being married off to a stranger, Mum and Dad's big fear was loss of face. I was not unsympathetic to their plight. I imagined myself standing at the altar in a white wedding dress and Indian people taunting my dad as he yelled, 'Just you wait, just you wait till *your* daughter grows up.' I imagined Indian women nudging each other, their breathy gossip drifting out from behind their hands as Mum and Dad quickly passed them in the street, heads lowered in shame. I imagined my parents' phone falling silent for lack of friends willing to call. I could frighten myself better than anyone else. I could summon guilt in a flash.

Things might have been different if my parents had been part of a mere handful of Indian migrants who came to Britain in the 1960s. They might have dissolved into British society seamlessly. But they were part of mass migration. At that time, migration from Punjab was so commonplace it was as if whole towns and villages had uprooted and transplanted themselves from India to Britain. Migrants brought with them entire social systems – the lock, stock and barrel of family hierarchies. Mores, norms and rituals were all part of the cultural baggage they carried with them – baggage they clung on to after they arrived. Because that's what migrants do – they don't just transplant their physical bodies to a new land, they bring with them their modes of operating, the structures that hold their communities together and the language that lubricates the whole machinery. Culture from the old country serves as a raft to hang on to in uncharted waters. But by the time they are settled in their new country and the raft is no longer needed, it's been around so long it's become a crutch, a habit, a comforter like a child's favourite blanket.

It's been an odd kind of reverse colonisation by the Indians in Britain: chicken tikka masala, Diwali, multicoloured saris, Bollywood movies, bhangra rap, the corner shop, IT companies, the steel industry. But any kind of colonisation has a dark side: unhappy arranged marriages, crippling pressure for larger and larger dowries, oppressive social policing of young people who don't toe the line, social coercion, domestic violence, honour killings.

Many Indian migrants of the 1960s had roots that went back to farming communities. Outside influences can badly disrupt the established order of things in such small, close-knit communities. Village life was about making the most of the land people tilled, within the confines of whatever Mother Nature bestowed or inflicted. From a brutally economic point of view, many sons meant many workers to farm the land, and therefore prosperity. Sons could even travel far and wide to cities to earn money, if necessary.

Women performed the role of producing and looking after the economic providers – men. Boiled down to the basics, a woman's womb is the vital vehicle through which labour, in the form of sons, is delivered. That labour can farm the land or even be part of an army to act as security. No wonder, in a patriarchial society, men would want to exercise control over women, and therefore their wombs.

So a woman must marry a man who is chosen not by her, but by those wiser and older than her, such as her parents and other older relatives – people who are charged with keeping her under control. It's not difficult to picture the problems that might arise in keeping order within a community if a woman were to have control over her life by choosing her own husband. She might choose a man and move elsewhere, making her womb redundant to that community, or she might marry an outsider who doesn't conform to that community's norms. These scenarios ultimately threaten the stability or survival of a small rural community by changing its make-up.

A system of morals that venerates family honour, especially if it links honour to the womb, acts as a useful device to keep women under control. Responsibility for protecting honour is placed on *their* head. So it is *they* who can be legitimately punished if there is any deviation from the moral code. Beating a woman keeps her fearful and under control. Disowning a woman by banishing her or destroying her through murder eliminates the threat to the community.

If women themselves can be co-opted to dish out punishment to other women, even better, because then rebellious women, who dare to exercise choice, cannot form a collective force against men. Harsh mothers-in-law and village gossips successfully police their gender's own oppression. One of the best ways to co-opt women is through a hierarchy that places married women who produce sons at the top and childless women at the bottom. A woman who produces no children may be considered a witch, a bringer of curses, by other women. This keeps the women divided and therefore weak. The whole community is then safe from internal threats (women who won't do as they're told) through fear. And we all know that fear is the mother and father of obedience.

There will be people who disagree with my interpretation of things, perhaps even dismiss it as radical feminist blathering. But what other explanation is there for such heinous crimes as honour killings committed by men, sometimes with the help of women? We simply can't dismiss such murders as rare. Globally, it's estimated that about five thousand women were the victims of honour killings in 2000 (the most up-to-date figure I could find). According to the United Nations, such killings are believed to be on the rise and they happen in many different countries: Bangladesh, Brazil, Ecuador, Egypt, India, Israel, Italy, Jordan, Morocco, Pakistan, Sweden, Uganda and the United Kingdom.

I know of one honour killing in Australia, and in Britain about twelve or thirteen people, mostly women, are killed every year to 'protect' their family's honour. (Men murdered in honour killings are more often than not the boyfriend of the rebellious girl.) These numbers suggest that the honour system is very much alive among some in the British South Asian community. Many Asians, such as my parents, migrated to Britain in the 1950s and 1960s. But many are born in Britain too, like my brother and sister. And if you think it's the older generation that is most likely to perpetuate the honour system, think again.

In 2012, a BBC survey about the honour system found it was strongly supported by *young* Asians in Britain. That's a surprising result since one would imagine a second generation to be more relaxed about anachronistic traditions. The survey interviewed 500 Asians between the ages of sixteen and thirty-four and found that 69 per cent agreed that families should live according to honour. A worrying 18 per cent felt that behaviour by a woman that could affect her family's honour, such as disobeying her parents or wanting to leave an existing or prearranged marriage, justified physical punishment. Frighteningly, 6 per cent of young Asian men said honour killings could be justified. That compares with 1 per cent of women who thought killings could be justified. On the face of it, these results are remarkable and inexplicable. Clearly, there needs to be a mindset change here.

In reality, nobody knows how many women are murdered in honour killings each year, whether it be at the hands of male relatives or male relatives in cahoots with their mothers-in-law. Britain's Crown Prosecution Service estimates there are about 10,000 forced marriages every year in Britain.

So is it possible to discern why people hold on to the honour system so strongly? Hatred of Western ideals is one explanation, because they threaten the normal workings of some non-Western communities. A global study by an American think-tank called the Middle East Forum found that 58 per cent of victims were murdered for being 'too Western' and/or for resisting or disobeying cultural and religious expectations. Being 'too Western' included being seen as too independent; not subservient enough; wanting an advanced education and a career; having non-Muslim, non-Hindu or non-Sikh friends or boyfriends; and wanting to choose one's own husband.

In countries such as Britain, Canada and Australia, which have significant numbers of Asian migrants, forced marriages and the emotional coercion that frequently lies behind arranged marriages can go undetected for years, particularly if the wider community sees such practices as foreign customs not theirs to judge.

When I was a teenager, the likes of Enoch Powell had been comprehensively shunned and multiculturalism was the new black – so to speak. It was only when media reports revealed brutality towards Asian women who tried to escape arranged marriages that the authorities stepped in. Yet there was little support for young women scared of what the future held for them, partly because they did not wish to expose their families' private lives to external scrutinisers and partly because there was an unwillingness by the wider British community to interfere. Multiculturalism at its worst.

Thankfully, the British government no longer sees forced marriages as a foreign custom in which it has no right to intrude. It views them as human rights abuses, and in 2012 passed a law to make them a crime. Years earlier it established the Forced Marriage Unit to help victims. In 2011 the unit dealt with 1500 cases, a third of whom were minors – schoolchildren who suddenly became wives. The youngest was reported to be just five years old. Every year the unit rescues hundreds of women (British citizens) taken overseas for forced marriages. The government has produced official guidelines for its departments on how to handle cases of forced marriage. These are positive steps forward but progress is always resisted by those who can't let go of the past.

In 2002 the British government wanted to start a discussion about arranged marriages and whether Asians could marry Asians brought up in Britain rather than importing marriage partners from places such as India and Pakistan. I'd say that's a perfectly legitimate topic for discussion. But when the then home secretary, David Blunkett, suggested arranged marriages *should* involve partners from Britain and not the Indian subcontinent, he was accused of 'attacking Asian culture'. These were his exact words: 'We need to be able to encourage people to respond particularly to young women who do actually want to be able to marry someone who speaks their language – namely English – who has been educated in the same way as they have, and has similar social attitudes.'

I believe there are many young Asian women brought up in Western countries who would prefer to marry an Asian man also raised in a Western country, rather than one raised in the subcontinent. But Blunkett was accused of causing offence, and the criticism came from interesting places. Habib Rahman is the head of a charity called the Joint Council on the Welfare of Immigrants. 'Everyone despises forced marriages,' he was reported as saying. 'But such an attack on the institution of arranged marriage is an attack on the whole communities of the Indian subcontinent'.

Rubbish! It should be possible to discuss arranged marriages without anyone being berated for daring to question the way the Asian community behaves when it arranges the marriages of its sons and daughters.

The arranged marriage cheer squad has sought the moral upper hand for some time, arguing that such marriages represent stronger family bonds, longer-lasting relationships and superior moral values. They use rising divorce levels in Western love marriages and the disconnectedness of the nuclear family from their wider family and community networks to support their case. They also frown on the higher priority given to individual self-fulfillment over family values. These are undoubtedly legitimate issues of concern.

But it is not arranged marriages per se that allow for strong family bonds, successful relationships and moral uprightness. It is *people* who make these things happen. Unquestioning support for arranged marriages wilfully overlooks the subtle manipulation and emotional coercion that can lie behind them. Multicultural sensitivity is one thing, but allowing cultural relativism to compromise women's human rights is quite another.

Guidelines for government departments on how to handle cases of forced marriages do not exist in all Western countries, including Australia, where the Indian community has been growing rapidly since around the turn of this century. In particular, there has been significant migration from Punjab.

Australia takes migrants from all over the world and while its recent policies of multiculturalism have served it well, cases of forced marriages come to light from time to time. In 2011, reports of a fourteen-year-old girl, betrothed by her parents to a seventeen-year-old boy whom she had never met and who lived in another country, horrified many people. The story surfaced after the Family Court confiscated her passport in a bid to stop her from being taken overseas to be married by her parents. She was reported to have told child protection workers that she had not been forced into the engagement and would not have to marry him if she changed her mind after they met. In the face of questioning by child protection workers, strangers to her family, a fourteen-year-old is liable to say what she *thinks* is the right thing to say to protect her family. Regardless of whether she was being forced into a marriage or not, she was clearly unaware that marriage at fourteen is illegal in Australia. The case is a reminder that children and adolescents, who often believe what they are told, are particularly vulnerable to mental manipulation and social coercion.

With increasing migration from South Asia, forced marriage has become an emerging problem in Australia. At the moment there is no law to ban the practice, although early in 2012 a bill proposing a ban was put to parliament. What's needed is education to reinforce the message that forced marriages are unacceptable. But the education must be backed up by legislation to make them a criminal act, as is now the case in Britain. Of course, no daughter would want her parents to go to jail, but a law banning the practice empowers a woman because at least she then knows that the state is there for her, even if no one else is.

There was no such law or even social support for girls who needed it when I was a teenager. Just before my twentieth birthday I felt more keenly than ever that Mum and Dad were intensifying their efforts to get me to accept their plans. I still had no plan of my own to escape.

'Sometimes you have to marry when you are told,' said Mum, speaking in Punjabi to lend her words authority.

'Why?' I asked.

'Well, if one parent becomes ill, he or she may want to see their child married off before dying.' This scenario had echoes of the Bollywood movie she'd been watching the night before: the ageing mother on her deathbed implores her son to marry before she leaves the mortal coil. He, hand in hand with the woman he loves (and whom his mother approves of), vows to fulfill her dying wish. Cut to scene of wedding where the old mother is frail but smiling, followed shortly by a scene of the now married couple weeping as they stand before a funeral pyre.

'Mum, you watch too many Bollywood movies.'

That evening I had another argument with my parents. Dad complained that Mum frequently suffered from migraines and that I did not talk to her often enough or try to establish a 'harmonious relationship' with her. Mum, for her part, referred to my sister and brother by their names, but had now taken to calling me 'the other one' – a situation that I thought was hardly conducive to a harmonious relationship.

'If something tragic happens in this house,' Dad warned, 'you will be to blame.' I figured he was watching too many Bollywood movies too.

By now I was beginning to get responses from universities asking me to come for interviews, but these letters sparked more rows. Mum and Dad simply didn't want me to move out to study, as this would delay their plans by at least three years. Most interview requests I received were from universities in the north of England and I needed Dad to drive me there. Sometimes he agreed, albeit reluctantly, and other times he simply refused. I was in his hands.

One day a letter arrived with a postmark from Hertfordshire – far enough from home to require moving out, but close enough to allow for regular visits home during term-time. I wanted to attend the interview, but Mum and Dad refused to drive me there. Angry and frustrated, I marched off to Twickenham train station and bought a ticket to Hertford. As the train pulled out, I felt galloping anxiety. I was nineteen years old and the furthest I had ever travelled on my own was to the neighbouring town of Richmond. Catching the train to Hertford, about 70 kilometres away, was at once liberating and frightening.

That week I received a call from the college in Hertford, which later came to be called Hertfordshire University, offering me a place on a three-year degree course. I told my parents I intended to accept the offer and that I planned to study social sciences and to major in political economy, which I assumed would prepare me for a career in journalism.

'You will not go. I will never let you go,' screamed Mum.

'I advise you to forget about further education,' said Dad. He begged me to at least consider delaying starting the course for a year and to get a job in the meantime. His request surprised me, but when I quizzed him further, he finally revealed his plan for my future.

Dinesh was going to apply to migrate to Britain with the intention of marrying me and Dad felt the immigration authorities would look more favourably on his application if I was employed. As an earning wife I could at least offer him temporary financial support while he looked for a job. So that's why Dad was trying to stop me from going to university, I thought. Obviously, his plan was predicated on the assumption that I would agree to marry Dinesh.

> Tuesday 18 September, 1984: *'Why should I shape my life and future around a man I don't even know, let alone wish to marry? Furthermore, what if the idea of marriage with him falls through? . . . I do not think my parents are being fair. They're playing games with my future because they're so concerned with that wretched marriage to a stranger.'*

The next evening, my aunt and uncle arrived to help my parents try to dissuade me from leaving home to study. I felt outnumbered and I knew that any unconventional action by me would affect my sister and brother's chances of having an arranged marriage, if indeed that was what they wanted when the time came for them. Raja wasn't even a teenager yet and remained largely disconnected from what was happening between me and my parents. I doubt he would have even been aware that he too would be expected to have an arranged marriage someday. Vin, on the other hand, looked on with a silence I often found exasperating. There were times when she would reprimand me for upsetting Mum and Dad. Increasingly she failed to back me up in arguments with them.

'Why don't you ever support me?' I once asked her.

'What do you want me to say? There's nothing I can say. You're always upsetting them. You behave selfishly sometimes. You make things worse for yourself,' she replied. I felt her slipping away. My friends were always there with a sympathetic ear, but Vin, who saw how upset Mum and Dad would become after a row with me, was not always willing to take my side. In my absence my parents would pour out their troubles to her and she was there to listen to them, absorbing their frustrations, taking on their woes, perhaps building a resentment towards me. I think it made her move away from me. Or perhaps it was I who was slipping away from her.

The evening that my uncle and aunt arrived, I don't recall Vin being in the room. Everyone lectured me on how I should put family priorities ahead of my own, how marriage was important for a woman, and why I should trust my parents to make the right choice for me. I cried and begged that they allow me to leave home to study, but they were adamant. By the end of the evening they had broken me down. I surrendered, exhausted by their marathon lecturing. 'Okay, okay,' I yelled through tears. 'I won't go.'

After a restless night I woke to find a world turned grey. Crushed, I came down to breakfast to find Dad was already at the dining table reading the newspaper. I sat down.

'Dad.'

'Yes.'

'Please,' I began, and words came tumbling out of my mouth as if it was not me speaking, but someone else inside me. 'You could tell people you didn't want me to leave home to study but you allowed it because you thought it was best for me. You could tell them that you wanted your daughter to have a good education; that in Britain, things have to be done differently. People won't think any less of you. They'll think you did a noble thing.'

Dad was silent. I kept my head lowered. I didn't look into his eyes, but the words kept coming out. 'If you love a child, you will do whatever makes that child happy. Doing a degree will make me happy.'

'And if you love your parents, you will do whatever makes them happy,' he said. I raised my eyes to look at him. His collar was unbuttoned and there was red-rimmed exhaustion in his eyes.

It was just me and him now. We had reached an impasse and we couldn't stay like this. I knew this was only a dress rehearsal. One day there would be another even bigger clash. That day was coming and we both knew it.

'Your mother and I are your parents,' he said quietly. 'Of course we want you to be happy. That's all we want.' He closed his newspaper as if he was closing an entire chapter on our lives. 'Go then,' he said. 'Go and do your degree, and we will always support you.'

I wanted to throw my arms around him and tell him that I loved him, but he would have recoiled at the physical contact.

'Thank you, Dad,' I said, standing up.

It was time to leave, time to pack my bags and walk out of the door – if only for three years.

CHAPTER 9

A Match at Last!

'"You will marry a boy I choose," said Mrs Rupa Mehra to her younger daughter.'
Vikram Seth, A Suitable Boy

'Your turn to put the fookin' kettle on,' said Bob, reaching for the cigarette papers on the coffee table and grinning at me. The other students had all objected to making the tea, arguing that they had already made it twice in the past month or that they had only just sat down after a marathon walk to the corner shop to get the fags. Everybody always had an excuse. I had moved to Hertford to start my degree course and clearly fallen in with what Dad would have called 'bad characters'.

For nearly three weeks at the beginning of the first term, Bob had convinced everyone he was allergic to washing-up liquid in order to avoid doing the dishes. 'Well, go on then,' he said with a note of irritation. 'Are you going to make the fookin' tea or what?'

Bob Taylor was from Birmingham. His inability to speak a single sentence without swearing belied his boyish face and rosy cheeks. I'd been ordered to make the tea all my life, so it seemed natural to do as I was told.

The kitchen was a nasty state of affairs. There were three dirty pans soaking in cold water in the sink and a teetering tower of unwashed plates and mugs on the drainer. A ring of congealed bacon fat marked the level to which the sink had been filled before water started seeping down the plughole. There was a grubby tea towel on the back of a chair and empty beer bottles and stinking ashtrays on the table. Somebody had scribbled a Hitler moustache on a picture of Margaret Thatcher that was hanging on the wall. A paring knife had been stabbed into her forehead. I was glad I didn't live at Springfield Lodge. Shared student accommodation was the pits. I'd found a room to rent on the other side of town. It was miles away from the campus and I didn't like it because I lived alone, but at least it wasn't filthy. I'd find somewhere closer soon.

I looked around for tea-making equipment. At home Mum and Dad always made tea in a pan. Once the water came to a boil they'd throw in some loose-leaf tea and sometimes some cardamom pods, cloves and cinnamon bark too. Then they'd pour in milk and bring the whole thing back to the boil again, before simmering it for at least ten minutes. Voila! Tea – Indian style.

In student shared houses things were different. With all the pans in the sink, I sought an alternative. Luckily, there was an electric kettle on the bench. Mum and Dad didn't have an electric kettle, probably for the same mysterious reason they didn't have an ironing board. I was traversing new territory. When the kettle came to a boil, I opened the lid, threw in some teabags, poured in the milk and pressed the button to make the whole thing come to the boil again. I took it into the living room and filled everyone's mug straight from the kettle, cord trailing behind.

'What the fookin' hell is that?' said Bob, throwing down the copy of a student newspaper he had been browsing and sitting upright in his armchair.

'Er, it's tea,' I said, without looking at him.

'Well, fook me dead. You call that fookin' tea? She's pourin' it straight out the fookin' kettle,' he said, to no one in particular. 'Are the fookin' biscuits in there as well?' Phil, Lou and Dave, who had been engaged in a conversation about whether punk started with the New York Dolls in New York or the Sex Pistols in London, stopped their bickering and looked over. 'Just ignore him,' said Lou kindly. 'Anyway, what the fuck *are* you doing?'

These were my salad days – so horribly green in judgment. Bob passed me the joint he'd been rolling while I was in the kitchen. 'Here, get your laffin' gear round that. I think you fookin' *need* it.'

For the three years of my degree course I was effectively out on parole. Dad had stood aside at last to grant me the tertiary education he had venerated in theory but had tried to block me from in practice. Had he come round because he knew his position was untenable? Because he wanted me to be happy? Because of my dogged pursuit of something he secretly wanted me to have but couldn't bring himself to admit? Mum had no choice but to fall into line with his acquiescence, for he always had the final word.

Both Vin and I were relieved that the arguing in our house had finally come to an end with my departure. And on campus no one was ordering me around, asking me questions about where I'd been or what I'd been doing. I was free to do whatever I wanted. I looked upon the world with fresh eyes and ridiculous optimism. The sun was shining and young people were everywhere. There were Geordie accents and cockney accents, southerners and northerners, boys and girls, all united in their private efforts to work out who they were as they elbowed their way to the bar.

Like so many other students, I was irresponsibly making adult choices. I opened a bank account and ran up an overdraft. I bought books and never read them. I found a decent place to live but rarely paid my rent on time. I knew how to cook but never fed myself properly. It's not easy managing newfound freedom. Even if somebody had shown me how to manage it I would still have carried on drinking, flirting, puking, wasting time and making excuses for late assignments. I fell in love with every tall, skinny guy in tight black jeans that walked past (though I was always too timid to do anything about it). If I could only have seen past the smoke, I might have worked out what I was supposed to be studying. But someone was always 'skinnin' up' and someone always had enough money for at least a Henry (Henry the Eighth – as in an eighth of an ounce of hash).

Off campus, in the real world, bad things were afoot and the fallout reverberated through the student community. Unemployment was over three million, football hooliganism hit the headlines repeatedly, AIDS was spreading and race riots broke out sporadically up and down the country. Handsworth, Brixton, Toxteth, Broadwater Farm in Tottenham – place names indissolubly linked to economic deprivation and racial discrimination.

Enoch Powell raised his head above the parapet to tell the country that the 1985 Handsworth riots were a vindication of the warning bell he had sounded in 1968. But, as had been the case for many years, nobody was listening to him anymore.

Unlike my school days, I felt no hostility from fellow students. In fact, these students were not unlike the students I had befriended at Richmond upon Thames College. Nobody called me a nignog or told me to go back to wog land. In the age of multiculturalism, everything 'ethnic' was to be celebrated.

'Oh, I love Indian culture!' enthused one of the girls in my class. Her parents were both English. She had never been to India but was planning to go backpacking there after finishing her course. India was a rite of passage for many students. 'I just love the saris, the colours are so rich. Do you know how to tie one?' I nodded yes. 'Oh, you must show me – I'd love to wear one. You're so lucky having a culture. I don't have a culture because I'm English.'

'Of course you have a culture,' I said. 'What about Christmas, or white weddings, fireworks on Guy Fawkes night, Morris dancing, for god's sake – that's all English culture, isn't it?' She blinked quizzically for a few uncomfortable seconds.

'Yes, I suppose so. But it's not the same, is it? English culture is boring. Indian culture is so exotic!'

If people weren't banging on about colourful saris and the rich tapestry of my ethnic exoticism, they were asking me for the recipes for lamb rogan josh or chicken tikka masala. I could certainly help them with lamb rogan josh, but maybe they would have been better placed than me to know how to cook chicken tikka masala since the dish was allegedly invented in Britain. (Lizzie Collingham, in her book *Curry: A Tale of Cooks and Conquerors,* says food critics dismiss this dish as inauthentic since it was the creation of an enterprising Indian chef who whipped up a can of Campbell's Tomato Soup, some cream and a few spices to make a gravy for the chicken that an ignorant customer had complained was too dry, thus producing 'a mongrel dish of which, to their shame, Britons now eat at least eighteen tonnes a week.')

There was a lot of love for all things Indian. While mostly bewildering and sometimes amusing, I was often infuriated by the blindness this love caused. This fawning, this cringe-inducing toadying, played a part in stopping British people from seeing what was happening right under their noses: Indian girls were struggling to have a say in their own lives.

The groups of friends I hung around with were pro-multiculturalism, but not soppy. They were angry, they were always angry. Mostly they were angry with racism, angry with Thatcher, angry with the police, angry about high unemployment. They hated all forms of social conformity and deference to the crown. They were deeply concerned that a generation of graduates would walk out of universities and polytechnics and simply join the end of the dole queue, and they weren't going to put up with it. They marched in the streets, held up placards and shouted. They wanted to change the world. They handed out leaflets, did volunteer work and picked coffee beans in Nicaragua. And I watched as if through cellophane. I was more of an observer than a participant. Always there in the crowd, watching my friends protesting, rather than actually protesting myself. I admired their anger and their refusal to accept defeat. They were Brits who could not, and would not, be suppressed.

Tony Wood, a vegan anarchist with dreadlocks, was a Londoner and sort of the leader of the pack. He was older than everyone else, wore a rubber coat and sold beer at the Glastonbury festival. When he talked about the inherent failings of capitalism and what was wrong with 'the system', it was as if he was coughing up all the grit and grime that had accumulated since the beginning of the industrial revolution. He hated the police more fearlessly than anyone else I knew, and I loved him for that! I recall him distributing a telephone number that people were to call for legal representation if the pigs arrested them at the demo they were preparing to attend. 'Write it on your arm,' he said. 'That way you won't lose it.'

In the big, grown-up democratic world of student demos, people had the right to speak out against the system. The very act of protesting was legitimate, not like at my mum and dad's house, where protesting against any parental rule was entirely illegitimate; where questioning the Indian system was objectionable, and more so if you were female.

Being away from home allowed me to think about things other than arranged marriage, and boy did I need the mental relief. But temporary relief was all it was, not a solution.

Mum and Dad would have been happy for me to marry an Indian boy if I'd met one while studying, but only if he met all the various criteria, and I knew very few Indian boys. Instead of focusing on my studies, I confess I wasted valuable, never-to-return time boring my friends with my conundrum or escaping the whole thing through whatever mind-bending opportunities came my way.

Some nights I barely slept for fear of the nightmares that visited me with terrifying regularity. One night I dreamt I was dying on the road outside my parents' house. Vin rushed to help me. She was on the ground with my head in her arms, Dad was looking down at me and a crowd was gathering. 'I think she's going,' said Vin, panicking. 'We're going to lose her, Dad. She's dying.' Two men dressed like tradesman approached. 'Let me see,' said one of them, kneeling on the ground. 'I can help.' He reached over and put his whole hand in my mouth. After a moment, he pulled it out again. 'Nah, mate,' he said, looking up at my dad. 'Too late. She's gone.' Vin laid my head on the ground and stood up crying. Dad looked at her and said angrily, 'Why did you let those men come near her? You shouldn't have let them touch her.' I woke up stunned. It was the first time I had dreamt I'd died.

In my first year in Hertford, I returned home to Twickenham every weekend because my parents expected me to. They had more control over me if I was right there in front of their eyes. But our weekends were too often filled with conflict. Why had I cut my hair? I looked far too Western. When was I going to wear sensible clothes? (I had painted my shoes banana-yellow using Dulux gloss.) Why did I have to wear such a large nose-stud? By the second year I went home less frequently, but even then Dad managed to exert his influence from afar. I'd come back to my digs at the end of a day of lectures to find my letterbox stuffed with reminders of overdue library books, rent bills and, from time to time, a buff-coloured envelope with a second-class postage stamp addressed to Miss. S. Das in Dad's unmistakable cursive. I'd open it and there would often be no letter, just newspaper clippings: '*Racism in Britain Today*'; '*Fears for Missing Student*'; '*Girl, 8, Graduates with Honours*'.

The engine of the arranged marriage juggernaut was idling while I was away from home. Efforts to find a match never actually stopped. But now that I'd started my course, Dad, true to form, wanted me to do well. He was always afraid that I'd fail my degree, or – even worse – come back after three years with more than just a degree. 'If you come home and tell me you want to marry an Englishman,' he once said, 'you will never see anyone as dangerous as me.'

Most of the time he suspected I was spending too much time with friends and insufficient time studying. I read newspapers a little more frequently, and Dad's clippings were always interesting, but like most students I got much of my news from the TV or radio and I didn't always pay as much attention as I should, because my new life held far too many distractions. Dad would use my trips back home at weekends to quiz me relentlessly on my knowledge of international current affairs.

'What's happening in South Africa?'

'I don't know. Apartheid?'

'Every damn fool knows about apartheid. I mean, what happened there this week?'

'I don't know. Tell me, Dad. Tell me what happened there this week.'

So Dad would explain the latest development in detail: that the P. W. Botha regime had declared a nationwide state emergency and what its implications were likely to be, or that the British had imposed sanctions and how this might play out.

'It is vital to read the newspaper,' he said. 'One day there might be a war and you won't know where to go for shelter because you won't have read the front page.'

'If there's a war, Dad, and there's not going to be, but if there's a war I'll know about it because I will have heard it on the radio.'

Living away from home gave me the confidence to exercise impudence when I returned. Once I had merely posed questions about the prevailing orthodoxy, gingerly probing the parameters of the world, but now I used retorts and sarcasm to try to shape that same world. Things had turned upside down. It was Dad who had not wanted me to leave home to study or to consider journalism as a career, yet here he was, wanting me to get good grades and read newspapers. It was I who had wanted to do a degree and become a journalist, yet here I was, without a care for my studies or the slightest inclination to pick up a newspaper. After one fraught conversation I found Dad staring at me with fixed eyes. 'You're a lion at home and a lamb outside,' he said, felling me with one blow.

In the summer of 1986, after two years of being away, I was at my parents' house during the end-of-year break. I had a summer job working as a clerical assistant in a car showroom. It was mindless work. The filing was brain-jarringly dull and the salesmen were lecherous, but I earned £100 a week and that was a lot of money for a twenty-one-year-old student. One sunny evening I came home to find Mum and Dad hadn't been to work. I smelt the familiar aroma of cumin seeds sizzling in oil as I entered the kitchen. Mum was standing over a pan wearing an apron she'd sewn herself, complete with frilly edge. Dad was folding plastic carrier bags for recycling. He never thoughtlessly scrunched them and shoved into a bag for later use. He always folded them neatly so they took up as little room as possible.

My parents both had a somewhat cheery disposition. Dad looked as if he was trying to suppress a smile and Mum was humming. I was instantly alarmed by their behaviour. Through the window I caught a glimpse of a stranger sitting in a chair on the lawn in the back garden – an Indian man enjoying the warm evening breeze. He looked vaguely familiar.

'Who's that in the garden?' I asked.

'That's Dinesh, the doctor from India,' said Dad. I looked around the kitchen quickly for clues about what was going on. Was Mum making one of her special feasts? Were more visitors coming? Nobody had told me Dinesh was in the country, let alone visiting us today. Upstairs I could hear Vin laughing with Raja and a radio playing. Why was her laughter always so bloody carefree? She would be confronting an arranged marriage too, one day. Didn't the dead weight of that impending horror crush the laughter out of her? Why was her breathing so free and easy, while mine was short and shallow?

For the years that I had been away from home, Vin had lived without my influence, perhaps even my bad influence. She disliked the fact that I would return home each summer to disturb the tranquility of the house with my rowing, sneering and seething, and then leave for the start of the new term, like a hurricane blowing through a dingle-dell cottage.

'I don't want to be like you,' she once said. 'You're the most irritating person in the world and you hurt Mum and Dad all the time. It's always either your way or the highway. Why don't you just stop causing trouble?' We weren't the same person anymore and we probably never would be again.

I put down my bag and stepped into the garden. Dad followed. Dinesh looked up and we greeted each other. He had light brown skin and looked younger than he had in photos I'd been shown. His hair was very black, as if dye was concealing its natural light and dark tones. He didn't smile much. Vin and Raja, I later discovered, had already met him. He had visited our house before, but I had been in Hertford at the time. So everyone in the family had met him, except me. Vin and Raja joined us in the garden and everyone chatted with ease, mainly about Dinesh's career as a medical practitioner. Dinesh was a match put forward by Dad's side of the family in India, most of whom were also doctors.

It's odd how memories of significant moments can only be recalled as disjointed snippets which, when pieced together, form the whole picture, but not seamlessly. Yet irrelevant and insignificant memories, like the hugeness of a doorknob in your child hand, or the smell of dry elm leaves on the way to school, can remain alive at the fore of your mind for no apparent purpose at all.

I can't remember exactly what I spoke to Dinesh about in the garden, but I know we talked about diabetes, and somewhere in the conversation I mentioned the islets of Langerhans, the part of the pancreas that produces insulin. There's no accounting for the bizarre details one absorbs from *Reader's Digest* articles. Dinesh looked at me, surprised.

'You know about the islets of Langerhans?' he said.

'Yes, I do.'

I recall that particular snippet of conversation not because I have a special fondness for pancreatic juices, but because, momentarily, there was the possibility that I might have impressed him. It was a bud of a moment that, if allowed, might have flourished into something more mature. I let it pass by because I lacked the will to capture it.

Later that evening while Mum chatted to Dinesh in the living room, I took Dad aside in the kitchen and we spoke quietly.

'No, Dad.'

'Why not?' he asked gently.

'He's okay. He's nice, but I don't want to marry him.'

'But what's wrong with him?'

'Nothing. Nothing at all. I just want to finish my degree. I have another year to go yet.' It was a legitimate reason.

'Love will grow,' said Dad in a half whisper, as if he was finally revealing one of life's hidden secrets.

'Dad, I could live with a smelly sock for the rest of my life, and grow to love that too.' He looked at me, bewildered. It was quite possibly the daftest analogy I had ever used. It simply fell out of my mouth. Words, especially unwise or hurtful words, once said, cannot be retrieved by the speaker. They exist as a form of regretful pain, if not in the ears of the listener, then always in the memory of the speaker.

Perhaps Dad took this imbecilic comment as a sign that he ought not to push the conversation further; perhaps he had expected me to say no. Perhaps he already had a contingency plan. At any rate, his earlier muted cheeriness evaporated and he said nothing more to me for the rest of the evening. I retreated to my bedroom. Mum and Dad stayed up late talking to Dinesh – much later than they would ordinarily have done with a visitor.

The next morning I was getting ready for work when I heard muffled conversation from the living room, directly below my bedroom. Mum and Dad were talking with Vin, but I couldn't make out what anyone was saying. As I went downstairs I noticed the living room door was slightly ajar. I could hear Vin's voice: 'He's okay, but I'm not sure. I don't really know him.'

I hesitated on the stairs and then decided to join them to find out what was being discussed. But at the bottom step, I found myself walking towards the front door. 'I'm off,' I yelled. 'See you tonight, about five-ish.' I closed the front door behind me and took the long way to the car showroom: up to the end of the curvy road, past the bus stop and across the main road, near the big roundabout. Was Vin the fallback? Were they going to try to marry her to Dinesh? Would she feel compelled to step in to avoid our family being humiliated because of my rejection? Would they be able to talk her round?

Since I'd been away in Hertford, she had left school and was building a career in fashion while still living with Mum and Dad. She managed a number of women's clothing shops in London and was proving to be a deft sales coordinator. 'No, that dress does you no favours,' she once told an overweight customer who came out of the fitting room, her rolls of fat stuffed into a tight white dress. 'Here, try this orange one. The kaftan look is all the rage this summer. Ever thought how glamorous you might look in orange?' I wondered if Vin had become bored selling clothes to women. And now that I had said no to Dinesh, had she seen an opportunity to move out of Mum and Dad's house and build a new life for herself with him?

Given that Dinesh was a match suggested by my paternal relatives, there was a great deal at stake for my dad. With two daughters approaching a ripe age for marriage, he had declared he was in the market for suitors for them. His family in India had dutifully put forward an eminently suitable boy, who had gone to the trouble of making a reconnaissance trip to Britain. Dad had welcomed him warmly as if he was in own son. The fact that I had rejected him was embarrassing enough. To have two daughters saying no would be catastrophic. And for such gross humiliation to be visited upon a man with a reputation in the community as impeccable as my dad's would be mortifying.

I spent the day at the car showroom agitated and distracted. Constantly looking at my watch, wishing I could fast-forward the day so I could rush home and talk to Vin. As the clock struck five I was already out of the showroom, running home the short way. I ran through the house calling for her, even though I knew she couldn't be there because the locked porch door signalled I was the first one home. As I was trying to regain my composure I heard a key turn. I rushed into the hallway and threw open the door. Vin looked smart in her work clothes – fashionable and classy, with her hair tied in a high ponytail.

'What happened this morning?' I asked urgently. She walked past me and up the stairs, straight into the bedroom without saying a word. She closed the door and kicked off her heels.

'They asked me what I thought of Dinesh,' she said.

'And?'

'I said he was okay.'

'What are you going to do?'

'I don't know,' she said, sitting on the bed. 'What are *you* going to do?'

'I don't know either.'

We both sat in silence for a while. 'Look,' I began. 'I have another year before I finish my course. There's no way I'm going to have an arranged marriage before or after it's finished. I'm going to marry who I want.'

'Who?' she asked.

'You don't know him,' I lied.

I didn't know him either, of course. I didn't even have a boyfriend. But two years of freedom in Hertford had confirmed in my mind that I would never be able to go through with an arranged marriage. And my decision had implications for Vin.

'One day I'm going to tell them,' I said urgently. 'I know I'm putting a noose around my own neck. I know I'm the eldest and I'm supposed to get married first, but as soon as I tell them I don't want an arranged marriage, our family's finished. Then no one will marry *you*. Do you understand? I don't want to destroy your chances of getting married, Vin – not if you *want* an arranged marriage. Don't wait for me. You have to make a decision. And if you really want to marry Dinesh you might be better off doing it before I drop my bombshell.'

She looked at me with a face devoid of emotion. She didn't share her thoughts with me much these days. 'Do you want an arranged marriage?' I asked her.

'I don't know. I suppose it could work. I'm not completely against them. The only thing is, I don't know what he's like.'

I honestly didn't know whether she would say yes or no to Dinesh, but I felt it was only right that I told her of my intentions.

Days later, Mum and Dad sought an answer from Vin. Would she marry Dinesh? They asked her to decide as he was about to return to India and they wanted to know whether to officially start talks with his family. They told her I was a lost cause and that only she could give the family a good name. Standing precariously between my impending bombshell and her desire to meet parental expectations, Vin agreed to marry Dinesh on the condition my parents allowed her a long engagement to get to know him better.

Mum and Dad were overjoyed and relieved in equal measure. Suddenly, there was a lightness in the air, as if someone had pulled back all the curtains in the house and let the sunshine in. My parents were floating with happiness and, from then on, things happened very quickly. By the end of the summer, Vin was formally engaged to Dinesh. He returned to India to await a date for the wedding and wind up his affairs before migrating to Britain, and I returned to Hertford for my last year of parole.

Many years later I asked Vin, 'Did you feel pressured to marry that summer?'

'Yes,' she said flatly.

'By Mum and Dad? By what they said?'

'Partly,' she said. 'But what you said about your bombshell was a big contributing factor.' It gutted me to know she felt pressured to marry because of me.

In my final year I barely went home at all – two, maybe three times. Mum and Dad were preoccupied with wedding plans that were becoming increasingly complicated. With our family being spread between Britain and India, it was decided that Vin and Dinesh should marry in both countries.

An additional concern was immigration technicalities. The days when a man in a Commonwealth country could simply apply for an employment voucher and get into Britain were gone. By the 1970s British authorities suspected immigration scams by spouses from India and Pakistan and embarked on a frightening and disgusting form of crackdown. Indian and Pakistani women hoping to emigrate to Britain to marry were subjected to intimate personal examinations by immigration staff to 'check their marital status'. Virginity tests were banned in 1979 after a British newspaper revealed that an Indian woman had been subjected to a virginity test at Heathrow by a male doctor. In 2011 the *Guardian* published reports showing that the practice had been more widespread than first thought, particularly in British high commission offices in India and Pakistan.

Since honour and chastity are of paramount importance in Asian communities, the practice horrified Indians in Britain and India, and I recall my parents discussing virginity tests in hushed tones with my uncle and aunt when I was a teenager. I remember the expression on my mum's face: a mixture of disgust and fear.

In the 1980s British authorities still suspected spouse immigration scams, but by now had become much craftier. There were rumours that immigration officials were subjecting married couples to intense questioning about their wedding day in an attempt to establish whether the arranged marriage was genuine. Undoubtedly, this would have been a strategy employed to sift out those who had engaged in sham marriages as an excuse to get into Britain.

Essentially, this is how it worked: British Indian girl (or boy) travels to India and marries Indian boy (or girl). Girl then applies for her Indian spouse to be allowed to migrate to Britain so they can live together. British immigration officials in the high commission in New Delhi interview the husband and wife separately, asking questions about their courtship and wedding day. The answers are then compared to see if they tally. Any husband and wife team whose answers do not match are presumably put in the 'sham marriage' category and the application to enter Britain is knocked back on the grounds of insufficient proof of a genuine marriage.

It was rumoured that just one small slip-up could ruin a new bride or groom's chance of getting into Britain. Couples felt under pressure to 'get the answers right'. Even those engaged in genuine arranged marriages started rehearsing their lines. Parents advised their sons and daughters to answer questions carefully, and kids, who'd been told for years that love would grow after marriage, were now being told to behave as if they were already in love.

The surreal summer of 1986, when I said no and Vin said yes, seemed to pass faster than other summers. When winter came round, Vin was off to India with Mum and Dad, where she had a small Hindu wedding and became Dinesh's wife. (They planned to have a ceremonial wedding in Britain once they returned for the sake of friends and family living there.) When Dinesh applied to migrate to Britain, he and Vin were asked by British immigration authorities in New Delhi to attend separate interviews.

In the waiting room at the British High Commission, fans whirred overhead as newly married couples waited to be questioned. Most women there wore brightly coloured clothes and plenty of heavy gold jewellery – as newly wed Indian women are wont to do. Vin wore a simple flowery dress and high-heeled shoes, and was the only woman wearing Western clothes in the waiting room.

Dinesh was interviewed first. When he emerged from the interrogation room nearly an hour later, he had the air of a shattered man.

'He looked like he'd been beaten up,' said Vin, recalling the day. When it was her turn, she entered the room with confidence, reaching out her hand to greet the official behind the desk – who she said bore a striking resemblance to Louis Mountbatten, the last viceroy of India. He rose to shake her hand. 'I don't think any of the other Indian women shook Mountbatten's hand,' said Vin, 'but I made that fucker stand up and shake mine. That's when I knew we were equals.'

He grilled her about her wedding day. Where did she get married? What was she wearing? When did she first meet her husband? Where did they go for their honeymoon?

'What will you do if your husband is denied entry into Britain?' he asked.

'It doesn't matter where we end up living. I don't care if we have to live on the moon, as long as we're together,' she replied.

'And what colour were the sheets on your wedding night?'

'I can't remember, it was dark.'

Vin was taken aback by that question. But she provided an excellent comeback, just as she had the day Dad had questioned her about the skip outside the dilapidated house she never visited in Teddington. A few months later, Dinesh got a stamp in his passport. He packed his bags, said goodbye to his family and flew to London immediately to start a love affair with his wife.

By the time Dinesh migrated to Britain, I was still in Hertford lurching from one panic attack to the next. There were just four months to go before I sat my finals and I was appallingly under-prepared. For two and a half years I had given insufficient thought to my studies. I had begged Dad to allow me to leave home to do a degree and promised I would study hard, but now I feared I would not meet his expectations.

I had already let him down by rejecting the men he'd proposed, and had justified doing so by telling myself I was entitled to choose my own life partner. But there could be no justification for doing poorly in my degree. I feared that what lay before me now looked like a straight path to failure. After three years of paid tertiary study there was no guarantee I would find work, let alone work as a journalist. The year was 1987, and though unemployment had begun to fall, there were still more than three million people trying to get by without a job.

Much of the partying died down as final-year students bunkered down to swot. Flowers peeping through garden fences signalled the reawakening of summer, yet I was unable to feel the optimism they normally brought, for the fearful gloom that had descended behind my eyes showed me a world in black and white only.

Then again, Vin and Dinesh were about to get married, and there's nothing to lift the heart quite like the joy of a riotous Indian wedding.

CHAPTER 10

An Arranged Marriage

'My family is my strength and my weakness.' Aishwarya Rai

It must have been late by the time I left my friend's place. There was no moon so the night was as dark as it could be. I took a shortcut through a park to my student accommodation. The grass underfoot felt damp and springy and I walked quickly even though it wasn't uncomfortably cold. I was about halfway across the park when I heard someone behind me, their footsteps squelching in the wet grass. I started running and whoever was behind me started running too. I ran faster and faster, taking great leaps as I went. Panic was pressing on my chest and my legs were an instant away from buckling under me when I heard a man's voice. 'Go on, go on,' he jeered, 'run to the comfort of your mother.' I kept running, the stamina coming from sheer terror. I don't remember opening the front door, only leaping up the stairs two at a time to my bedroom, where I slammed the door shut behind me. The phone started ringing and I looked about the dark room. There was no phone there, yet it sounded as if it was right next to me.

I opened my eyes. Light poured in through the gap in the curtains. My legs were quivering and my T-shirt stuck to my chest as I lay in my bed. I was exhausted. The phone was still ringing. I got out of bed, still shaking, and hurried downstairs to answer it.

'Hi, it's John. Hope you don't mind me ringing – I know it's earlyish.'

'Hi.'

'You okay? Sorry if I woke you.'

'It's fine.'

'Hey, I was just wondering – fancy going out for a coffee today or just catching up, or something?'

Was he asking me for a date? I looked in the mirror hanging opposite. My eyes looked puffy and there were small beads of sweat above my top lip. It couldn't have been a side effect of the antidepressants the doctor had prescribed because I'd thrown them in the bin as soon as I'd picked them up from the chemist. I didn't need drugs – not that kind anyway.

'Sure,' I said. 'Why don't you come over to my place about two o'clock.'

I'd known *of* John Hobson for about a year because I'd seen him around the campus many times. He was a singularly peculiar-looking student, who tucked his jeans into his thick woolly socks and walked with a purposeful stride. He had extraordinarily large swimming-pool eyes and long, dark eyelashes – longer than a man's normally would be. His bee-stung pink lips were always ever-so-slightly apart and there was a sharp demarcation where his high forehead ended and his hairline began. You couldn't forget a face like his because the default expression was one of harmless curiosity, like a three-year-old looking into a camera lens.

He had a good rapport with Sanjeev Bhaskar, a fellow student who, after he finished his degree, went on to become a household name with the success of his comedy TV shows *Goodness Gracious Me* and the *The Kumars at No. 42*. In the late 1980s Sanj was already wowing students as one half of a duo comedy called *The Bhaji Boys*. They used to perform at the Boathouse – our student bar. Sanj had a remarkable talent for mimicking accents that John found very impressive. Being a scholarly type, John had started a PhD at the London School of Economics. I first met him when he returned to Hertford to give a one-off lecture. We had swapped telephone numbers then and now he was coming over at two o'clock.

It was raining when he arrived. His soft, zippered leatherjacket smelt faintly of roast beef. I was supposed to be revising, so we didn't bother going out. We sat in my room and talked over a cup of tea instead.

'What do you think of the political economy course?' he said, flicking through my revision notes.

'It's okay, I suppose.'

'What do you know about it?' He asked the question seriously, like a teacher might speak to a pupil.

'Not much. I'll probably fail.'

'No, you won't. I'll tell you everything you need to know.'

It was an odd thing to say, but that's exactly what he did. He spent the next four months travelling from Camden in London, where he lived, to Hertford, taking me through the course in summary form, step by step. Whether it was at my place, his place, in a café, at the Boathouse bar or walking down the street, he engaged me in lively conversation about the theories, the arguments, the counterarguments and the big thinkers that I needed to know about. He read my essays, asked me questions, checked and double-checked that I understood the concepts. He was a masterful teacher: patient, committed and curious to hear my thoughts.

'The history of all hitherto existing society is the history of class struggles,' he once said, sitting in a café mimicking the archetypal nutty professor, and then he burst into laughter with his mouth so wide, I could see he had no amalgam fillings at all. I looked at him warily. 'Marx, Karl Marx,' he said, in the tone he would have adopted if he'd been saying, 'Bond, James Bond.' 'We can learn a lot from Marx, even though he's so bloody reductionist,' he added.

John was the great-grandson of the famous economist and critic of imperialism J. A. Hobson. John's father was a capitalist who, no doubt, would have liked to have seen his son become a successful businessman. But John had rebelled against capitalism by becoming a Marxist. He was twenty-four years old and the only person I knew who had read all three volumes of *Das Kapital*. 'I just sat in my room with the curtains drawn and read them. It took me six months,' he told me.

But that was the past. 'The problem with Marxism is that it's too neat,' he said. 'Marx simply doesn't have all the answers. I found myself increasingly unable to argue my case. That's why I'm not a Marxist anymore.'

'So what are you then?' I asked.

'Not sure.'

'Does that mean you're a wishy-washy liberal?'

'Ah! Now, it depends on what you mean by liberal.' Whenever he started a sentence with 'Ah! Now . . .' it usually signalled that he was about to take a complex subject, condense two hundred years of history pertaining to the particular topic and then explain its relevance. Whether he was tossing around the ideas of Marx, Weber, Nietzsche, Machiavelli or Thatcher, he would become animated to the point of virtually exploding. He would leave me mesmerised by his very intonation, if not the ideas themselves, and then he would ask for *my* thoughts on the matter.

If John had any venom in his veins, he saved it all for Margaret Thatcher. Unlike his father, John believed 'Maggie' was destroying the country. Social unrest, industrial strife, cripplingly high unemployment, the doubling of inflation, the collapse of the manufacturing industry: these were the features of her rule that he despised. 'There's only one word to describe Margaret Thatcher: cruel,' he thundered, marching around my bedroom, running his hands furiously through his hair and bringing down clenched fists against his thighs. His tendency to exhibit excessive nervous energy and supreme agitation simultaneously made him a charming confusion of Basil Fawlty and George Costanza.

I have a delightful old photograph of him standing next to Margaret Thatcher in a London street, his trousers tucked into his socks, with one arm around her shoulder and the other gently pulling her towards him in a loose embrace. Thatcher is wearing a navy suit and holding a handbag and has her arm around John. Both are looking at the camera and smiling. Behind them, graffitied in block letters on a wall is the word LIFE. There is no one else in the shot.

'How on earth did you come to be hugging her?' I asked when I first saw it.

'Look carefully. The old trout's a cardboard cut-out,' he replied. And indeed, if you look at the photo closely, you notice Thatcher *is* a cardboard cut-out. But the pose is so natural, and the lighting so exquisite, the pair of them look as though they are intimate friends.

John and I spent a great deal of time together, during which he never seemed to tire of teaching me. I got used to the smell of roast beef on his leatherjacket and his obsession with playing U2 cassettes on a loop. I told him about my fear of going home after the finals and the arranged marriage that my parents were expecting me to go through. I told him about the tyranny of the Indian mother-in-law, the social hierarchy of Indian families and how so much hinged on honour, and he was horror-struck that such a subculture could exist in Britain. He was raised in what one might call a very English family, and while he had a handful of male Indian friends, such as Sanj, he had little insight into arranged marriages and what they entailed. He asked endless questions, as if he was an anthropologist discovering the living habits of a new tribe. His studious curiosity, which he employed in a determined bid to dissect and understand the sociology behind this cultural phenomenon, gave me the opportunity to consider it more closely too. And when it was time to sit my finals, John was by my side till the very moment I went in for the first exam. He had done all he could and the rest was up to me. The last thing he said before I went into the exam hall was, 'You can do it.'

When the results arrived by post a few months later, I was shocked to discover I had passed with a very respectable grade. John was delighted and Mum and Dad were relieved. My three years of parole were over and I returned to Twickenham, to find Vin had become quite enamoured with the idea of marriage and was actively participating in wedding preparations. Raja had grown into a strapping fourteen-year-old who lived in his own world of pop music and mates, and was hardly ever home. If his friends called round at the weekend, Raja would take them to his bedroom, where they would spent entire afternoons. He'd emerge in the evening to tell Mum and Dad he was going out. Vin and I had never been allowed that level of freedom, and privately I was disturbed by my parents' double standards.

The end of the academic year was always the beginning of summer, which meant Mum would look forward to the *Rakhi* festival, usually observed according to lunar movements around June, July or August. The ceremony is a celebration of the bond of love between brothers and sisters, and is probably my favourite Indian ceremony because if its simplicity. Sisters tie a thread around their brother's wrist as a gesture of affection and the brother in return presents his sister with a gift to symbolise his promise to protect her from life's hazards. As with any Indian festival, the ceremony involves a certain amount of feasting and merrymaking. But in our house Mum always kept it simple, perhaps to distinguish it from bigger celebrations.

Mum and Dad would go 'Indian shopping' and buy several ceremonial wrist threads that had attached to them in the middle a small round tinsel decoration or colourful disc. They looked like glittery kitsch watches. 'Come and choose a *Rakhi*,' Mum would trill, and Vin and I would peer into the box on the kitchen bench and each choose a thread. We delighted in choosing the gaudiest ones, knowing Raja would have to wear them on his wrist for the rest of the day. Mum would beam as I tied my thread around Raja's wrist and then stepped aside to allow Vin to do the same. After that, Raja would pull out of his pocket two £5 notes that Mum had given him earlier, and present one to me and one to Vin. We didn't engage in elaborate gift-giving on this day. In our younger days Raja would complain the ceremony was unfair because he received no money, only a tacky wrist decoration, and Mum would laugh and relish explaining the meaning of it all. Everyone in the family enjoyed *Rakhi* day because it brought us together and momentarily allowed us to put aside our frustrations and troubles with each other.

Within days of my return to Twickenham I went back to my vacation job at the car showroom, where the salesmen were still vulpine and the cars still overpriced. But this summer I had a lightness in my step. John and I had started a relationship that held all the illicit thrills of secrecy as well as the fear, for me anyway, that Mum and Dad might discover I *had* returned from college with more than just a degree. I'd come back with an Englishman, of all things. Well, at least I didn't want to be a poet. I decided I would continue seeing John on the quiet and refrain from bringing discord into the house. As Vin had said, I needed to stop causing trouble, especially since Mum and Dad were happier than I had ever seen them because Vin and Dinesh were about to marry for the second time – this time with a ceremonial British Indian wedding.

All weddings are complicated, maddening affairs, but nothing beats an Indian wedding for sheer bedlam. Punjabis are especially gifted at organising friendly chaos. Planning and preparations can drag on for months and still there will be shocking pandemonium on the day. In contrast to Western weddings, where things are planned to the minute – where even the bride's late arrival is factored into the programme – Indian weddings seem deliberately organised to make a mockery of the word 'schedule'. That said, everything is carefully planned, just randomly thrown together. Details of the ceremony are endlessly discussed yet allowed to unfold as they please on the day. And along the way there will be an awful lot of shouting, a hullabaloo that would be a riot were it not for the celebratory smiles and hearty back-slapping.

As Punjab is home to Hindus, Sikhs and Muslims, Punjabi wedding traditions vary but also have similarities. The Hindu wedding ceremony is elaborate and long, and usually conducted in Sanskrit. The couple encircles a fire to seal their union. A Sikh wedding is considerably shorter, conducted in Punjabi and requires the couple to circumambulate the religious text of Sikhism, rather than a holy fire. Vin had a ceremonial Sikh wedding for pragmatic reasons.

But before the wedding there were numerous pre-wedding rituals to observe. The *Roka* ceremony, to formally mark an engagement, is only the start. When the time nears there is the *Sagan* ceremony, during which parental blessings are given to the engaged couple and gifts are exchanged. Essentially it is a ritual that marks both families' acceptance of the proposed match, part of which involves the girl being presented with a long red scarf, her *dupatta*, by her in-laws as a welcoming gesture. *Sangeet*, or singing sessions, are held in the homes of both families every evening till the day of the wedding. This usually amounts to an awful lot of partying in the run-up to the wedding day.

Then there is the *Mainyan* ceremony, in which the bride is bathed in a paste of turmeric and gram flour to give her a fairer glow. This is followed a day or so later by the *Mehndi* ceremony to decorate her hands and feet with henna (henna is a symbol of an inner glow). Last, there is the *Chooda* ceremony, in which handfuls of red and ivory bangles, washed in milk and rose petals, are placed on the girl's wrists. (Ivory has been replaced with white plastic these days.) Now, finally, the girl is ready for her big day, the day her mum and dad have been waiting for since she was born.

On the morning of her wedding day, Vin wore an ornate red and gold sari. Her bracelets extended almost as far as her elbows, and on her hands, each resplendent with henna patterns, she wore a *punja*, a gold bracelet attached by five intricate chains to five rings on each digit. Around her neck was a necklace of woven gold threads. Her fingernails and toenails were painted pillar-box red.

But the zenith of bridal gold jewellery is saved for a girl's face and head. It is unbelievably elaborate and smoulderingly exotic. A significant part of Vin's dowry was the jewellery she was given by Mum and Dad. She looked like a Bollywood star wearing it. An intricately woven gold chain starting at the crown of her head flowed down the central parting in her hair and came to rest in a round *tikka* (disc) at the top of her forehead. From there the chain split, flowing to the right and the left, following her natural hairline to her ears. Just below the *tikka*, in the centre of her forehead close to her eyebrows, sat a teardrop bindi in blood red.

All women look beautiful wearing a bindi. It is a unique, surprisingly erotic and captivating symbol: a third eye, a drop of sensuality, the focal point of a woman's wisdom. Vin's face was instantly transformed into a countenance of powerful dignity. Above each black eyebrow ran an alluring arc of small alternating red and white dots that curved around on to her cheeks, framing her dark eyes as if with confetti. A large gold nose-stud was connected to her left ear with a loosely hanging chain and her ears dripped with gold bell-shaped earrings. Tiny paisley petals quivered from the rims. Her lips were an exquisite pout of intense red.

It was barely possible to absorb at once all the colour and radiance from Vin's bridal costume. Her make-up masked her expression and I couldn't tell what she was thinking. Was she happy? Was she frightened? Was she relieved? She was about to marry the man I had turned down.

Since she'd accepted the match, we hadn't talked much. She was about to do what I could never bring myself to do. By the end of the day she would have *sindoor* in the parting of her hair – the mark of a married woman.

Should I have been standing in her shoes that day? There is such a small space between the words yes and no. It could have been me wearing red and gold that day. It could have been me preparing to leave my father's house. I tried to picture myself in Vin's bridal outfit. But I couldn't muster the mental image. There had been such a small space between me and Vin as little girls, only just making us two people. But now, in her bridal outfit, she stood as a distinctly separate person.

I hadn't asked her how she felt about Dinesh; she probably wouldn't have told me anyway. Once she had accepted him, she was effectively honour-bound to treat him with the utmost respect, and no doubt that would have included not discussing her private thoughts about him with me. I was confident that the family would have chosen well, that Dinesh would be a good husband and she a good wife. I was confident that she would always stand by her man. What I could not be confident about was whether she would be happy. I felt my emotions being tossed around like corks in the sea. I was delighted she was moving into the next stage of her life – perhaps she would have romance and love would grow. But I would see less of her, and, even though we had moved apart, she remained my most treasured friend. It was going to be a joyful wedding day, but I couldn't help feeling the sting of self-hate. Why? Because I was relieved. Relieved that it was not I who was preparing to marry. And something about that relief made me dislike myself.

Outside, I heard the sound of men's voices. I looked out of the window to see the arrival of the *barat* – the collective term for the groom's male family members and other accompanying men. Dinesh was wearing a grey Western suit. My dad greeted him at the front door with warmth and respect. By now our English neighbours were aware that something was up and were looking through their windows as wedding guests snapped up every available parking spot down our road.

Traditionally, each side of the front door is anointed with a drop of oil before the groom is received. So there was Mum, the proudest Indian mother in all of England, standing on the doorstep of the porch, a plastic one-litre bottle of vegetable oil from the kitchen cupboard in her hand, waiting to greet the man into whose care she was going entrust her youngest daughter.

The *barat* eventually left for the local Anglican church hall where the Sikh wedding was to take place, and Vin followed shortly afterwards. As the bride's sister, it was my job to stay near her, help her adjust her sari, give her tissues when required, dispose of the scrunched-up old ones, bring her a glass of water, tell her if there was anything untoward visible in either nostril, and other such things. But once we arrived at the hall, I couldn't get within a two-metre radius of her because of the throng of guests aching to see the bride. Dumpy middle-aged Indian women, with their polyester cardigans and fat elbows, formed the front rank of the phalanx bearing down on her.

Vin married before three hundred guests, and like any other Indian wedding I've ever attended, few of them paid attention to the words uttered by the holy man. They organised themselves so that men sat on one side of the hall and women and children on the other. The women instinctively pulled their long, colourful *dupattas* or saris over their heads as a gesture of respect while the men, who all appeared to have come equipped with clean white handkerchiefs, proceeded to knot them over their heads as a gesture of respect. Most people had removed their shoes before entering the hall, so the entrance foyer looked like the bargain basement section of a second-hand shoe shop.

While the priest went about his business chanting holy words, small children ran up and down the sides of the hall wailing for their lost mums. Others sat eating crisps and tittering. Teenagers slouched about while women gossipped. Occasionally a seated man would grab a child running around in circles and send him over to his mother on the other side of the hall, whereupon she would pull him over to her seat, give him a sharp clip around the ear and thrust a bag of salt and vinegar crisps in his lap. There appeared to be, on the face of it, a serious paucity of decorum, but then that's nothing new at an Indian wedding.

On the stage where the ceremony took place, I sat cross-legged near Vin, but I couldn't tell whether the ceremony had started or whether the priest was saying pre-wedding chants. Then a mutter went through those assembled on the stage that the coconut had been left behind at the house. Not *a* coconut, but *the* coconut. Mum, looking anxious, bounded off the stage, so I followed.

'What's going on?' I asked over the din.

'We've left the coconut at home,' said Mum. 'We need it. It has a red ribbon round it. It's on the kitchen bench.'

'What do you need it for?' Realising she would need to explain five thousand years of Hindu custom, I didn't let her begin. 'Never mind. Get Dad or Raja to go home and get it.'

So off went someone, I have no idea who, to get the coconut. None of the guests had any idea what was going on, so it didn't matter that everything was behind schedule. *How much* behind schedule was anybody's guess. The coconut, Mum explained later, was a gift sent by Vin's parents-in-law as a symbol to ward off evil. When it had been fetched, it was passed gingerly through the crowd as if it was the Kohinoor finally retrieved from the crown jewels. Once it was in Mum's grasp she instantly relaxed.

The wedding ceremony took place around the holy text. As is customary, Vin sat cross-legged to the left of Dinesh. Over one shoulder he had draped a pink sash and when the time came, my Dad performed his fatherly duty by tying a knot between one end of Dinesh's sash and a corner of Vin's sari *pallu* – the loose end that is draped over the shoulder. Apart from the obvious symbolism involved in *literally* tying the knot, the gesture also symbolises a girl being passed by her father from his care to that of her husband's. Connected like this, Dinesh led Vin around the scriptures four times in a clockwise direction. During their circumambulations, the holy man spoke words seeking god's blessing, emphasising the couple's loyalty to each and reminding them of their family and religious duties. After the fourth round Vin and Dinesh were formally husband and wife.

There was much feasting, singing and dancing for the rest of the day, until, somewhat exhausted, we returned to my parents' house for the final post-wedding ritual, the *dholi* ceremony. This was the last time Vin would set foot in Dad's house still a daughter of the household. Once gone, she would return only as a member of her husband's household.

Many of the wedding guests came to the house to witness this final, heartbreakingly sad moment when Vin tearfully bade farewell to everyone. Mum could not stop the flow of her tears and nor did she try. The cacophony of the wedding celebration had evaporated and there was a hush in the front garden as the afternoon turned to evening. The car was waiting as Dinesh said his last goodbyes to guests waiting to shake his hand. Vin walked towards the car and then turned to Mum, Dad, me and Raja, embracing us all as if she no longer belonged to our family. And indeed, technically speaking, she did not.

CHAPTER 11

The Ice Age

'Usually when people are sad, they don't do anything. They just cry over their condition. But when they get angry, they bring about change.' Malcolm X

John and I continued our illicit relationship, which became more difficult as the days passed. He spent most of his time in the British Library and was difficult to contact as these were pre-mobile-phone days. Dating took careful planning and involved John driving from Camden in his beat-up Mini across town to Twickenham. It was a tedious, sometimes two-hour-long journey through congested traffic that ate away at valuable time. Sometimes we met for no more than an hour during my lunchbreak. (I still worked at the car showroom.) Other times, I would lie to my parents, fabricating some story about going to the movies with girlfriends to get an evening out with him. It was absurd and deeply frustrating that at the age of twenty-two

I was scurrying around, ducking and weaving through life to hide my relationship with John from Mum and Dad. Soon John and I began to realise that the secrecy was unsustainable. We talked loosely about marriage, but both of us remained hesitant to charge into the unknown and bring down upon ourselves all the attendant consequences.

On one occasion I learnt that Mum and Dad would be away one evening, probably until late. Seeing an opportunity, I rang John and we arranged to meet. He would drive to Twickenham and park his car halfway up the road (so it wasn't too near my parents' house) and I would join him around six o'clock once my parents had left. Unfortunately things didn't go quite to plan – they never do. As my parents were getting ready, my *nanni* arrived. Had they arranged for her to effectively 'babysit' while they were out? So I couldn't go out as planned because *nanni* was there to guard the front door. Around six, while she was watching TV, I told her I was popping out to post a letter. I found John sitting in the Mini halfway up the road as planned. I explained why I couldn't leave the house.

'I don't know how long *nanni* is going to stay,' I said, standing on the pavement leaning down to the driver's window. 'She might leave in a short while or she might stay the whole evening till my parents get back. I can't leave while she's here.'

'Don't worry, I'll wait,' said John. I returned to the house. An hour later, *nanni* was still watching TV. I crept out of the house and sprinted up the road to John's car again.

'She's still here. I'm sorry. You'd better go back to Hertford,' I said.

'It's okay. I'll just carry on waiting.'

'You can't sit in your car waiting for me – you could be here all night.'

'I'll wait. I'll wait for as long as it takes,' he said softly.

The evening light was already fading. His blue eyes were steadfast, looking at me with ageless wanting. I felt like crying. I wanted to stay with John forever. Instead, I kissed him and left him sitting in the car. I don't know how long he sat there waiting in the dark, but I felt that I could spend my life with him and I didn't care about anything else in the world.

So, a month or two after Vin's wedding, John and I decided we had to come clean and tell my parents we were having a relationship. They most certainly would not approve. They might even try to separate us. But we couldn't continue with our illicit rendezvous; it was too difficult. In fact, the whole relationship was becoming untenable and that enraged me. We were adults, having a relationship that would have been acceptable in anybody's eyes but my parents'. We could not move in together, as leaving my parents' house an unmarried woman would have hurt the family's *izzat*, and possibly been more catastrophic than actually marrying. There was only one way forward: to stay together in a legitimate relationship, we had to stop pussyfooting and get married. I'm not sure either of us really wanted to get married immediately, but we felt we had no choice. Escaping an arranged marriage meant forcing ourselves to have a love marriage.

Now that Vin was safely married to a respectable Indian doctor, the time had come for me to drop what I had once referred to as my bombshell. I wondered whether I should write a letter and leave it for Mum and Dad, or tell them face to face. I decided to tell Dad that I wanted to marry an Englishman and let him break the news to Mum himself. For weeks I sought the right moment, but there were always distractions. The phone would ring, or the doorbell, or Mum would call Dad to help her in the kitchen.

So one Saturday night in September 1987, I made an appointment with my dad.

'Dad, I'd like to speak to you on Tuesday, at about eight o'clock. Is that okay?'

'Yes,' he said. He didn't ask me what I wanted to talk about. He didn't even express surprise that I was making an appointment to talk to him. Perhaps he assumed it would be bad news. Perhaps he had willed all those earlier distractions in the hope of avoiding the confrontation we had been heading towards for years.

In the ensuing days I tried to steel myself. I imagined there would be a huge argument accompanied by terrible shouting and tears. Dad was a calm man, not given to wild displays of emotion, but I feared he might lose control, unleash anger he had restrained for years and perhaps even hit me. Or perhaps he and Mum would turn me out of the house, telling me they didn't recognise me as their daughter anymore. I would spend the night at John's if that happened.

Strange as it may seem, I still had my small brown runaway's suitcase. I had taken it with me when I left home for three years to study, and I'd brought it back when I returned. I was twenty-two years old and I'd never unpacked it. Inside were still all the things I'd stowed in it many years before: a toothbrush, a few clothes, sanitary pads, a pen and the stolen photos. I opened it, looked at the photos and put them back. The letters inside the lid stared up at me: SIOUX. I took out the old clothes and replaced them with new ones, clicked the case shut and slipped it under the bed. I might still need it.

Despite being a fully grown adult, I didn't think things through with agonising pedantry as, say, a forty-year-old might: weighing up the pros and cons, balancing the financial cost against the benefit or considering and reconsidering the emotional, moral and ethical fallout of my actions. I thought I'd thought it through, and my youthful enthusiasm would certainly see the project through, but I hadn't really thought it through *properly* – with wisdom. I knew this meeting with Dad would be the confrontation to beat all confrontations, but I didn't know what was going to happen or how I would handle the fallout.

I understood what it meant to have a love marriage. I understood I would be the first in my family to break the tradition of arranged marriages. I understood that I was putting my interests before those of my parents and my extended family. I was defying my parents' culture. I understood that if my marriage failed, I alone would be responsible; and that my actions would hurt my parents because they would be the ones who would suffer condemnation from the Indian community. I knew I would have to forgo the warmth of family to pursue my own dreams and I knew that to free myself from my parents' stranglehold, I also had to throw off their embrace.

When Tuesday evening came, Dad was waiting for me in the dining room at eight. It was an ordinary weekday, but everything after this day would be anything but ordinary for him and me. He wore a look of haggard patience. My heart felt too big for my chest and my mouth was dry. 'Don't be scared, don't be scared,' I repeated to myself. But I was scared. How do you muster the strength to break your parents' hearts?

'Dad, I've been thinking about this arranged marriage thing,' I began. 'I'm really sorry, but I don't want to go through with it. I don't mean I don't like the guys you've been considering. I mean that I don't actually want an arranged marriage.'

'It's all right,' he said softly. 'You don't have to get married straight away. We will wait until you are ready.'

'No, that's not what I mean. I mean I don't want an arranged marriage – ever. I want to choose someone myself.'

'That's all right as well, you just tell us who he is, and we can make the necessary arrangements.' How peculiar that we were conversing in the same language yet we were so far apart in understanding. Was Dad deliberately facing away from reality?

'I've already met the person,' I said. I couldn't bear to say the word 'man' or 'boy' in his presence. Ludicrously, it seemed inappropriate.

'Who is it?' he asked. I thought I heard a note of mild but invariable irritation in his tone. I hesitated momentarily before I spoke.

'His name's John. He's English. I'm sorry.' Even as I said the words I felt cheap. Ashamed that I was not a virgin. Chastity is meant to be an Indian woman's most priceless possession and the loss of it to anyone other than her husband equates, mythologically speaking, to the eternal damnation of her soul. I looked down at the tablecloth so Dad could not sense my writhing discomfort, and waited for his response. He was silent, and he stayed silent for so long I thought he could hear my own shrill thoughts: 'Say something. For god's sake, say something.'

'Is it the same John I met in this house?' he finally said. I wondered which John he was talking about. I didn't look him in the eye; I couldn't bear to. Then I suddenly remembered he was talking about my old friend John. John who had sat smoking in the living room all those years ago. The John whom Dad had met by a mistake, when he was meant to meet Paul the drummer.

'No, not him,' I said, my shame multiplying exponentially, as if there had been many men in my life. Dad fell silent again and still I could not raise my eyes to look at him. We sat like that for some time, until I couldn't take it any longer. When I finally looked up, uncertainly, and saw my father's noble, angular face, he looked tired, so tired and thin. His gaze was fixed on me, not in anger, but with crushing despair in his eyes. He seemed, all of a sudden, so far away. His tears fell onto his light grey trousers, spreading into small dark drops of parental anguish.

'I'm sorry, Dad. I'm so sorry,' I said, and burst into childish tears.

Later that evening, when he told Mum, she lashed out and tried to strike me, but Dad held her back until she fell to her knees and broke down. She beat her head with her clenched fists and cried deep, breathy sobs of disappointment and pain.

From that day on, everything changed. At first Mum cried a lot. Vin and Dinesh, who lived in a neighbouring town, would call over and try to console her day after day, but her tears seemed endless. Through ajar doors I would hear them talking gently to Mum, soothing her frayed nerves, trying to retrieve the cheery, optimistic mother she had once been, celebrating her enthusiasm for life through her unfailing commitment to festive religious ceremonies. If I entered the room, they would all look at me with expressions of disgust and consternation.

Raja, whose existence till then had been very much at the fringes of home life since he spent so much time with his friends, re-entered the family fold and unleashed his anger at me for the misery I had wrought. 'Look what you've done to Mum and Dad,' he roared. At the age of fifteen he was a towering figure of mounting testosterone and self-righteous ire.

I learnt to stay out of people's way, retreating to my bedroom when there were others in the house. John was my only source of comfort. We met occasionally, but it was mostly on the phone that I kept him abreast of the tumult at home. My parents never asked to meet him. Eventually I arranged for John to visit us for tea one afternoon. He dressed smartly in a suit and tie. Dad and he spoke civilly to each other, mostly discussing John's studies. Dad asked him a little about his family but Mum stayed very much in the background and barely said a word. John didn't stay long, perhaps three-quarters of an hour. After he left my parents didn't make any comments. It was as if he had never been there.

As the days passed, communication between me and the rest of the family simply ceased to exist in any meaningful form. It was the beginning of our Ice Age. If I met Mum in the hallway, she would walk past me without looking at me or saying anything. If our eyes ever met, she would look away quickly. Her lips seemed permanently pursed. Her once open features were now a closed knot.

Communication between Dad and I became perfunctory, and Raja barely spoke to me. I was in a hitherto unknown zone: I was living in the same house as my brother and my parents, yet I was alone and shunned. I had tried to brace myself for frightful shouting and possible expulsion from the house, but what I now confronted was a crushing silence. I had not expected to be cold-shouldered within the warm confines of family. They had sent me to Coventry and I didn't know how to get back.

A week or so later Dad took me by surprise: 'Your mother and I have no say anymore. So, go. Go and marry whoever you want. There's nothing we can do about it.' He spat the words out bitterly and I was unsure what he expected me to say or do.

'Dad, I don't want it to be like this. I don't want to get married without your blessing.'

'Marry who you want,' he snapped. 'But you don't have my blessing.'

'Well then, I will carry on living under your roof until I do.'

He looked at me sharply and left the room.

Three months went by and still Mum didn't speak a single word to me. It was crippling. She had sent out Lady Capulet's directive: 'Talk not to me, for I'll not speak a word. Do as thou wilt, for I have done with thee.' If she wanted to communicate with me, she passed messages via my dad, as if he were her official spokesman. Every night she made dinner and set the table for Dad, Raja and herself but not me. I stayed in my bedroom until I smelt the aroma of her cooking and heard the others going into the dining room to eat, and then I would skulk down the stairs and lay my own place at the table.

Dinner was always in total silence, not like the old days when Vin and I would indulge in uncontrollable giggling fits and Dad would glare at us and make threats about how we wouldn't be laughing so much in our husband's houses. Obviously, Mum didn't want me to join them for dinner each night, but I silently insisted on having my presence noticed, if not acknowledged.

It was a truly unbearable existence – familial persecution, day after day. I wondered how long we could continue this charade.

Autumn had come and gone. Winter had already settled, and though red robins perched on the garden fence, they never sat long. It was dark by about four in the afternoon and the evenings dragged interminably. A week or so before Christmas, Dad addressed me in Punjabi: 'Your mother and I are going to pay a visit to a Hindu temple. We would like you to come with us.' I immediately agreed. Who cared for what purpose, he had spoken to me.

That weekend Mum, Dad and I drove to a suburb on the outskirts of London to a gaily coloured temple decorated in tinsel. Shoeless, people were milling around as a holy man chanted mantras on a raised platform in the central part of the temple. The repetitive, baritone chants, like the heady incense, were mesmerising. We didn't spend long there. Mum made an offering at what I presumed was a shrine, where two colourful statues of Hindu deities stood. I had been inside a suburban temple before, but Mum and Dad were not overtly religious in that they made regular visits. In our house a temple was only visited in times of crisis or thanks.

After Mum and Dad had said their prayers, we drove to someone's house. Dad briefed me on what we were doing: 'We're going to visit a priest to talk to him. He is an old man; some say he was a pilot in his youth.'

'A pilot?' I said, wrinkling my nose. 'What kind of pilot?'

'We don't know. But he is an old man and he might speak to you.'

'Okay.'

When we entered the house, an old woman greeted us at the

door and offered us tea. The living room had been converted into a mini temple of sorts. There was no furniture, save for a couple of armchairs that had been pushed against a wall to create space. A white sheet was spread on the carpet and a small group of middle-aged Indian women sat on the floor listening to a holy man who was sitting cross-legged in the lotus position before them. He was bare-chested apart from a saffron-coloured cloth wrapped around his lower half with the loose end thrown over one shoulder. He had long dark hair that fell to his shoulders and a dark, brushed beard. His skin was as fair as a Caucasian's but his dark eyes were unmistakably Indian. He certainly didn't look like an old man. Aged thirty-five, tops, I guessed. I imagined him piloting a jumbo jet in his saffron garb.

He stood up when my parents entered the room and led them to another room while I waited in what I assumed was the temple part of the house. The women on the floor gave me a welcoming smile and I joined them. Mum and Dad were gone for no more than about ten minutes. When they re-emerged, Dad called me over and ushered me into the room with the pilot guru. Dad closed the door behind him as he left me with him. There was brown and cream chequered lino on the floor. The guru was sitting at a formica table with four chairs around it. He gestured for me to sit down.

'What is your name?' he asked in English.

'Sushila.'

'Your parents are troubled.'

'Yes,' I said nervously. I had no idea what was going on. I wondered if he was going to give me a religious telling-off.

'I have spoken to them and told them all will be well in February. What must be, must be. They have nothing to fear.

You too have nothing to fear.' He opened a carved wooden box on the table beside him and took out a small brown bead and a silvery ring. 'This ring is for you to wear.' He handed it to me and I placed it on my little finger 'Take this bead, also. It has a small hole. Your mission is to thread it. Be patient as you try.'

I took the bead and examined it. It was about half the size of a pea and had a tiny, barely visible hole in it. 'It is time for you to go now,' he said, leading me out of the room to where Mum and Dad were waiting.

We drove home in silence, bewildered silence on my part. I rolled the bead around in my hand all the way, wondering about the significance of February; wondering what we had achieved. For a week I tried to thread the bead. A thin chain I had was far too thick. Even the finest needle in the house was too thick. Cotton thread lacked the stiffness it needed to get through the hole. Fishing line might have done the trick, but I didn't have any. After several exasperating attempts, I opened my bedroom window and flung it out as far as I could.

It's hard to know what my parents were thinking, but many times I found my mum sitting alone, staring out of the window at the park opposite the house, elbow on the table, chin resting on her palm. My parents had sought guidance at the temple because they were lost. Things had been certain once, but now all was filled with doubt. Mum and Dad felt the tectonic plates of their lives shifting, but they didn't yet know what the new landscape would look like, or their role within it, and it frightened them.

One day, Dad came home with a bundle of papers. They were application forms for civil service jobs. Jobs within the tax office, specifically. Jobs like the one he had. Of course, I still dreamt about being a journalist, but I had no idea how to realise that dream. There were three million unemployed people in Britain, so the chances were that there would be hundreds of people ahead of me in the queue. Dad suggested I apply for a job at the tax office.

'I don't want to work in the tax office,' I protested.

'Why are you so confident they will offer you a job? Why don't you fill in the application form and see what happens? You need a steady income.'

'But I can't work in the same office as you.'

'You wouldn't be in the same office as me. I work in income tax. This is an application for the inheritance tax department.'

'The death tax?'

'Fill in the form. You have nothing to lose.'

So I sent off the application and they called me for an interview.

'Dad, I don't want to work in tax.'

'Why don't you attend the interview? You have nothing to lose. They may not even offer you the job.'

So I went to the interview and they offered me the job.

'Dad, I don't want to be an inheritance tax officer, taking money from the dead.'

'You have no other job offers. Why not take the job till something better comes along. At least you will have a decent income. You need a decent income.'

So I took the job. I went from helping car salesmen lie to hounding the relatives of the dead for money. But my home life didn't change. Mum continued to ignore me. We still passed each other in the house, eyes downcast. We ate at the same table without a word. We folded each other's dry laundry and left it in neat piles. I tried to talk to her but she simply turned away from me.

In total, Mum didn't speak to me for five months. It doesn't matter how old you are, the withdrawal of parental love is always agony. I couldn't undo what I had done. Words, once uttered, cannot be retrieved. I don't know how much longer I could have lasted. Then, in the first week of February, while winter stubbornly hung all around, Dad came and sat with me at the dining table where I was reading the newspaper. He and I were the only ones in the house.

'We have all suffered,' he said in Punjabi. I looked at him, unsure of what to expect next. 'Your mother and I are not young anymore. We cannot be happy unless you are happy. And you will not be happy until you are married to John.' It was the first time he had spoken John's name. He stood up, looked down at me and then placed one hand on my head with the softest touch. I felt the warmth of his palm. 'You are my child. I want you to be happy. Marry John. You have my blessing, now and forever. Live long.'

'Thank you, Dad.'

He left the house, maybe to get some fresh air, I don't know. I went upstairs to my room, buried my head in my pillow and cried.

CHAPTER 12

Paradise Road

'Full of Eastern promise.'
Fry's Turkish Delight advertising slogan, 1950s onwards

What was it that Mickey Rooney said? 'Always get married early in the morning. That way, if it doesn't work out, you haven't wasted the whole day.'

Had there not been a legal minimum period of twenty-one days to give 'notice of intention to marry', John and I might have simply walked into the local registry office and married the morning after Dad gave his blessing. My parents didn't think I was wasting the whole day. They thought I was wasting my whole life. They didn't actually say so, but I could tell by the way their faces refused to smile.

So John and I were forced to take twenty-one days to plan our wedding. He was busy buying a house in London for us to live in and I had nuptial arrangements to make. By choosing my own husband I had, under the Indian system, forgone my right to a grand ceremony organised by parents, so it fell to me to make preparations for the big day – or perhaps I should say the small day.

I bought a packet of pre-printed wedding invitations from the local newsagent and sent them to our friends. I had an old pair of white shoes. So I replaced the laces with satin ribbons and bought a knee-length wedding dress in my lunch hour. Done.

Well, overdone actually. The biggest mistake was the wedding dress. It was what could be described as a modern 1980s wedding dress: knee-length, ivory silk, hexagonal neckline, leg-o'-mutton sleeves, fitted bodice, dropped waist, puff-ball skirt. I wasn't just a fashion victim, I was a fashion casualty. Unlike other Western brides, I was not surrounded by a clucking clutch of hens advising me on something old, something new, something borrowed, something blue. I assumed that because I was not an Indian bride I must be an English bride in white. There were simply no cross-cultural signposts for me to read.

I hired John a dark morning suit that he wore with a wing-collar shirt. He looked like a cross between a stage actor from a 1920s movie and Count Dracula. I don't like to dwell too long on how we appeared standing next to each other.

Naturally, there was no dowry for me, but kindly Dad had booked lunch at The Winning Post – a local hotel up the road from our house. I didn't deserve, and nor did I expect, any gold jewellery from my parents. But some traditions are almost impossible to relinquish. As a gesture, they did give me a gold chain and John a gigantic gold ring that any gangster would have worn proudly. And so that John and I had rings to exchange on the day, he sold his much-loved fretless bass guitar and bought me a diamond-cluster ring.

I wish I could say that 26 Februray 1988 was the happiest day of my life. But the temperature never rose above five degrees Celsius, which is about as warm as my parents' hearts could get that day. Mum wore one of her oldest saris: a turquoise and orange checkered one that she had told me countless times she disliked, and Dad wore a dark suit with a red tie. Raja didn't turn up because he said he had to sit a test at school. Dinesh looked suitably smart. Vin, who wore a lilac silk sari, was the only one who had a remotely celebratory tone to her attire, and even that was subdued by Indian standards.

John's parents looked exceptionally smart and were courteous and friendly. They were outside their normal comfort zone and they did their best. They were happy for their son and that was the most important thing. Altogether, John's family, my family and a handful of close friends formed a group of about twenty-five people at the registry office, which happened to be on Paradise Road. We were hardly on our way to Eden. Still, life has a funny way of throwing in a dose of poignancy when you least need it. On arrival, everyone was keenly aware of the cross-cultural sensitivities and the stated approval hiding the barely concealed disapproval, and no one knew quite what the etiquette at a mixed marriage was supposed to be. This is what happens when customs are broken: no one knows how to behave anymore. No one knows how to celebrate. No one knows what to say to whom.

On the way in I noticed an attractive girl with auburn hair, perhaps in her twenties, wearing a red dress waiting in the corridor with an anxious expression. Perhaps I should have worn a red dress that day – it might have been a conciliatory gesture to my parents' heritage. But it hadn't occurred to me to make conciliatory gestures. Unthinkingly, I had picked a white dress. White: the colour of mourning for Indians.

We milled around in the waiting area until the registrar's assistant approached me. 'Excuse me. Awfully sorry, but there's been a bit of a delay. There's a lady who's booked to be married before you, but her, er, the groom has not arrived yet.' The assistant turned to look at the girl in red who was still standing in the corridor. 'We can continue waiting, or perhaps you and Mr Hobson might like to go first.' John and I looked at each other and decided to go first.

The registry office was housed in a listed Georgian building and the ceremony room was suitably decorated in dignified tones. There was a pale-blue carpet underfoot and cream-coloured wallpaper. A couple of large gilt-edged mirrors stood above the fireplaces and flowers on the mantlepieces added a little understated cheer. Everyone bustled in and the registrar, a smartly dressed, middle-aged woman with the wonderfully appropriate name of Mrs Lusty, introduced herself as we stood before her.

'Hello, John; hello, Thootheela,' she said. I noticed she had lipstick on her teeth.

'Sorry to interrupt,' said John politely, 'but her name's Sushila.'

'Thorry, Tootheela,' said Mrs Lusty, correcting herself.

John looked at me, but I dared not look back for fear that I might start laughing. Behind us I could hear a kerfuffle. I turned around to see John's dad, a large presence in a camel-coloured wool coat, fussing over 'the ruddy camera'. He was in a last-minute panic, struggling to get the loose end of the film through the slit. A picture of Vin's missing coconut wrapped in a red ribbon flashed through my mind. I turned around again and Mrs

Lusty smiled, revealing the full extent of her lipstick mishap. A few minutes later, somewhere between Mrs Lusty reading vows and whispers of, 'There, hold that bit down and grab the end of the film,' John and I became huthband and wife.

There was a smattering of applause that died out quickly as our friends realised they were the only ones clapping. John and I signed a piece of paper before leaving the room to have our photos taken outside on the lawn. An arctic February blast blew through the corridor as someone opened the door and I noticed the girl in red was still alone. Had she been stood up on her wedding day? Somebody threw a handful of confetti in my face. I shivered. John had arrived in my life just in time to save me and I was immensely grateful.

On the lawn, someone took photos. I can't remember who. But, again, no one knew the etiquette of mixed-marriage photo expressions. No one knew whether to smile or frown, whether to express joy or offer commiserations, or whether to just look neutral. My parents opted for the funereal expression. John and I went for the uncomfortable smile. Family members adopted a look of profound discomfort, while friends brandished faces that said nothing more than what-the-fuck!

When we arrived at The Winning Post for lunch, the manager, upon seeing my posy, screeched, 'Oh my goodness me, I didn't know the booking was for a wedding party.' Turning to my dad, she said, 'Mr Das, why didn't you say?'

I didn't mind that the tables had not been decked out in the manner befitting a wedding luncheon. After all, there would be no mischievous or boring speeches, no three-tier cake to cut, no champagne or dancing in a marquee. There were just twenty-five people eating a warm lunch on a winter's day. But there seemed to me to be a surreal quality about the way the sun was setting on my long teenage rebellion: a dash for Paradise Road, an encounter with Mrs Lusty, before, finally, remarkably and bizarrely, I reached The Winning Post.

John and I moved into our new house in North London to start our married lives. He ploughed on with his PhD and I spent my days administering inheritance tax.

Now that I was a married woman, I no longer came under Dad's jurisdiction – so to speak. Under the Indian system I would have come under my husband's jurisdiction now, but because my husband was a Westerner and I had formally taken up a Western life, I did not have to come under anybody's jurisdiction. I was, technically speaking, a free woman. (Proviso: the West does not require a woman to come under her husband's control. However, it sometimes expects her to act as his appendage.)

John and I had only known each other for about ten months before we got married, so, as would have been the case in an arranged marriage, we spent the next few years getting to know each other. Often we would be invited to Sunday lunch at John's parents' spectacular Edwardian house just outside London. His mother would pour me a glass of sherry before lunch and ask after my parents. I never saw anybody play the baby grand piano in the dining room but I noticed one year that John's parents' Christmas card list included the names of several peers. John's famous great-grandfather and his father had been awarded knighthoods, which both had turned down for similar, political reasons.

John learnt things about me too – mostly things that left him asking more questions. 'Why is it that every time we meet an Indian person, they want to know where in India you come from?' he once asked. He was thinking about the old Indian man in the cornershop near our house who had asked me that question.

'Because Indians are always trying to pigeonhole other Indians. The man in the cornershop was trying to work out my caste.'

'What is your caste?' asked John, blinking like a baby. I recalled my dad once telling me never to ask anyone their caste as it was an offensive question. Dad was vehemently anti-caste. It degraded humans, he said.

'Sit down young man,' I said, mimicking my dad, 'and I will explain.' John slumped onto the sofa, dangling one leg over the side. He wore pink suede boots. He always wore suede boots. I began my story. 'A long time ago, when I was about fourteen years old, I needed pocket money to buy a Boomtown Rats album. So I went to the newsagent and asked for a job as a newspaper girl. The lady behind the counter was Indian. She asked me my name and my age and then she said, "What's your caste?"

'Well, I didn't know my caste. Mum and Dad had never told me, but they had told me no one should ever ask anyone their caste. I knew the woman had asked me something she shouldn't have, so I legged it out of her shop and ran home. I told Dad what this woman had asked me and Dad said to me, "Sit down, young lady, and I will tell you your caste."

'So I said to him, "No! Don't ever tell me my caste. I don't want to know." I figured that if I didn't know my caste, I could never judge other Indians and they couldn't judge me. And to this day, I don't know my caste and nor do I want to know, because as long as I don't know, I can't pass it on to my kids, if I ever have any, and that's the only way to put an end to this vile system.'

'Very good,' he said. 'Very good indeed. I'm proud of you.'

'And I'm proud of my dad for never telling me.'

I thought about my parents frequently after I left home. Sometimes I imagined them sleeping soundly at night, glad to see the back of me, relieved they no longer had to stay up late waiting for me to come home. Perhaps I was projecting my own relief. Other times, I imagined them avoiding shopping in Indian areas for fear they might run into someone who would cast disparaging looks their way, or cross to the other side of the road to signal their disapproval. I tried not to think about the fallout from my actions that Mum and Dad might be suffering, but even when I didn't think about it, I could still feel the guilt ossifying in my bones.

I would have given a great deal now to fall about laughing with Vin like we used to. But all that was over. We were married women now. She to a man chosen by Mum and Dad and I to someone I had chosen. I wondered if she was happy. I would have liked to have asked her but we didn't communicate much. We were both too busy feeling the parameters of our new roles.

On the occasions when Vin and Dinesh and John and I visited Mum and Dad, we all got along well. Everyone was civil and I felt no discomfort talking to Dinesh and he showed no signs of feeling any discomfort talking to me. All very pragmatic. Sometimes, but not frequently, John and I visited my parents alone. Again, everyone was always polite. We marked birthdays and Christmases with muted fanfare, but even then there would be a light dusting of tension on everything.

I recall John and I visiting my parents once, perhaps for someone's birthday. Mum greeted us shyly at the front door and ushered us in. I walked in first and John followed behind. We had barely got as far as the kitchen when Mum turned to me and said, 'You should let John walk before you.' I looked at her quizzically. 'He should enter the house first. He is the man.' I let her comment slide past me. I could have started a row right there in the hallway, but it wouldn't have been a good look.

After lunch that day, I started gathering the dishes to take them into the kitchen. 'Give us a hand,' I said to John, who helped me with the plates at his end of the table. Mum shot me a sharp look. Later, in the kitchen, when John wasn't there, she said, 'You shouldn't ask John to help you with the dishes.'

'Don't tell me, because he's the man,' I said, rolling my eyes. 'Mum, we always do the dishes together.'

This time Mum rolled her eyes, tutted and busied herself at the sink.

'Iss the *Kurwa Chauth* ceremony next week,' she said. 'Are you going to keep the fast?'

'I don't need to fast to show John I'm a devoted wife.'

'Iss good thing to do. Good for marriage,' she said, as John entered the kitchen.

'Mum wants me to keep a *Kurwa Chauth* fast for you,' I said turning to John.

'Why not?' he said. There was a note of resignation in his voice that suggested perhaps I should keep the fast just to make Mum happy.

'Yes, why not?' repeated Mum.

'Okay, I tell you what. I'll keep a fast if John keeps a fast. That way we're equal.'

Mum put her hand to her chest, aghast. '*Hai!* Man no need to do,' she said, looking at John kindly.

'It's okay,' said John. 'I don't mind fasting.'

'*Hai, hai!*' she said to the pot plant on the windowsill in front of her and plunged her hands into the sink.

I sensed Mum was, despite herself, beginning to like John. He had time for her and never corrected her crooked English. I once found the pair of them standing in the kitchen talking about the economy.

'The interest rate's far too high,' John was saying. 'You simply can't rely on rates to bring the economy under control. They're too blunt an instrument. Monetary policy, you see . . .'

'Oh, I know, John,' said Mum. 'Iss terrible, isn't it?'

'Yes, well,' continued John, looking at her distractedly, 'You're not wrong there. Certainly the impact on the ordinary family is frightening.'

'Yes, frightening,' said Mum.

I suspect, but perhaps I'm wrong, Mum had little idea what John was talking about, but she was enjoying his attention, enjoying his company – enjoying being English, I dare say.

The following Wednesday, as promised, John and I fasted. Around mid-morning I was contemplating my rumbling stomach when he rang me in the office.

'Sorry, I had a Mars Bar,' he announced. 'I was starving.'

'Never mind. I didn't think you'd last. I suppose I can eat something as well now.' That was the first and only time we attempted to keep the *Kurwa Chauth* fast. It was no big deal that we didn't succeed, but I confess I felt a pinprick of dejection knowing that John had been unable to discipline his physical self with the mental rigour required to achieve spiritual devotion. But the feeling didn't last long. After all, I might have succumbed to a Mars Bar too. He'd just got there first.

Communication between my parents and I fell away silently over the next few years. They didn't call me very often. I didn't call them. It wasn't so much that I didn't want to keep in touch, it was more that I continued to struggle with my own feelings of guilt. Every time I saw Mum and Dad they looked older and more fragile. And with every visit they seemed to have less to say to me. Or perhaps it was I who had less to say to them. I never asked them how they were coping. I suspect that even if I had, feelings would have been too raw for them to talk about it. I couldn't bear to see the disappointment in their eyes. I had done an ugly thing and I didn't want anyone to look at me. Quasimodo. I didn't want to continue offending Mum and Dad with my presence. I needed to put myself into voluntary exile.

It's hard to believe that it took me more than twenty years to ask my dad what he went through after I left home. The day I picked up the phone and rang him to ask, my heart's ferocious pumping was reverberating in my head. I didn't want to hear what he might tell me.

'Dad, how did the Indian community react towards you after I married John?' I asked him nervously. There was silence for a while and then a small sigh.

'Nobody said anything to my face,' he said. 'They don't talk face to face. People talk behind your back. They didn't say good things.'

'But how can you be so sure if you never actually heard what they said?' I asked, hoping he had been mistaken.

'You, Sushila, were the first person to marry someone outside our community. It was very shocking to everyone. Others followed the trend after you.' He paused. I thought he wasn't going to say anymore, but then he continued. 'People did not say good things. Some people I knew – they simply did not call me anymore. Other people called less. I did not receive as many invitations to functions and other social things as I did before. People didn't ask me for advice anymore. Our family lost standing.'

He said everything I didn't want to hear. And he said it with the disconnected straightforwardness of a man describing someone else's experience. Guilt had its hands around my throat. Would there ever be a time when the past would simply be the past? Or would the sea keep washing ashore the debris of years gone by?

The first four years of my marriage were superbly tumultuous – like riding on the waltza at a fairground. Right from the outset it was clear there was a third person in our marriage: Margaret Thatcher. John was unnaturally obsessed with her. She had smashed the miners and bombed the Falkland Islands but her work was not done yet. There was still the poll tax to come – a community charge that took no account of people's income and therefore their ability to pay.

For the next few years John and I watched helplessly as interest rates rocketed and our monthly mortgage payments soared into the stratosphere. The rate went from 9 per cent when we married to 15 per cent the following year to 14 per cent the year after. John was still completing his PhD and on my income alone we could barely survive. John's parent's came to our rescue several times.

'It's like taking a wage cut every bloody month,' yelled John, stomping around the house. 'This is going to kill us. No wonder it's called a mortgage. It's a gauge of our mort!'

We stopped griping about the mortgage to our friends after vegan Tony with the dreadlocks called us 'a pair of capitalist home-owning shits'. Indeed, we were luckier than most – we had a house in central London. But the mortgage was strangling us. For John, every financial blow was personal and the government's policies were to blame.

The late 1980s and early 1990s had a surreal quality, because so many mad things were going on. My memory of that time is dominated by two explosive events that affected me deeply: the publication of Salman Rushdie's *The Satanic Verses* and the introduction in Britain of the poll tax. They made the world feel like a bad place.

Being an unhealthily nervous person, I suppose a level of bearable anxiety pulses through me on any given day. But when Ayatollah Ruhollah Khomeni, the supreme leader of Iran, issued a fatwa calling for Rushdie's death on Valentine's Day 1989, my anxiety levels rose. Some Pakistanis in Britain were very vocal in their criticisms of Rushdie's book and I feared this might lead to a backlash against brown people. I feared a fresh round of racism on the streets. But that's not what happened.

A British-Indian author was the epicentre of a gigantic earthquake that sent shockwaves around the world. It was almost certainly the first time Britons (and anyone outside the Muslim world) became aware of the meaning of the word 'fatwa' or the idea of a religious edict. There were pictures of burning books on TV and animated conversations at dinner parties. Suddenly multiculturalism was back on the table.

Just as the Enoch Powell era had, unintentionally, paved the way for life in the time of multiculturalism, now I feared the Salman Rushdie affair would pave the way, unintentionally, for life in the time of cultural relativism.

While I joined the throng of wellwishers signing petitions and postcards in support of the right to free speech, John was signing petitions against the evil poll tax. All around us scary things were happening. A Pan Am flight exploded over Lockerbie in Scotland, killing everyone on board. The agriculture minister appeared on TV feeding a child a burger to show that Mad Cow disease couldn't be transferred to humans. Nelson Mandela, who had been in prison since I was born and was still there, turned seventy. I found myself signing a birthday card for him at a stall at a shopping centre. John and I seemed to be forever on an endless procession of protest marches singing 'FREEEE-HEEEEE, NELSON MANDELA!'

Anger and cynicism were everywhere all the time, but never more so than at the poll-tax protest demo in London on 31 March 1990. John and I went along, as did thousands of other people, including families with children. Many of our friends were wearing 'Fuck the Poll Tax' T-shirts. Mine just said: 'Can't Pay, Won't Pay'. It was a beautiful sunny day and from where we were in the crowd things were going along fine until the police stopped everyone near Whitehall. At that stage we didn't know they were trying to control the numbers of people flowing into Trafalgar Square and nor did they bother telling us. Everyone was jittery and before we could get a sense of what was going on, police on horseback were charging into the crowd. Sticks and cans were thrown about by the protestors. Singing and chanting quickly turned into screaming and shouting. John grabbed my hand and yelled, 'Run!'

He was virtually dragging me along as he tore through police ribbon and kicked down barriers. I could hear horses thundering behind us but there was no time to look back to see how close they were. Eventually John let go of my hand and scaled a wall as quick as a lizard. From the top he reached down, I grabbed his hand and he pulled me up in one swoop as my feet scrambled along the wall trying to get traction. We sat on that wall panting, along with god-knows how many other people and watched the horses charge by. It was the singularly most frightening moment we'd experienced at a demo, which the following day's newspapers described as the poll-tax riots.

Later, having become separated from the friends we had gone with, we walked around the streets in disbelief. Shop windows were smashed, cars had been turned over, a building was on fire. People were sitting on the kerb with shocked faces. The social and industrial unrest of the past decade had become a tinderbox that burst into flames that day.

A lot of young people left Britain around that time. We had a friend who left to find work in South Africa. Another moved to France. America was a destination for the disillusioned, too. Young people had lost hope. For many Generation Xers, hope was crushed into the dust, just like the 'Kill the Bill' badges and the 'Ban the Bomb' badges had been a decade before.

Back home in our corner of London, the social dysfunction was becoming unbearable. We were burgled twelve times in four years, mostly by teenagers looking for drug money. They'd smash down our door, break windows and go through our drawers and even our casserole pots. The police were useless. Eventually we took down our wooden front door and replaced it with a solid steel security door – similar to the type you see on bank vaults.

An arsonist burnt twenty-three cars down our road. We woke up in the middle of the night to find flames climbing 12 feet high as windscreens exploded and tyres burst. The police caught the arsonist but he was out on parole within six months. Around the back of our house, on a vacant plot of land on which British Rail wanted to build a concrete factory, rats roamed. Mice ate our muesli more often than we did. A stray cat often came prowling around our back garden, so we held it hostage for a while with the lure of milk, hoping it might eliminate the rodent problem, but it turned out to be the coward of the feline neighbourhood. Travellers set up camp on the land behind our house for weeks at a time and frequently stole our TV aerial.

John was livid that life was so desolate in Thatcher's Britain. There was always maintenance to be done around the house, the Mini was constantly breaking down and money was flying out of our pockets. When John put his foot through the rickety bottom stair one evening, his face was so red with anger I thought his head would burst. But it wasn't until a rat died under the floorboards of our 117-year-old house that things really came to a head.

We couldn't remove its reeking carcass because the floorboards ran across the six terraces down the road, rather than along each house (don't ask why), so they couldn't be lifted. The local council advised us not to panic as the problem would be gone within a few days after the 'maggots deal with it'. In the meantime, would we like someone to come and deodorise the area? John told them where to stick their deodorant and slammed the phone down. 'I can't take it anymore,' he cried. 'I can't live like this.'

Maybe that was the day he started thinking about escaping London, and Britain. He would devise a plan he said, to get us as far from the Tories as we could possibly get.

CHAPTER 13

Sparse End of the World

'To live in Australia permanently is rather like going to a party and dancing all night with one's mother' Barry Humphries

John's plan to escape Thatcherite Britain involved finishing his PhD and applying for every available academic job anywhere on the face of the globe. I imagined his chances of finding employment outside Britain were about as promising as my chances of shedding my reputation as the black sheep of the family (pardon the pun). I had quit my job as a death-tax officer after just two years, following a rather unsavoury incident. I had been forced on two occasions, as stipulated by regulation 52b, subclause 2.1, to call an eighty-two-year-old woman and tell her that if she didn't pay the £11,000 of inheritance tax she owed following the death of her twin sister I would have to call in the 'enforcement department'.

On both occasions she had wept bitterly, telling me that to meet her financial obligation she would have to sell the house that she and her sister had lived in for forty years. On the second occasion I had, somewhat unprofessionally, wept in sympathy. I resigned the next day.

When John announced he had been offered a job as a lecturer at a university in Australia, I dug in my heels. I had just found a new job in publishing as an editorial assistant. It was a step down from being a tax officer and it wasn't quite journalism, but at least I wasn't robbing the dead anymore. But more importantly, I had, during my married years, thrown off the handcuffs of Indian culture and was enjoying carving out a clearer British identity – or so I thought. It was like coming out of jail and starting over. For the first time I felt no pressure to behave or look Indian. Nobody was hounding me to speak in Punjabi or constantly reminding me to protect the family's *izzat*.

I spoke English, wore jeans, ate fish and chips and was married to an Englishman I had chosen. Life in Britain was far from easy and John was fuming with rage much of the time. If you weren't a stockbroker, financial analyst or property developer, life was nightmarishly expensive. From billboards to the pages of the weekend magazines, we were mocked by advertisements for fast cars, quality watches, granite kitchen benchtops and tropical holidays – luxuries we had no hope of attaining. But flushed with the romanticism that accompanies the early years of married life, we were confident we could scratch our way out of our darkness. I was, for the first time, beginning to feel comfortable in my British skin. The last thing I wanted to do was go to Australia, where I imagined nothing exciting was going on because it hardly ever featured in the evening news.

Australia was not a country I spent a great deal of time thinking about. I only knew three things about the land Down Under:

1. The prime minister's name was Bob Hawke.
2. It was the natural habitat of a certain bouncing marsupial.
3. The British had stolen the country from black people and the White Australia Policy had been established to stop any other blacks getting in.

For six months John and I argued about it and in that time I was unable to mount a cogent argument for staying in Britain. My job was fine, but it was hardly where I wanted to be. Communication with my family had virtually flatlined. And British Rail looked set to win the battle against local residents to build a monster concrete plant right behind our house. (A supply of concrete was needed to build the Channel Tunnel.) Our future in London looked bleak. Besides, who was I to stand in the way of John's career? We had undoubtedly reached a juncture in our lives. So we packed the measly contents of our house and started thinking about koalas and Foster's beer.

My parents appeared to take the news well. Their response was disturbingly pragmatic. Did John have a secure job? Did we have somewhere to live? Would I be able to work? Were our passports up to date? I recall no long chats about how we would miss each other or reminiscences into my childhood to tease out memories of joyful parent–child connectedness. I didn't feel I was moving far away from my parents, perhaps because I felt I had moved away from them a long time ago. Anyway, John's contract was only for four years. We'd be back.

When I visited them for the last time Dad said, 'Look after each other and be careful. Remember who you are. Australia has not always been a welcoming place for some people.' Mum hugged me on the sofa and I found myself stiffening against her warmth. She was hugging me as if I was a baby, playfully squeezing my cheeks and holding my face with both hands. Her affection was, I thought, an attempt to savour a final moment with a child she was about to lose all over again. But memories of her refusal to acknowledge my presence in that same dining room just four years earlier still stung, and I was embarrassed by her baby-cuddling, the way pinched middle-class British people are privately discomfitted by the easy-flowing emotion of continental Europeans. To display emotion is to lose control of oneself, I thought. And I wouldn't have thought that had Dad not absorbed the lesson from the English and successfully, yet unknowingly, passed it on to me.

At the airport, Mum cried till all the tissues in her hand were dense balls of white paper. Everyone was smartly dressed – Vin, Dinesh and Raja, even my uncle and aunt, and my cousins Twinkle, Peen and Ash. Indians always dress smartly for the airport and only they know why. There were endless jokes about kangaroos and Kylie, sharks and crocodiles; a cheery veneer over airport anxiety.

Dad was the last person I hugged. He returned the embrace with one hand placed momentarily on my shoulder and all the warmth of a folded ironing board. He looked into the middle distance as if checking the flight monitor and sniffed softly just once before giving me his parting advice, 'Look after yourself. Take care of your health. Do your best. And keep in touch.'

I waved a final goodbye from the departure gate and still my eyes were dry. That day, even I was shocked to find I had no tears in me at all.

Nearly thirty years earlier another goodbye, this time in northern India, had generated significantly more tears. It was a bitterly cold February morning. A packed and labelled suitcase stood by the front door of my grandparents' house. Dad, crying and barely out of his twenties, embraced his mother, who threw her arms around him and sobbed uncontrollably. The pull of blood is a mighty force. He bent down and touched her feet. 'Stay happy,' she said, placing her hand on his head.

His father too was struggling to control his tears. This was his first son, still climbing the early rungs of manhood yet ready to fly off to seek his fortune. Dad, dressed in a dark suit, turned to his father and embraced him. Then he bent down to touch his feet too. When he rose his father took him by the shoulders and said, 'Look after yourself, son. Take care of your health. Do your best. And keep in touch.'

Then, at Palam Airport (now Indira Ghandi International Airport) in New Delhi, Dad embraced his wife of just three months. 'Don't cry,' he said. 'We'll be together again soon.'

Palam Airport, that storehouse of grief in the 1960s, must have been a terrible place to work. From clerks to cleaners, to witness daily other people's pitiful loss would have made men weep who otherwise had hearts of stone. Even the optimism of adventure does not temper the sorrow of migrant goodbyes. And because migrants cannot know for certain when they might see their family again (for none of us knows the day nor the hour that death might come knocking), they must necessarily say goodbye as if it were for the very last time.

It was three o'clock on the morning of 16 December 1991 when John and I landed at Melbourne Airport. There was hardly anyone there, just a handful of people milling about. Had it been three in the morning at Heathrow, the place would have been teeming with people from all over the world. Spectacularly stupid as it may seem, I imagined Melbourne's airport must be in the outback.

A few days later, when I woke and looked out of the window of the granny flat where we were temporarily staying in Greensborough, an outer Melbourne suburb, I saw no humans at all. I felt as if I had arrived on the opening pages of a post-apocalyptic novel. There were signs that life must have existed: parked cars, washing flapping on a line; and there was the familiar drift of nature: moving clouds, wind through the trees, a baking sun. But not a single visible human anywhere. And all around the air was thick with silence.

Within twenty-four hours we had been transported from a foggy and damp London winter with the temperature close to zero to the height of an Australian summer whose temperature hovered around 32 degrees. Every day the sun shone shamelessly. We ventured out to look for people, only to find we had to walk for fifteen minutes in the roasting heat before we saw what we thought must be a mirage: a tatty corner shop labelled 'Milk Bar'.

We wandered the streets looking at single-storey weatherboard dwellings. 'Bungalows made of wood,' said John. By the afternoon a hot wind was billowing all around us. It was as if a hairdryer on full blast was constantly blowing hot grit in your face. There are better ways to exfoliate your skin than by sandblasting it. By the time we got back to the flat my contact lenses had dried on to my eyeballs like two bits of sticky tape. It must have been three days before I stopped swearing.

Australia was the land of the giants. Everywhere seemed intimidatingly large: huge sky, big cars, wide roads, spacious houses, gigantic fridges. Even the people were bigger. Sure, wide open spaces and room to move sound like luxuries, but when you've lived most of your life in a city squished for space, driving a Mini and peeping at slivers of sky between tall old buildings, bigness can make a person feel very small. And feeling so small, I felt I exerted no power on my environment – or my life, for that matter. Where once I had confidently strode around in my miniature world, blissfully unaware of my size, I was now a Lilliputian scurrying about for a place to hide.

I had imagined that the move to Australia would be culturally fairly straightforward. It was not unlike Britain: it was largely an Anglo-Celtic country where people spoke English. It had a functioning democracy with a similar legal system and comparable schools and universities. In fact, there would probably be lots of British people in Australia. And the chances were there would be very few cultural hurdles to jump. It wasn't as if I was moving from a Western country to an Eastern one, or vice versa, as my parents had done before me.

Well, I was right about everything except the hurdles. Australia, like Britain, might have been a largely white, English-speaking country, but boy did I have a few things to learn.

I recall going into the North Carlton post office within the first two weeks of arriving and trying to buy two postage stamps. I had no idea how my accent sounded to Australians and I most certainly didn't expect to be confronted by the brute force of Australian pride. I mean, how was I supposed to know egalitarianism was the opiate of the people here? They don't tell you that kind of thing in travel books.

'Two first-class stamps, please,' I asked the man behind the counter, who looked up and stared at me as if I was from Neptune. His face was a mixture of disgust, exasperation and pity, like a high court judge about to sentence a teenager for killing his mother in a drink-drive accident. He leant across the counter slowly and deliberately, and, straightening out a gnarled finger uncomfortably close to my face, said, 'In Astraya – we yonly have one claass.'

The little queue of people behind me stopped chatting and a middle-aged blonde woman stacking shelves turned around to look at me. In the silence I thought I heard the wind whistle through a keyhole and a gate swing on its hinge. There's nothing like learning a lesson the hard way.

Failure to read social and cultural signposts in another country often leads to exquisite humiliation. But there is some knowledge that only the citizens of a country can instinctively understand because the shine on the fine threads of meaning that are woven through their country's unique history are immediately visible to only their eyes. National identity is therefore a vast tapestry of fine threads brought together to create a picture with which the majority identifies and recognises effortlessly. Outsiders too can see the larger picture. But it's only when the light falls in such a way, or the tapestry is viewed from this or that angle, that the outsider can see the shine on those finer threads and therefore catch the meaning that, to the native, comes instinctively.

Migration means being an outsider, at least for a while. Feeling like a foreigner is uncomfortable – the very antithesis of being a social animal. But for a period of time all migrants must be foreigners and they feel it every time they fail to understand an 'in' joke, when they can't comprehend what is being asked of them, and when they mispronounce words. I died a thousand embarrassing deaths when I was corrected for pronouncing it the river Yaara (as in the name Lara) and not the river Yarra (as in barramundi). But at least I didn't thank the lady behind the counter for the recee-p-t and not the receipt, as Dad had done once. And Mum – well, she's always going to irrren the clothes and polish the vindows. Nothing anyone can do about that.

There were quite a few times John and I didn't get things right, more often than not in front of his colleagues.

'Thank you for the invitation to the barbecue. We'd love to come.'

'Great, we'll see you in the arvo, then.'

'In the arvo? Where's that exactly?'

'Where? No, see you in the *arvo*. See you in the afternoon.'

'Oh, yes, of course, in the arvo.'

'And bring a plate, if you like.'

'A plate? A dinner plate?'

'A plate of food, a contribution. A salad, or dessert – something like that.'

'Oh, yes, of course – a plate in the arvo.'

Life was hard at first. Our belongings had yet to arrive (by ship) so John and I had nothing but our clothes and a few books when we moved into a big empty house in the inner-city suburb of Carlton. Life had to be rebuilt. We bought two garden chairs so we wouldn't have to sit on the floor and most nights we ate baked beans on toast and played backgammon. Eventually I bought a little transistor radio and we huddled around it every night listening to the BBC World Service. (The Australian Broadcasting Corporation would switch to the BBC overnight.)

In those early days, my attempts to understand Australian political news usually ended in frustration and boredom since all the names, places and events were unfamiliar to me. Mostly I found the news dull and parochial, although Paul Keating's toppling of Bob Hawke as prime minister four days after we arrived in the country was quite exciting. (Years later Keating would not deny Hawke's revelation that during a private conversation, Keating had referred to Australia as 'the arse end of the world'. Man, how Australians hated him for saying that!)

John started work as a lecturer in international relations at La Trobe University and I envied him having a purpose in life. I spent all day in the flat pacing up and down like a maniac or leafing through the local paper looking for a job. But there seemed to be no jobs I could actually apply for. Hairdresser, typist, dental assistant, bricklayer – I was qualified for nothing. One day John came home to find I had ringed Sandwich Hand, Leaflet Deliverer and Home Help on the jobs pages.

'You don't have to do jobs like that,' he said. 'You have a Bachelor of Arts degree and several years' experience in the workforce. You have enormous potential and lots to offer. Have confidence.' As always, John was there to support me, but I felt my confidence slipping away.

The phone hardly ever rang and even when it did it was usually somebody who had dialled the wrong number. On one occasion

I succeeded in making a complete goose of myself. The phone rang and I ran to answer it, half-hoping it might be Vin.

'G'day. Can I speak to Bruce, plaise,' said a gruff but nasal male voice.

'Bruce?' Surely there weren't actual people called Bruce or Sheila in Australia? 'John? Is that you?'

'No. Is Bruce there?'

'Stop mucking around,' I laughed, and then, getting into the spirit of the joke, added, 'Yeah, mayte, Bruce is roit here eating a Vegemite sandwich. Wanna speak to him, do ya? He'll be down the pub this arvo.'

'Look, who is this?' said the voice, clearly irritated. 'Is Bruce there or isn't he?' Realising that it was not in fact John on the other end of the line, I winced.

'Er, sorry, I'll just check if he's here,' I said, and covered the phone with my hand, bit my bottom lip and allowed a bit of time to pass. 'No, sorry, I'm afraid Bruce isn't here.'

'Well, why the bloody hell didn't you just say that in the first place so we could have avoided all this piss-farting around?'

That was a most unfortunate exchange but at least the phone rang that day. The doorbell never made a sound and nobody ever walked past the front window. Each day was filled with the ugly cawing of crows and the unfamiliar medicinal smell of eucalyptus leaves. Time passed. My confidence continued to shrink and my alienation grew. I now understood how Mum must have felt washing nappies in cold water and pushing me around in a pram in the park all day.

One Saturday our neighbours, Arthur and Janet, invited John over for a beer. They didn't ask me so I stayed in the flat. John returned after an hour looking perturbed.

'How did it go?' I asked.

'It was a bit weird.'

'What do you mean?'

'Well, Arthur drinks a lot of beer. He told me to be careful of Asians because they can't be trusted.'

'What did he mean?'

'I don't know,' said John, shrugging his shoulders.

'Is that why they didn't invite me? Because I'm Asian?'

'No, I don't think they think you're Asian. Asian in Australia means Far Eastern.'

'So what am I?

'You're Indian.'

'No, I'm not, I'm British. My passport says I'm British.'

'Yes, I know, but you're still Indian. Anyway, count yourself lucky. I suspect being Indian is better than being a Pom in Australia.'

I encountered little overt racism in those early days, but there were plenty of occasions where my 'difference' was pointed out to me. Once in a while someone would mimic an English accent in my presence, which varied from Arthur Daley's cockney to an exaggerated snooty haw-hawing. A woman I used to see regularly in a local shop once said, 'You look different with your hair tied up – more foreign.'

The most confronting experience I had was in the State Library. John was browsing the shelves while I took a book to a nearby communal table and sat next to a woman, possibly in her fifties or sixties. She turned to look at me. 'Don't sit next to me,' she said loudly, so that other people on the table looked up. 'You're disgusting and you smell.'

Suddenly, something the size of a golf ball expanded in my

throat and I immediately felt tears in my eyes. Memories of the two bikers sniffing the air for the smell of curry filled my head. John, who had heard the exchange from where he was standing, immediately came over. 'What's the matter? Why don't you want this woman to sit next to you?' he demanded of the old lady.

'Because she's disgusting,' she replied. She stood up, picked up her bag and coat and walked off. By now everyone at the table and onlookers nearby were staring at me, in silence. John asked me what had happened.

'Nothing, nothing happened. She just said she didn't want me to sit next to her. I want to get out of here. Let's go, please,' I said fighting back tears.

Sitting in the car on the way home John expressed his anger at the woman. I sat wondering why I hadn't responded to her offensive remark. We were about halfway home when I suddenly said, 'Turn around, go back to the library. I should have said something to that woman and I didn't.'

John immediately did a U-turn and drove back to the library. When we entered, the old lady had returned to the table and was sitting in the same seat. I approached the table and she looked up. 'Not you again,' she yelled. 'I don't want you to sit next to me. I don't want people like you to sit next to me.'

Everyone around the table looked up again. I stood frozen to the spot. Words were stuck in my throat at unhappy, awkward angles and I couldn't cough them out. John leapt in. 'Why don't you want to sit next to her?' he demanded. 'Is it because of the colour of her skin?' I couldn't bring myself to say anything. The woman stood up, grabbed her bag and started marching towards the library counter. John followed her. 'Turn around and answer my question,' he yelled. But she ignored him and continued towards the counter. 'You haven't got the balls, have you?' shouted John. 'You haven't got the balls to answer me.'

By now, it seemed everyone was craning to get a glimpse of the exchange that had disturbed the hush of the library. The old woman finally reached the counter and we heard her tell the librarian, 'That man is harassing me.' She turned and pointed at John, who halted in disbelief.

'Me? Harassing you?' he bellowed. Before he said anymore I grabbed his sleeve and he turned to look at me, eyes wide open.

'Let's go,' I said. 'Let's get out of here.' And so we left.

Many times over the next few months I shared my experience in the library with people I met, and the circle of friends John and I were becoming part of, and each time their response was almost exactly the same.

'God! She sounds like she was a bit crazy in the head.'

Quite possibly she was mad. And quite possibly she was racist too. What interested me was people's immediate readiness to address her possible insanity rather than her possible racism. I suspect the woman was probably nuts, but I'll never forget how her comments made me feel: small, humiliated and very far away from safety.

I was never quite sure who or what I was meant to be in this new country. Perhaps it was just as well I was in Australia – a nation of people constantly trying to work out who they were, apart from Aboriginal people, who all had a very clear idea of who they were, except nobody seemed to be listening to them.

John and I found Australians fiercely friendly and shockingly suburban. They lacked the gritty edge of Londoners, preferring to live their lives in a comfort zone of conformity. Curiously, they were always looking for endorsement. Wherever John and I went, people wanted to know what we thought of Australia. They would be overjoyed to hear positive remarks and go cold on us if we were less than effusive. They were maddeningly oversensitive to criticism by outsiders, we found, and so we learnt to keep our thoughts to ourselves, which only served to deepen the alienation.

All new migrants feel alienated. And all migrants have some negative feelings about their new country. Voicing that negativity uncoils the intolerably tight knot that develops through homesickness, isolation and unbelonging. But in Australia, where migrants are expected to be grateful for the opportunities offered to them, any negativity is met with flinty faces. So migrants to Australia learn the mantra that Australia is god's own country, where it's beautiful one day, perfect the next. Woe betide anyone who doesn't stay on message.

Settlement of the physical self can come relatively quickly. The body adjusts. But settlement of the mind takes longer because the mental self must negotiate the three stages of culture shock: the early romance of arrival, the resentment of the new country, and finally reconciliation through the passage of time. Romance, resentment and reconciliation – they're always the same, no matter which generation. And, just as Mum did when she moved to England, I leapfrogged stage one and went straight to stage two. 'I don't like it here,' I complained to John. 'I haven't got a job and haven't got any friends. I want to go home.' But he insisted we give it a chance, at least a year.

Lack of work leaves time to think – too much time to think. For the first time since I had left my parents' house I was enveloped in genuine silence, which forced me to reflect on what it meant to marry out. As the first in my family to break the tradition of arranged marriage I had opted out of my family's community.

I had no right to draw on them for support now. And anyway, my family was far away – not just emotionally, but physically too.

Memories from the past intruded on my thoughts daily. Mum and her 'bastard bloody!' I shouldn't have pulled away when she tried to hug me that last evening together. Dad and his undesirable elements! They had both meant well, hadn't they? They hadn't cast me out. They could have done. But they hadn't. They still considered me their daughter. They had done their best, hadn't they? Perhaps we all needed time away from each other. Perhaps, despite my protestations, I had come to Australia to put myself into voluntary exile. It was better for everyone that I got out of their hair. Yet now, on the other side of the world, they seemed before my eyes all the time.

So I decided to send them a letter. Not a letter with words on paper but a cassette recording of my voice and John's voice. I wanted it to be real. John and I talked to them as if everyone was in the room with us – Mum, Dad, Vin, Dinesh, Raja – all the while recording ourselves. The next day I put the tape in an envelope and sent it to Twickenham.

Then, a month later, a small parcel arrived in the post for me – with a London postmark. I ripped it open quickly and a cassette fell out. I rushed to the hi-fi, stuffed it in and pressed play. At first there was silence, then muffled sounds. Then suddenly Mum's voice burst into the room: 'Hello. Hello, Neelum. Iss the mummy here.'

She'd used my other name, the name only my family used. I felt a tsunami in my chest. That same feeling when I came out of the school gates and Mum was standing there with all the other mums, waiting to collect us – that huge, unmistakable wave of relief that she was there for us. Mum, with her lovely red lipstick – she'd smiled when she put it on. Mum, with the plait down her back, the mole on her chin. Mum!

Then there was Dad on the tape. 'Hello, Sushila and John, your dad here. I love you both. Thank you for your tape. It was very nice. Sushila, you still have that cough.' And it didn't end there. There was Vin and Dinesh and Raja, and Twinkle, Ash, Peen and my uncle and aunt too. All of them laughing, giggling, joking about Kylie and kangaroos again. Weakened by the sounds of their happy voices, I burst into tears – lots and lots of big silly tears.

The tape marked the beginning of the end of the Ice Age. Australia is nearly 11,000 miles away from Britain. Intensity of signal strength usually falls off with distance. But signal strength between parents and children, as measured in love, does not obey that rule. In fact, distance, while it has the annoying propensity to deepen nostalgia, can also soften memories of hurt. Australia's tyranny of distance, so often maligned for the ills that it brings, wafted my way a boon of warm family feelings that created the first cracks in the pack ice.

After that, letter-writing seemed easier, phone conversations warmer. Even breathing seemed less laboured. Perhaps it was the thaw, or just the passage of time that relaxed the fibres of our life in Australia. The following year I completed a postgraduate course in journalism at the Royal Melbourne Institute of Technology (now, bizarrely, the Royal Melbourne Institute of Technology University) and I was ready to apply for jobs.

I sent my CV everywhere, including to the Australian Associated Press, a national news agency, which responded with a flat rejection. But someone had told me that news-agency work was the fastest way for a new journalist to learn the trade so I rang the Melbourne bureau chief and begged him for a job. He said he had nothing available so I offered to work for no pay for a week (work experience to some). He said that might lead to issues with the journalists' union, so I offered to work for free for just one day. Clearly a patient man, he eventually asked me to come in for 'a chat' the following day.

Tom Hyland was a slow-speaking Tasmanian with an eyebrow masquerading as a moustache. His blue, unblinking eyes stared through his rimless glasses and his white shirtsleeves were rolled up above his elbows. He studied my CV as I chewed my nails on the other side of his desk. I couldn't tell what he was thinking – his face gave nothing away, partly because his mouth-mat was obscuring minute southerly facial indicators.

He asked some general questions. His manner was robotic, but only very slightly, so that anyone communicating with him would still be satisfied he was human. The gaps between his words seemed so long, it was hard to know whether he had finished speaking or had simply paused to think. At the end of the meeting he said, 'Okay. Come in for one shift. Next Monday.'

'Oh, thank you, Mr Hyland, I really . . .'

'. . . at nine o'clock.'

'Yes, thank you.'

When I arrived for my day of employment he asked me to check whether there was any truth in the rumour that drivers were concealing their car registration numbers from traffic cameras by rubbing them with dry handsoap. By five o'clock I had finished my 'investigations', which revealed that the rumour was not true, and had written an eight-paragraph story focusing on the police's denial of the scam's success. The reporter at the desk next to mine said, 'How many yarns did you do today?'

'One,' I replied. 'Why? How many did you do?

'Six.'

I felt suddenly nauseous. Then it struck me. This was a news wire service, not a short-story workshop! I was supposed to be churning out reports by the hour, not taking all day to investigate a minor rumour. I cursed myself for misunderstanding my role. I had had a chance to prove to the boss that I could be a good journalist and I had blown it by being a slowcoach. I filed my story and approached Tom's desk, half-crippled with embarrassment.

'I've filed my story,' I mumbled.

'Good. Thank you very much,' he said, looking up briefly from his computer screen. I wondered if he was being sarcastic. I couldn't tell.

'Okay. I'll be off then.'

'Yes. Goodbye,' he said continuing to type. I walked towards the door, hastening my step as I went. There was a burning sensation behind my eyes and I could feel I was about to start crying. I swallowed to hold it all in. Then I heard my name called out and I turned around to see Tom craning his neck over his computer.

'Yes?' I said thinly.

'Can you do a shift? This Thursday?'

I sniffed the tears back up my nose before they ran free.

'Yes, er, yes. Yes, I can.'

'Good. See you then.'

Within thirty seconds I went from being at the bottom of a trough, my confidence crushed, to flying high above a mountain, jubilation bursting my heart. Had I known that the rest of my journalistic life would follow the same cycle of screeching highs and despairing lows, I might have walked away from it all there and then. But this was a huge moment in my life: I was going to get a second shift at AAP, and many more after that. Tom Hyland had given me my first break in journalism and I thought he was the greatest man alive.

I worked at AAP for a year before I said goodbye to Tom and his team and joined *The Age*, a left-leaning quality broadsheet where I really *didn't* have to file a story until the end of the day. Things were looking up again. My arranged marriage issues were a thing of the past, my family was back on board and John and I, despite our ups and downs, were chugging along fine in our new country.

Dinesh, like John, had also tired of the Tories and decided to leave Britain. He and Vin moved to New York, so now Mum and Dad had only my brother left – their future welfare state. Raja, in his early twenties, a handsome young man with a leatherjacket and the gift of the gab, was forging a career in the music business, working as a sound engineer. He had a rock 'n' roll life but Mum and Dad were sure he'd come good in the end. If there was a moment when everyone in my family seemed to have a relatively stable and happy life, it was then. If only it could have stayed that way.

CHAPTER 14

They Told Me So

'You have brains in your head. You have feet in your shoes.
You can steer yourself in any direction you choose.
You are on your own, and you know what you know.
And YOU are the one who'll decide where you go.'
Dr Seuss, Oh, the Places You'll Go!

My marriage lasted exactly twelve years and nine months. There is never one reason for marriage breakdowns and it can take many years, if not the rest of your life, to work out exactly what went wrong when they happen. John and I simply grew in different directions, always together, but moving outwards from each other, like two separate branches on the same tree. For us, once the decision to go our separate ways had been taken, there was no going back.

Five years after arriving in Australia, John moved to Sydney to take up a senior lecturing post at Sydney University and I carried on working as a journalist in Melbourne. But we stayed in touch, crying down the phone, trying to work out where it all went wrong. And even after we had exhausted ourselves looking for the answers, we stayed in touch, primarily to make sure the other person was managing on their own.

I was in my thirties and childless when we separated – an appalling time for a woman, in particular, to start life again. We hadn't tried to start a family, always thinking we would do that soon, but not yet. Now I had a car, a job and I eventually bought a flat. Well, actually I had a reliable car, an enviable job and a comfortable flat. I tumbled out of my marriage straight onto the heap of thirty-something single professional women with all the scaffolding required to hold up the appearance of a liberated and independent life, but none of the scatter cushions of inner comfort.

Reminders of John jumped out from the most unlikely places and the memories were welcome as often as they were unwelcome: suede boots on shoe-shop shelves, U2 playing on the radio, Sanj Bhaskar on the TV. Although I never again came across a leatherjacket that smelt of roast beef. These small reminders were enough to undo me, but on the whole I thought I was managing fine, until a senior colleague on the newspaper took me aside one day and asked, 'What's the matter?'

'Nothing.'

'Something's not right,' he said. 'I can tell by the look on your face.'

I reluctantly told him I was dealing with the breakdown of my marriage and he shared with me his own similar experience some years earlier. I felt relieved to have spoken about my angst with him, and though I knew 'talking' helped to alleviate burdens, I nonetheless could not bring myself to tell other colleagues or many of my friends. Most of all, I could not bring myself to tell my parents.

A year after John and I separated, I still couldn't find the courage to tell them what had happened. I had once shattered their hopes and dreams with my refusal to have an arranged marriage. I had insisted on marrying the man of my choice. I, their firstborn, had inauspiciously brought shame upon their heads, hurt their *izzat* and damaged their standing in the Indian community. Surely they had suffered enough. One day I would have to tell them. But I was tarrying because I didn't have the strength. They would almost certainly see it as a vindication of their warning years earlier: *'These English boys, these Angrez boys, they go when they finish with the girl.'*

Had I had an arranged marriage, perhaps love would have grown and my marriage to whomever my parents had chosen would still be going strong. Who knows. Certainly my sister's marriage was proving to be successful – she even had a child now. My marriage would inevitably be compared to hers and I would be the loser. The facts would speak for themselves. I had had a love marriage to an English boy and it had gone wrong, just as they'd said it would. What a disaster.

One night I was sitting at home alone when the phone rang.

'Hello Sushila, how are you?'

'Hi Dad, I'm fine.'

'How's John? Is his job going well?'

'Yes, he's fine too. His job's going really well.'

'Are you both keeping good health?'

'Yes, we're both doing really well.'

There were many phone calls like that. Sometimes Mum would ask to speak to John, and I'd tell her he was working late or had gone shopping or was visiting a friend. After all these years, my parents had reconciled to John. Mum even asked if we were contemplating starting a family soon, to which I responded by telling her if there was any news to report, she would be the first to know.

At the end of every phone call I would be simultaneously overcome by relief that I had managed to lie my way through it, and shame that I had been too spineless to tell them that John and I had separated, that he lived in Sydney now, and that I was lonely and adrift. But I simply didn't know *how* to tell them, and how I would handle what might come afterwards. The feeling was not unlike the anguish I'd felt when I was trying to work out how to tell them I didn't want an arranged marriage, except this time the agony was laced with fear of humiliation.

I spent weeks and months in a madness of my own making and shared my thoughts with no one. I looked at photos of Vin's cherubic child and wondered whether I would have had a similar-looking baby had I married Dinesh. In the background, biological clocks were ticking everywhere: in women's conversations, in cultural studies books, in newspaper articles and in the bedrooms of commitment-phobic men. I lurched from week to week hoping that something would happen to make that inevitable phone call to my parents slightly easier.

By the end of that year, joyless madness had taken over and I was focusing on my work ever harder, spending long hours at my desk, for there was nothing to go home for. I decided to work through the Christmas period that year – taking leave felt pointless. I drove to the office along empty roads on Christmas morning. The sunshine bounced off the top of cars parked along the leafy streets bordering the Botanic Gardens. Melbourne's

Shrine of Remembrance stood bold and strong. The summer air, still morning-fresh, would be suffocatingly hot by the afternoon. The streets were empty. This was a Melbourne Christmas – sunny and glaring, all hairdryer hot. This was not the Christmas I grew up with.

I hankered for a winter chill in the air and brussel sprouts with a pinch of Mum's garam masala. I wanted to scrape the ice off my car windscreen with my credit card, like I used to. I wanted the weatherman to warn of more cold fronts and hazardous driving conditions, not of northerly desert winds. So hard to adapt. At least being in the office took my mind off things. Later that day, taking the same route home, I remembered I hadn't been shopping and there was barely anything to eat in my flat, just the usual fridge stalwarts: half a bottle of wine and a tub of olives.

I pulled over by a 7Eleven, that overly illuminated beacon of convenience, and went inside. The woman behind the counter had a remarkably heavy brow and five o'clock shadow. I guessed she was Lebanese, maybe Greek. Perhaps even Turkish. You can be anything in Melbourne. I asked for a hot meatpie, which she placed in a paper bag for me. 'Merry Charissmas, love,' she said, handing me the change. I ate the lukewarm pie in the car on the way home. It didn't feel like Christmas, it really didn't feel like Christmas.

When I got home I thought about calling London, but the time difference wasn't good and they'd probably still be asleep. 'I'll ring them tomorrow,' I thought. 'Maybe I'll tell them about me and John too. Nah, probably not the best day. Maybe some other time.' I studied my last bank statement. I had enough money in my account for a trip home. I would have paid double the price to be able to go home for a while, but I knew I was stuck here. How would I explain John's absence? They would ask me why he had not come with me. They would ask me if everything was all right.

I can't remember when I finally told my parents, or what motivated me to call them on that particular day, but I remember the conversation.

'Dad, things have not been going very well with me and John. We've tried our best but we're not happy. We've talked about it a lot and we've decided to separate. I just wanted to let you know.'

'What do you mean?'

'We've decided to finish things. We're separating.'

'This is all very sudden. You must take time to consider these things. What is the problem?'

'Nothing – I don't really want to talk about those kinds of things. We're separating because things are not working out. I'm sorry, Dad.'

'Is there somebody else?'

'No. Neither of us has found anyone else. It's a decision we've made together.' There was silence as Dad absorbed the news. After a long pause, he finally said, 'There is no need to rush. There is plenty of time for reconciliation. You must try to reconcile your differences.'

'Dad, there is no chance of reconciliation. It's over.'

'It's all right,' he said kindly. 'Everything will be all right.'

There were many more conversations like that with Dad and Mum. They encouraged me to try to keep my marriage together, to work out what was wrong and put it right. If only it was that easy to rewind the passage of time and undo the knots of a relationship. The idea of relationship breakdown simply did not register on my parents' radar. They could never visualise their own marriage falling apart. There was no such thing for them.

Their philosophy was quite different: people hit hard times, but they get through it. Everyone's life has some struggle and pain, that's no reason to pack your suitcase and leave. A wife should forgive and forget – it's her duty. A marriage is not good or bad, it just *is*.

Please, they begged, couldn't John and I work it out? Here they were pleading with me to stay with the Englishman that they had not wanted me to marry in the first place almost thirteen years before. But now, for them, divorce was the least desirable outcome. Theoretically speaking, within the traditional Indian social structure, a divorced woman belongs neither to her father nor her husband. In India, there is a strong religious, cultural and social stigma attached to divorce and this still informs the thinking of diaspora Indians. Widows are often shunned in India, but a divorced woman does not even have the dignity of a widow. A divorced woman is damaged goods.

I waited for my parents to tell me I had ruined my life, that if I had only listened to them and allowed them to choose a husband for me, I would still be a respectably married woman. But there was no reproach. They never reprimanded me for refusing an arranged marriage, nor taunted me for the breakdown of my love marriage. They didn't say 'we told you so' or claim any type of victory. They didn't need to.

But did I feel I had made a mistake? *Should* I have had an arranged marriage? Would I have been happier? Did I regret my decision to have a love marriage? Well, of course I wondered what life with Dinesh, or any other man my parents might have chosen, would have been like. Of course I wondered whether an Indian husband would have taken me gently by the shoulders as I rose from touching his feet during the *Kurwa Chauth* ceremony. And, yes, I regretted that relations with my parents had been damaged because I hadn't followed Indian tradition.

Regret is surely the worst of all emotions. By its very nature it can never go away. It must linger forever. It's quite unlike anger, for example, which can be eliminated from one's system through the pressure cooker vent of verbal or physical expression; or grief, which necessarily loses its agonising edge with time. Regret is an altogether very different animal. Quite simply, regret would not be regret if one didn't rue forever.

So is that how I felt? Did I regret refusing to have an arranged marriage? No, absolutely not. It all comes down to choice and control. Like so many women before me, I wanted a say in my future, even if others *thought* they knew better or *did* know better. Every individual must be free to make her or his own mistakes. That's the nature of freedom.

Months later my mum was on the phone again, as she had been nearly every week.

'Are you sure you and John can't be together anymore?'

'Positive.'

'Then come back home. Come back to England. Why live in Australia anymore, with no family, no husband? Iss no good for you.'

'I know I need to rebuild my life.' But I had rebuilt my life after marrying John, then I had rebuilt my life again in Australia and now my mum was asking me to rebuild my life in London. How many times can a person rebuild their life?

'If you come back home, me and Dad can look for someone for you, if you want,' said Mum.

'What do you mean "look for someone"?' I asked.

'You know, maybe we find Indian boy for you.'

'Mum, I don't think so,' I said, bemused that she thought I might entertain the idea of an arranged marriage at this stage of my life. That really would have been the cherry on the cake for my parents: I marry an Englishman in a love marriage that falls apart. Then Mum and Dad marry me off to an Indian guy of their choosing and it's a rip-roaring success. No way.

I continued living and working in Melbourne and in many ways it was all downhill from there. I was binge-drinking, binge-smoking and binge-dating. If it wasn't for the memory loss that accompanies depression, those years would be easier to recall. All I know is that the seasons came and went because the leaves on the trees outside my flat changed from green to red to yellow and then fell to the ground several times over.

Life was empty and soulless. I seemed to be forever sitting on a barstool on my own, booking weekends out of town on my own, eating dinner on my own. Sometimes whole weekends would go by without me leaving my flat, getting out of my pyjamas and barely eating. I couldn't shake the melancholy; I could sometimes scarcely recall what I had done the day before.

I do, however, have an alarmingly vivid memory of having to complete an official form that required me to name my next of kin who should be contacted in the event of an emergency. It didn't make sense to name anyone in my family – they were all in England or America. Even John – Professor John Hobson by now – had moved back to England. I couldn't think of a single person whom I would not be imposing on should I be run over by a bus. I locked myself in one of the cubicles in the ladies' loos at work and stayed there for a long time.

'Are you all right?' asked a young reporter when I finally emerged.

'Yes, thanks,' I said. 'Just a bit tired of life.'

'Yeah, I know how you feel,' she said. 'This job gets to you after a while, doesn't it?' At work I carried on as best I could. I interviewed pillars of society, networked, made snap judgments and met deadlines. I told none of my colleagues that sometimes I sat at home staring at the wall for hours; that I spent weekends on my own lost in the fog of depression; that sometimes I just didn't feel like living anymore.

I rang my sister, who was now building a house in New Jersey, as well as my brother in London, in a hopeless attempt to feel connected to my family, but both sounded busy with their own lives. However, Raja must have heard a note of desperation down the phone, because something persuaded him to visit me.

He arrived at the peak of summer that year. By day I drove him around Melbourne showing him the sights, but in the evening and into the night we talked – and that's all I wanted to do.

He was no longer the boy he'd been when I had left England almost a decade earlier. He was now a tall man with broad shoulders, still able to talk the hind leg off a pony, but more restrained, perhaps even cautious. As a boy of about eight or nine, he'd had neat black hair, clear honey skin and a passion for football. He still had all those things, except his hair was now long and he sported a carefully crafted unshaven face. His leatherjacket completed his rock 'n' roll look. He was still a sound engineer working in one of London's few remaining small recording studios, and he spent a lot of time with rockstars.

I showed him newspaper clippings of articles I had written and he showed me his name on the back of the latest Robert Plant CD. 'I did backing vocals on that one,' he said with thinly veiled pride.

'Which other famous people have you met?' I asked.

'Not that many, really. Had a fag with Brian Ferry once – does that count?'

Raja had been outside my life for a long time and I had been outside his. My most vivid memory of him was his angry face shouting, 'Look what you've done to Mum and Dad,' after I'd broken the news that I would not have an arranged marriage.

It was all different now. He had an English girlfriend and he didn't have to hide her from our parents – he was living with her! I could never have lived with a boyfriend in my twenties – that would have been unconscionable. Clearly my parents were changing – or was it that Raja, being a son, was receiving special treatment?

My experience of traditional Indian families is that, metaphorically speaking, boys are given the cream, while girls get the milk. (In my mum's day, boys *literally* got the cream, while girls were given thinner milk.) The men of the family are fed first, women eat later. A 2010 American study of child gender and parental investment in India found boys received on average 10 per cent more parental time than girls. They were also more likely to be breastfed for longer, and given vaccinations and vitamin supplements.

Vin and I received as much or as little of everything as Raja ever did. But certainly in terms of our parents' moral strictness towards us, their grip on Raja was much looser. Was he allowed to do whatever he wanted? No. But he had greater freedom to associate with friends, including girls, outside the home. Didn't Mum and Dad want him to have an arranged marriage? 'Yeah,

Mum gives me the telephone numbers of Indian girls,' Raja told me. 'I met one once. She worked in a bank. She was nice and all that, but not my type.'

I asked him if he was prepared to have an arranged marriage.

'Yeah, well, I suppose if Mum and Dad found someone and she was all right, I suppose I would, but I'd have to get to know her and all that. But that won't stop me finding someone myself,' he said. A picture of him in his leatherjacket leading a demure Indian girl around the holy fire popped into my head. I couldn't imagine him doing things the traditional way and nor could I see him marrying a girl with whom a relationship had not naturally evolved. What he wanted was what is these days known as a semi-arranged marriage, where parents allow their sons and daughters to find their own match. If the match is deemed suitable then the couple is free to 'date' until marriage.

As far as I am concerned a semi-arranged marriage is merely an arranged marriage with the word 'semi' attached for the purposes of appearing modern. A girl, at some stage, is still required to marry someone her parents have vetted, whether she's picked him herself or not. And what if she chooses her own husband, secures her parents' approval, dates him and then dumps him because he isn't Mr Right? Would that be acceptable? I don't think so.

Raja wanted to please Mum and Dad, just like Vin had, but perhaps it was life experience that led me to believe that, despite his good intentions, the likelihood of him taking a course of action that would simultaneously please our parents and keep him happy was highly unlikely. I too had once aspired to an outcome that satisfied all parties, only to quickly realise that no such avenue existed. I felt sorry for my parents – they would probably have to tolerate a love marriage one more time.

During his stay, my brother and I, for the first time, talked about growing up in Britain. We both had lots of English friends, although he also had a few Indian ones, which I never had. His friends were a merry band of lads, who would spend time at each other's houses talking about football, laughing and eating crisps. I told him about my playground nignog experience and he was pensive.

'I got beaten up once,' he said suddenly. 'I was in the foetal position on the ground trying to protect my internal organs.'

His use of the words 'internal organs' made me feel panicky.

'What! When? What happened? Where?' I asked. So he told me his story.

'I was coming home from school one day – I must have been about eleven or twelve years old. I remember it was a hot day, I had my blazer on and my rucksack was full of books. There were two bigger boys on the other side of the road. I recognised them from school, even though they weren't wearing their uniforms. I think they must have been about fourteen or fifteen. Anyway, they crossed the road and came towards me. Then one of them hit me in my chest. Just completely out of the blue. I lost my balance because the rucksack was so heavy and I fell on the ground. They called me Paki and wog, and kicked me while I was on the ground. They told me to go back to my own country and then just walked off.

'It was a life-changing moment, really. I felt bruised when I got up; it hurt when I breathed. Anyway, I went home and Mum opened the door. I told her what had happened and she was pretty upset. She told Dad and he said, "Some people are frightened of things they don't know anything about." '

'What did he mean?'

'Well, he was trying to tell me people who don't know any better are either scared or angry about things they don't know about, and that's why they do stuff that doesn't make sense. Dad told me not to get angry and, you know, start thinking about revenge and all that. He told me to try and understand why those boys did it.' Raja paused. He'd started telling me the story slowly but as he spoke his words had tumbled out faster and faster. He paused to step out of the moment.

'Why was it a life-changing moment?' I asked instinctively, slipping into journalist mode. He took a beat of time to think before answering.

'I felt a lot of anger at the time. I wanted to take revenge on them for doing that to me. But that anger was immature. It was Dad who stopped me from taking revenge. It was life-changing because Dad made me see things from a different point of view. There were other incidents, but that's the one that sticks in my head. What gets me is that it was unprovoked.'

'How do you feel about it now?'

'I just think there are some people who don't have enough life education. They're not experienced enough to know that I'm no different to them.'

Having finished his story, he got up and went to the kitchen to make a cup of tea. His tone had been direct, as if he was giving me directions to the nearest train station. Neither of us said anything after that. We just sat and drank our tea.

By way of comfort, I might have been inclined to tell Raja that his was an experience from the past – that the world had moved on – had I not encountered a discomfitting experience of my own in the office just weeks earlier. I had leant my earplugs to a fellow reporter at the newspaper and needed them back so I could listen to an interview I had recorded. When I asked him for them, he opened his desk drawer, pulled them out and sniffed them. 'They smell of curry. They must be yours,' he said as he handed them to me.

Mortified, I took them and quietly returned to my desk. But later, seething with anger, I demanded an apology in writing – and I got it. No covering my face with my hands this time, no shouting swearwords into the air, no lump in the throat – not anymore.

On the day of Raja's departure I drove him to the airport and we hugged when they called his flight. 'You should come back home now,' he said. 'Mum and Dad want you to come back, and so do I.' And with that and a final wave, he was gone, his leatherjacket disappearing into the crowd as he went through the departure gates.

Perhaps I should have gone home straight away. I don't know. I was an experienced journalist in Melbourne and I enjoyed my job. I worried I wouldn't find an equivalent job in London. Newspapers all over the Western world were laying off staff as more and more people turned to the internet for news, and advertising revenue leached away. I missed London, heartily, but returning with no job, no partner and no property made me feel uncomfortable. Already I could hear the Indian gossips: 'Did you hear about Das's eldest daughter? Married a white man and ran away to Australia. Lost everything, came back with nothing. Too Westernised, huh! Too Westernised.'

Looking back now, I don't think anyone would have said that. I was a migrant to Australia, and like every migrant to any country before me, I was trapped in a slice of time from the past. Many migrants stay frozen in the pocket of time they existed in when they left their home country.

Mentally, I was aware that Britain's Indian community had moved on, become less restrictive of their daughters and better integrated into British life, but emotionally I still existed within the framework of the 1970s and 1980s – when Indian girls feared bringing shame on their families or dreamt of running away. My fear, of course, was induced by my parents' conservative morality, a hangover from 1960s India.

I felt trapped in a cage within a cage within a cage. Imaginary though my incarceration might have been, the iron bars of my mind were as strong as those of any real cage.

I finally decided to visit my parents in London in December 2000 – four years after I separated from John and a month after I was officially divorced. I was thirty-six years old.

There they were: Mum, Dad and Raja, waiting for me at Heathrow. Airports are such horrible places, full of crude emotion. Mum was crying even before I got out from behind the barrier that separates the travellers from the collectors.

'You are so thin,' she cried. 'Only your bones I can see. You lost too much weight.' Apart from occasionally wondering how my clothes had become so expanded, I hadn't noticed I had become so much thinner. I'd always been a slim person, but now I looked like a whippet. The best way to lose weight, other than by contracting a life-threatening illness, is to live through a divorce, no matter how amicable.

It's unsettling to see age catching up with your parents, if only because it's a forewarning of sorts. Mum and Dad had both taken to dyeing their grey hair black, yet they appeared older because of it. I was shocked to discover that Mum had had the black mole on her chin surgically removed, leaving behind a small shallow crater. I was cross. She had no right to stop looking like my mum. Dad was the same as ever, except he'd upgraded to a digital camera. 'Film always gives an excellent picture,' he said, 'but digital has some very superior qualities.' I felt a small burst of pride that he had so willingly embraced modern technology, rather than hankering for what he'd always known.

'You should come back to England now,' said Mum. 'Iss time to come home. Nothing left for you in Australia.' Perhaps she was right. What else was there to return to in Australia but journalism and childlessness? Next year, at the age of thirty-seven, my fertility would start its steep and merciless decline. What were the chances of meeting a new life partner and starting a family now? Grey hairs were appearing at my temples. Cynicism had gnawed its way into me. The world and I were getting older.

Dad wondered if I might find a job on a newspaper in England. It was an overt acknowledgment that he had reconciled himself to my career, and it pleased me. Ever since my teenage years we had been discussing world politics in one form or another, and though he never sat me down and specifically taught me about abstract concepts, I know my understanding of compassion and justice arose from the conversations we had.

Dad was proud and fascinated by my career. He never said so, but that was the obvious conclusion to draw from his interest in the workings of my newspaper. Where did it stand politically? How broad was its foreign coverage? Who owned it? What kind of man was the editor?

Most times Dad was across the news better than I was. He even knew what was going on in Australia – the BBC World Service, ever his friend. Every now and again I would present him with a new angle on a story, but it wasn't often that I had something to teach him. After all, what can you teach your father? What can you teach the man who assured you fairyfloss would not get stuck in your throat like a ball of cotton wool? What could you teach the man who took his five-year-old daughter into the garden one morning, just as the sun was warming the trees, and crouched down to carefully point with one finger to a glistening teardrop poised on the end of a blade of grass. 'Dew,' he had said. 'It comes in the morning.'

Comfortingly, nothing in Mum and Dad's house had changed, except Mum had her own TV now, on which she watched Indian soap operas in the living room at the front of the house. Dad used his TV to watch the news in the living room at the back of the house.

'He watch the news all day,' complained Mum, bustling about, crashing pots and pans in the kitchen. 'In the morning he watch the Pakistani news. Then he watch Indian news. Then he read the newspaper whole the day. In evening time he watch the news on BBC. All day iss same news.'

'Why do you get so worked up about it? You have your own

TV now. He's not stopping you from watching whatever you want,' I said.

'Yes, but he cut the newspaper and leave in every corner. His junk everywhere. Have you seen the garage? His junk in there. He never clean it. I ask him so many times, but he busy watching the news. He is not bread-winning anymore. He watching the news.'

'He *is* watching the news,' I said.

'See? Wor I tell you, he never stop. Bloody news.'

At least she had better command of her swearing these days. Later, in the living room at the back of the house Dad said, 'Your mother is obsessed with these Indian soap operas. Zee TV,' he put a mocking emphasis on Zee. 'She gets it on cable. I don't know how to stop her.'

'Just leave her, Dad. If she enjoys them, what's wrong with that?'

'You don't understand. They are affecting her thinking. She becomes too emotional.'

Be it an arranged marriage or a love marriage, bickering is presumably a universal phenomenon. But Mum and Dad, despite their needling, sometimes looked at each other with an expression that exhibited equal helpings of bewilderment, capitulation and curiosity. An expression that said, 'I understand you, but sometimes I *really* don't understand you.' Their love had grown and grown over thirty-seven years and there would be no end to it. They had their own language. If anyone inadvertently threw out Dad's newspapers, Mum would be the first to retrieve them from the bin, and any suggestion that Indian soaps were rubbish would be met with a flat response from Dad: 'Yes, but your mother enjoys them very much.'

No matter what, they would always be together because they believed fate had brought them together, and they accepted their fate. All Hindus accept their fate. The longer my parents were married, the more they baffled each other, but there was love and a calm acceptance of destiny: this is not a good life or even a bad life, this is just life unfolding, as it is meant to.

CHAPTER 15

The Triumph of Hope Over Experience

'I'm as free as a bird now, and this bird you cannot change . . . Lord knows, I can't change.' Lynyrd Skynyrd, 'Free Bird'

On the night of Saturday 12 October, 2002, terrorists detonated bombs on the island of Bali, killing 202 people: 38 were Indonesians, 88 were Australians. I was a news editor at the time and rostered to work the following day. It was going to be a big news day, so I got to the office early the next morning and began commissioning reporters to fly to Bali, keeping an eye on further breaking news and coordinating reporters on the ground in Melbourne. I had to work closely with the foreign editor, who was in touch with our foreign correspondents.

Some years earlier, Tom Hyland, that slow-speaking moustachioed Tasmanian who had given me my break in journalism, had quit his job at the wire service and moved to *The Age*, where he eventually took over as the foreign editor. His once brown hair had turned completely white by then. The day after the Bali bombings, Tom and I worked together to coordinate the newspaper's coverage of what was, at the time, the world's single biggest terrorist incident since 9/11.

Tom guided anxious reporters, spoke calmly and offered leadership and assurance. He was a steady pair of hands: dependable, experienced and utterly unflappable. I recall the day, not only because watching a professional at work was illuminating, but because we worked well as a team and I learnt a great deal from him. But if somebody had told me that I would one day marry Tom, I would have thought them barking mad. He was ten years my senior and by then I was most certainly not looking for a partner, let alone a husband. I had given up on men and had decided that living alone, an existence that is 50 per cent joy and 50 per cent guerilla warfare with oneself, was actually the best option for me. Thoughts of having children had faded. I was ready for a life of childlessness.

Most of my interaction with Tom was at the daily afternoon news conference, at which the various section editors would gather to brief the editor on the stories and pictures of the day. It was a relatively small conference room and with the doors closed the unlaboured breathing of the fifteen or so people gathered around the table would quickly cause an oxygen deficit, leaving previously compos mentis individuals in either a soporific torpor or a bizarre state of professional hysteria. Occasionally the decorum of the conference would collapse into low-grade one-upmanship about Australian Rules Football, that game of base thuggery in which players are required to run about as if in a schoolyard, spitefully snatching the ball off one another and punching each other in the head – all under the guise of manly sportsmanship. The room would become unnecessarily animated, discussing which team had won at the weekend, which player had gouged out whose eye and whether so and so's cruciate ligament injury would debilitate him for the remainder of the season. I despised those moments because I despised this babyishly named 'footy'. The only other person in the room who I'd heard also had little time for the sport was Tom. I'd look at him wearily across the table and pull a cross-eyed cartoon character's face, tongue hanging loosely out of one side of my mouth. He'd stare at me unblinking, his moustache acting as a disguise to conceal his expression. I could never tell what he was thinking.

Once conference started in earnest, the editors ran through their lists of stories for the day one by one, each vying for one of their own yarns to be the front-page splash. As the foreign editor, Tom's stories usually involved tongue-twisting foreign names of mass murderers, brutal dictators and far-flung war-torn cities, which he would pronounce with eyebrow-raising aplomb.

'I practise the pronunciation for at least an hour before going in to conference,' he confided to me. He was a solid performer who disliked being interrupted. When on one occasion the editor started a random conversation with the person sitting next to him during one of Tom's briefings, as he was wont to do sometimes, Tom stopped recounting his news list and continued seamlessly on an entirely different path: 'Meanwhile, in other news,' he announced, 'German armoured columns have crossed the Polish frontier. The British prime minister has issued the chancellor with an ultimatum and the Australian prime minister is about the address the nation. It looks like there's going to be another war. And the other story we're keeping an eye on is the Oscars.'

The dozy elite of Melbourne journalism stirred from their slumber and sniggered as the editor acknowledged Tom with an apologetic nod. *The Age*'s foreign editor had a way of commanding attention with sarcasm.

But Tom didn't need to use sarcasm to command my attention. I found him rather fascinating, not unlike a paleontologist discovering the fossil of a hitherto unknown dinosaur. His ever-so-slightly robotic manner eased when he was away from the office, as if somebody had oiled his joints, and he leant back comfortably in his chair when he talked about his son and daughter from a previous marriage. And while talking about his kids, who were both in their late teens, he'd find himself chasing memories of his own childhood growing up in a small town in Tasmania.

'My mum and dad both migrated from Ireland and came to Australia on the same ship. In fact, they fell in love on that ship and got married a year after they arrived,' he said. A romantically quaint story, so different from my own parents'. 'My father had a rich, expressive Irish brogue,' Tom continued. 'There were five kids in our family and we would cluster around him when he sat in his armchair to read to us every night.'

'Didn't you ever rebel against your parents?'

'Yes, I had a rebellion. I was a dope-smoking, long-haired hippie, but I still went to Mass – had to really. There are some things you can only rebel against slowly. Catholicism, I'm afraid, is one of them.'

Had we not enjoyed hours engaged in random musings, we might never have discovered that we harboured a mutual respect for fountain pens, had a penchant for anchovies and savoured unforgivably bad language. He was a welcome companion at a time when I needed some human company.

One day, after the war on Iraq had started and my working days were angsty-fast, Tom popped over to my flat for a cup of tea and to debrief. He had with him a brown paper bag that he handed to me, saying, 'Here, these are for you.' I peered into the bag and saw three small tomatoes and two brown eggs. 'The tomatoes are from my garden and my chickens laid those eggs today,' he said.

They were humble products, the results of his daily nurturing, and he was proud to show me his achievements. Indeed, his achievements were a gift for me. Journalism is a fierce business. Our lives, dominated by our careers, were a blur of deadlines, complexities, pressure, time poverty and brutal cynicism. In the midst of this madness, Tom brought me these simple unadulterated gifts of friendship.

We got married one autumn day in 2004. This wedding day was different. Mum, Dad and Raja flew over from London. For my first wedding, my brother couldn't make it; this time my sister couldn't attend because she was heavily pregnant with her third baby. I'm not sure *why* we married; after all, as Robert Louis Stevenson said, marriage is just a sort of friendship recognised by the police, and we really had no reason to put ourselves on their radar.

But this time around I was determined to acknowledge my roots and make a conciliatory gesture to my parents. So Tom and I arranged a wedding that could best be described as an amalgam of Eastern and Western ideas. It was a small event in a posh restaurant in Melbourne, with no cake and a solo harpist. I wore a red and gold sari that Mum helped me tie and Raja helped me with my Indian wedding make-up of red and white dots above my eyebrows. Tom wore a black jacket with a Nehru collar and a red silk cravat. Some days earlier Mum had said to him, 'Tome, you like maybe I dye your white hair?'

'Thank you for offering, but I think I'll just leave it as it is,' he'd politely replied.

She thought him too old for me. But when I reminded her there was a seven-year difference between her and Dad, she simply said, 'That's different, he's your father.'

It wasn't easy finding an established *mehndi* artist, but I found one miles away in one of Melbourne's rundown outer suburbs. Her flat was neat but sparse and I could hear a couple of children in the back room. On a shelf a small statuette of Ganesh the elephant god sat surrounded by an open sewing box full of cotton reels, Bollywood DVDs and a pack of Huggies baby wipes. She didn't talk much, so we sat largely in silence for two hours while she painted my hands and wrists in intricate patterns using a small icing bag of wet *mehndi* with a thin nozzle. At some point she looked up and, smiling, asked in a heavy Indian accent, 'What is the name of your fiancé? I am writing in your hand. It will take him long time finding. I will write very small for you.' And somewhere between the swirling lines and patterns at the base of my left thumb, in minuscule letters, she hid the letters T-O-M.

On the wedding day, nobody wore funereal expressions. Mum dressed in a bright turquoise and hot pink sari and Dad wore a little red flower in his lapel. My parents were smiling and it made my heart bleed with joy. Perhaps they thought Tom's seniority might bring wisdom that would put me on the straight and narrow. Perhaps they were charmed by him because, as Tom told me later, in my absence he had told them that I spoke highly of them.

Against a backdrop of multicoloured flowers strung on long threads like a bead curtain, Tom and I exchanged the marriage vows that we had written ourselves. We didn't exchange rings, we swapped garlands of fresh red and white carnations instead. The food and music were Western. And when it was all over, we went to India for our honeymoon, to see the world's biggest monument to love: the Taj Mahal, of course. It was a different sort of wedding, because this was a different sort of time and my parents and I had become different sorts of people.

I suppose I might have said goodbye to Australia and returned to London, the place I will always consider home, if I hadn't met Tom. But I would never have opted for an arranged marriage the second time around. I'd like to think the paths I chose with both my marriages left the door ajar for my younger relatives. I hope I legitimised love marriage, so that other younger members of our extended family felt more comfortable opting for free choice, with all its attendant responsibilities, over bondage within an honour system that subjugates women.

I am talking in absolute terms here. I'm not suggesting every woman who enters an arranged marriage is a slave. Most right-thinking people agree that forced marriages are absolutely unacceptable. Not everyone agrees that a law to make them a criminal act is the way forward, and that is a debate for another day. But arranged marriage is a feminist issue. If parents wish to help their children find marriage partners and their children want their parents' help, then that is mere matchmaking. In an environment where finding the right life partner is not always easy, this might even make sense. Whether this matchmaking by mutual consent is done through matrimonial websites, word of mouth or ads in newspapers, it makes no difference. As long as the couple to be married has the freedom to reject or accept the match, then there's nothing objectionable in that.

There are no doubt bright, enlightened young women who are in favour of arranged marriages, or 'semi-arranged' marriages, and perhaps have entered into one themselves without feeling they were unduly pressured. One could argue Vin was one such woman – sort of. I just don't know any others, which is not to say they don't exist.

But if a woman does not have the genuine freedom to reject a match without fearing the repercussions for herself or her family; if social coercion or emotional pressure is applied even in the subtlest form (and often it is subtle); if free choice *cannot* be exercised, even though a woman is outwardly *told* she is free to say yes or no – then there is surely a rot at the heart of arranged marriages.

Knowing what we know about the honour system, countries to which Indians have migrated, such as Britain, America and Australia, cannot consider arranged marriage a foreign custom in which they have no right to intrude. This particularly applies to Australia, where Indian migration is rising fast and there is little or no awareness of Indian culture other than cricket and curry.

Multiculturalism is all very well, but if feel-good policies that promote the so-called melting-pot theory of people living side by side, sharing each other's cuisine, is all that it has to offer, then it's not much.

Change has swept through my family these days and made it a multicultural and multiracial joint venture. My cousin Twinkle eventually married a British-Vietnamese man, and she and her family went through everything my family and I went through. Raja, having split up with his English girlfriend, went on to marry a British-Chinese woman. He had a traditional Hindu wedding followed by a traditional Chinese tea ceremony. My parents accepted his wishes. I have two other cousins in Britain who also chose their own husbands. All we need now is for someone in my family to declare they are gay and we will have traversed all territory known to man, and woman.

Mixed marriages, it seems, are on the rise everywhere. In Britain the rate of mixed marriages for second-generation Indians is about 14 per cent and the expectation is that this will rise in future generations as family pressures to marry someone approved by the family will almost certainly be weaker.

In America, mixed marriages made up a little more than 8 per cent of all marriages in 2012 – an all-time high. And in Australia, less than 20 per cent of first-generation Indians (those born overseas) married out. These figures indicate a heartening breakdown in racial barriers and a pleasing celebration of love across the racial divide.

Of course, mixed-race babies will be the result of these mishmash marriages. Ethnic ambiguity is the way of the future. Twinkle has two children and Raja has one. When I became pregnant at the age of forty, I welcomed the news with cautious delight. Learning that you are finally pregnant is like being told you have a winning lottery ticket. You're delighted, but you're not going to celebrate until you have that cash in your hands.

I knew I was carrying a girl because I had an amniocentesis test, and I was thrilled because that's what I had hoped for. Not only because I wanted the chance to raise a daughter, but because giving birth to a girl baby was the ultimate rebellion. Mum and Dad were beside themselves with excitement. They cared little that they had no say in the choice of my second husband, all that mattered now was that they would have another grandchild and the family would continue for another generation through *all* their children.

In my family we have become accustomed to big news being announced over long-distance phone calls.

'Hi Mum, it's me.'

'Hello, Sushila, how are you feeling?'

'I'm fine, no morning sickness or anything.'

'That is good. I am very very happy for you. I pray every day that god give you little baby and he listen my prayer.'

'Thanks, Mum. By the way, I know the sex of the baby.'

'What is it? Tell me, what is it?' she said eagerly.

'It's a girl!'

'Oh, never mind,' she said, deflated.

'Mum! It's fantastic that it's a girl. I'm happy that it's a girl.'

'Yes, yes, of course. I am happy too. Iss very good news. I get your father.'

My mum's immediate reaction was not a cruel response, it was merely instinctive. I wasn't angry or shocked by her comment. I understood it. She grew up believing that the birth of a boy is better than the birth of a girl because that's what her culture taught her. More often than not we don't see our culture. It's everywhere but it's invisible. We just absorb it.

And so, at the ripe old age of forty-one, I gave birth to a girl. She is part of a generation of mixed race children who, I hope, will grow up having a firmer sense of self than I did, instead of feeling she must slot herself into an identity imposed by others. But more importantly, my daughter, I hope, will grow up and fulfill her potential without having to waste half her life distracted by the struggle to be treated the same as men. Betty Friedan said it best in a letter to her daughter published in *Cosmopolitan* in 1978: 'I hope there will come a day when you, daughter mine, or your daughter, can truly afford to say "I'm not a feminist. I'm a person" – and a day, not too far away, I hope, when I can stop fighting for women and get onto other matters that interest me now.'

Around the time my daughter was about a year old, and I was just becoming accustomed to a child who could now walk and wreck the house simultaneously, I received a call from Vin. For years I had thrown around the idea of a big family reunion and we discussed it from time to time, but neither of us had managed to organise it. Now she had a plan.

'This family reunion – let's do it,' she said. 'Whenever we visit each other, we all do it in shifts. We never meet in the same spot at the same time.'

'Great idea,' I said. 'But where exactly do you think this reunion is going to take place? And what are the chances of everyone being able to get annual leave at the same time? And even if we manage to sort that out, what are the chances of coinciding the dates with the American school holidays? Remember, we're dealing with Indians here. It'll be like herding cats.'

'Yeah, I know it'll be tricky. But think about it. It's Dad's seventieth birthday next December. If we could only just get everyone together in December, we could celebrate his birthday and have Christmas together too.' I could hear her excitement down the phone line. 'I've spoken to Raja and if we all pitch in we could get Dad a camera – you know, the latest whiz-bang thing.'

'Yeah, okay. But we're talking about Mum and Dad, Raja, his wife and child, you, Dinesh and your three kids and us three. So that's thirteen people. Where are we all going to stay?'

'Actually, it's fourteen because my father-in-law is visiting us from India next year,' she added.

There was a silence as both of us contemplated the magnitude of the task. Then she shouted, 'We could do it at my place! Yeah, everyone could come to New Jersey and we could all stay at my house.'

Vin was sure she could pull it off. She was also happy for everyone to stay at her place because by now she and Dinesh had finished building a nice little house in New Jersey. Actually, it was more than a nice little house. It was an eight-bedroom mansion on an acre of land with plenty of bathrooms and a huge swimming pool. Maybe I should have married Dinesh after all.

CHAPTER 16

In the Land of the Free

'Another world is not only possible, she is on her way. On a quiet day, I can hear her breathing.' Arundhati Roy

When our baby was small I would lift her out of her plastic bathing tub each evening and Tom would carry the tub carefully into the garden and throw the water at the feet of the old sycamore maple tree, in a pitiful attempt to keep it alive during the height of the drought in Melbourne.

He was a tender, attentive older father, hanging tiny socks on the washing line, changing nappies and patiently prising his glasses out of her tight fist when she snatched them off his face. When I lacked confidence with the baby, he'd step in: 'Hold her over your shoulder, like this – they prefer it like that sometimes.' Or, 'It's okay, leave her be, she'll fall asleep by herself.'

One day, without prompting, he said, 'My kids, they just grew up so fast. Lovely little things. I should have spent more time with them when they were small. I was always at work – I don't know where my head was. It's good to be given another go at it all. Mind you, it's not like it was the first time round. Me and the little one were in a shop the other day and the lady behind the counter looked at her in the pusher and said, "Oh, how lovely to spend a day with granddad." I didn't think I looked *that* old.'

Early one morning, because every morning is an early one during toddlerhood, the phone rang. I knew who it was – there was only one person who never seemed to get the time difference right.

'Hello Neelum, Mummy here.'

'Hi, Mum.'

'Are you making the plans to go to America?'

'Yes. I can't believe we're doing this! I think Tom and I will be the first there. We were lucky getting the flights – it's not always easy around Christmas time.'

'We will all enjoy! How is the little one?'

'She's fine. She can say some words now. But it's hard, Mum. It's really hard going to work and doing all the mother stuff at the same time. I don't know how you did it with three.'

'Aaah,' she said slowly. 'Now you are learning what is the motherhood meaning. It is making sacrifice for children. This is the meaning of the parent love.'

Most unexpectedly, I had a picture of Dad as a young boy in my head, squatting in the chicken punishment position, holding his ear lobes.

'Hey, Mum, do you remember when you told me that story about Dad and how his nickname at school was the Saint because he took the blame for something he didn't do?'

'No, I don't remember that story.'

'You said his nickname was the Saint, I remember. You told me the story ages ago, when I was little. Don't you remember? He made a sacrifice to save all the kids in the class.'

She paused. 'No, I said his nickname is *Saieen* [pronounced sigh-een, with a nasal n],' she said. 'I don't remember the story you talking about. Everybody remember differently the past.'

'*Saieen*? Are you sure? What does it mean?'

'It mean person is very quiet, very pure. His heart is clean. He is near the god.'

'Huh? Is Dad there? Put him on.'

So she handed the phone to him.

'Dad, when you were young, Mum said they called you the Saint or *Saieen* or something, because you admitted doing something you didn't do to save the class and so the teacher gave you the chicken punishment. Is that true?'

'Yes, I had that nickname, *Saieen*, when I was a boy. That was a long time ago. It means someone who is very quiet and focused on god. Spiritual. But I don't know which story she is talking about. Usually I don't know what she is talking about these days. Perhaps she is thinking of the teacher who hit me.'

'What happened?' I asked, and he told me the story.

'I was in sixth grade, so I was about nine or ten. I was in an English class and the teacher gave us a spelling test. I had a few buddies in that class and they got the spellings wrong. Then the teacher asked me and I got the answers right. He was angry with my buddies for their wrong answers so he asked me to slap them as punishment. I did not want to slap my friends. But he ordered me to do it. So I simply touched their faces lightly. After that, the teacher became angry with me for not slapping them hard. So he said to me, "I will show you how to slap." Then he slapped *me* very hard with his large hand. I was a young boy and he had a very big hand. It was painful because he slapped across my ear. For some time after that my hearing was damaged. But it returned in later years. I still remember that teacher. His name was Mukund Lal.'

It was as if I had opened a box looking for something, and found something else more intriguing instead. Dad had been in a bind. He knew what was expected of him but he had felt uncomfortable doing it. So he had done what he thought was right instead, only to find himself punished for his humanity.

Had he not faced that same dilemma as an Indian father in Britain? People in his community had expected him to adhere to old traditions, but he had been left in an invidious bind when I demanded a love marriage. In the end he had done what he thought was the right thing for me and they had punished him for it. *This is the meaning of the parent love.*

'That's terrible, Dad.'

'Yes, he was not the finest teacher. Now I will put you back to your mother – she's right here.'

After I'd hung up I stood thinking for a moment, till my thoughts were interrupted by shuffling and dragging sounds coming from the living room. I went to investigate and found my nearly-two-year-old daughter hauling behind her a little brown suitcase: the suitcase with the two silvery clasps that snapped shut with a satisfactory click – the one I had planned to run away with in the panic of my youth. It had been my dad's, then mine. Now it was hers and she used it as a plaything, opening and closing it, stuffing it with soft toys and knick-knacks, and then taking them all back out again.

One day when she grows up, she'll probably ask me why it says SIOUX inside the lid.

Within weeks Tom and I were sitting with an excited little girl at the departure gates in terminal two at Melbourne Airport waiting for Qantas flight 93 to Los Angeles. It was nearly lunchtime and my daughter would be hungry soon. Tom had her peanut butter sandwiches in the Hello Kitty backpack on his back. In about twenty-four hours we would be at JFK Airport in New York. A night and day to fly to the other side of the world; half a lifetime to acclimatise.

'I can't believe Vin's managed to coordinate this reunion,' I said. 'I feel a bit nervous actually. It's been twenty-four years since we all lived under the same roof.'

'Why? What's there to be nervous about?'

'Don't know. What if it's awkward? What if we start arguing with each other? I don't think I could bear that.'

'What if you all just carry on from where you left off?'

It was late in the evening and frosty when we arrived in New York. The airport was warm and Christmas baubles dangled in the duty-free shop. Dinesh, who came to pick us up, looked almost no different to the way he had when I'd first set eyes on him in my parent's garden. Unlike Vin, who was a fast driver, he drove slowly and cautiously all the way to New Jersey, where Vin was waiting in her extraordinarily large house with her three kids.

Within days everyone had arrived. Mum and Dad, both wearing sneakers, looked like a pair of American tourists. A floppy map and self-darkening sunglasses would have completed the picture. Raja and his wife had with them their seven-month-old baby girl – a little half-Indian half-Chinese honeyball. It was the first time I'd met her. Vin's father-in-law was also there, a quiet old man who mostly kept to himself.

All the kids, once they'd finished staring at each other, became instant friends, rummaging through toys in the rumpus room and watching TV together. It was the grown-ups who needed a little help relaxing. We spent our first few days together being terribly polite, passing the salt, helping to put the dishes away, all smiling tentatively. That came to an abrupt end one evening when Vin pulled out a bottle of Grey Goose Vodka, placed it on the island kitchen bench with a loud bang and said, 'Right, who wants a cocktail?'

Within a couple of hours our shyness had evaporated and everyone was laughing and chatting loudly. It was like being at a house party where most of the partygoers bore a physical resemblance to each other.

Most evenings Vin and Mum prepared the evening meal. One night Vin asked me, 'Can you put some of this bayzel on the salad?'

'Bayzel?' I mocked. 'Bayzel? You're really American now, eh?'

'Well, you change, don't you?' she replied.

'I haven't.'

'That just shows there's something wrong with you. There's always been something wrong with your head.'

'She's changed, all right,' said Raja. Then he said to me, 'You sound like an Australian.'

'I most certainly do not,' I said, exaggerating my English accent to push back against a comment that perturbed me.

'You most certainly do. You go up at the end of all your sentences? Like this? Like you're asking a question?'

'No, I don't.'

'Yes, you do.'

'Don't.'

'Do.'

I looked at Vin for support. 'G'day, Sheila,' she said, raising her glass to me and grinning.

That evening after Mum and Dad had gone to bed, and the kids were sound asleep, Vin and I found ourselves sitting on the couch watching the TV on mute.

'Do you think you'll ever go back to England to live?' I asked without looking at her.

'Nah,' she said without hesitation. 'I've made my home here; the kids are settled at school. America's good, it gives people a chance. The country code for America is number one, you know. I'll always miss England though. What about you? You ever gonna go back?'

'I hope so. I don't want Australia to be the country I die in. It would be like dying miles away from home – where you should be when you die. But I have to consider Tom and a child now, so it's not straightforward. I might go back for a quick visit next year though. I have some business to attend to. I've got to give Mum and Dad something. Well, *return* something actually.'

'What?'

'Just some old black and white photos.'

Vin turned to look at me. 'I nicked them when I was a kid,' I said.

'Why?'

'I don't know. Probably because there's something wrong with my head.'

'I could have told you that.'

We sat in silence for a while, staring at the TV.

'Do you think you'll give your kids an arranged marriage?' I asked.

'No,' she said flatly.

'Nor me. I don't think Raja will either.'

'Mmm,' she said rubbing an eye. 'I'm tired. I'm gonna go to bed now. Got laundry and kids' stuff to do in the morning. We'll cut Dad's birthday cake at lunchtime. Don't forget to turn the lights out.'

She got up and took some empty glasses into the kitchen. She had Mum's shoulders from behind: slightly rounded. She had her skinny ankles too. I had my dad's height and angular features and Raja was somewhere in between.

Vin had an open-plan house so I could see her as she climbed the stairs and walked across the long landing to her bedroom. When we were kids, people used to say they could tell we were sisters. We didn't look anything like each other now.

After I heard her close her bedroom door, I sat for a while looking around me at the comfortable L-shaped couch, the fireplace without a mantelpiece, the large flatscreen TV, the twelve-foot Christmas tree standing in the hallway.

The era of arranged marriages in the family was dead now, I thought. How quickly it had happened – just one generation to end a centuries-old tradition. 'Still, the family's all together,' I said aloud to myself. 'The firm's still going strong.' Hauling myself off the couch, I made my way to the pink bedroom that Tom and I had been allocated.

The next morning I awoke to find my daughter standing near the bed like a silent child ghost, and weak sunlight passing easily through the fabric blinds. Downstairs I could hear cupboards being closed and plates clanking. I sat up and yawned. 'Good morning, my lovely little thing. Let's go downstairs and see what everyone's up to.'

When I opened the bedroom door I saw Vin on the landing wrestling with laundry.

'Good morning,' she said, folding a large white towel that had yet to go grey. 'I've got to go out, I forgot the flipping candles.'

'It's Sunday. Where are you going to get seventy candles?'

'This is America, baby. You can get anything you like, any time of the day or night. I could buy a whole lounge suite at midnight if I wanted.'

'Yes, very impressive. I'll come with you.'

I dressed and went downstairs with my daughter one step at a time to avoid rushing her. I found Mum having breakfast with Vin's kids, Raja and his wife feeding their daughter and Dad sitting on the couch, his head buried in the *New York Times*, reading all the news that was fit to print.

'Happy Birthday, Dad.'

'Thank you,' he said looking over the top of the paper.

'Will you give her breakfast, Mum?' I asked, helping my daughter climb on to a chair. 'Me and Vin are just popping out to get something.'

Mum gave my little girl a kiss, looked up at my face and then stared down at my knees.

'Your skirt look too short,' she said, disapprovingly. 'Haven't you got long one? Iss very cold outside. You need long skirt. Why don't you wear the jean?'

'Mum, I'm not sure if you've noticed but I'm forty-three years old and I'm a mother now. I like this skirt and I'm going to wear it. And I won't be cold.' She rolled her eyes. I rolled mine.

'Where are you going?' asked Raja.

'Nowhere, just got to get something,' said Vin. I blew the air as if blowing out candles. He looked at me quizzically, raised his eyebrows questioningly and put two straight fingers to his mouth as if he was holding an imaginary cigarette. I shook my head to indicate he had misunderstood.

'Whatever,' he said. 'Just be back before lunchtime for you-know-what.'

Vin and I left through the back door and climbed into her four-wheel drive parked in the garage. The air was bitterly cold.

'Bloody hell, it's freezing,' I said, rubbing my hands together vigorously.

'You should have worn something warmer.'

'I know, I know. I should have worn my jeans.'

Vin pulled the driver's side door and it closed with a soft thud, the way expensive car doors do. She turned the key in the ignition as the garage doors opened magically, and we drove out into the bright wintery sunlight. Once we were on the road she leant forward to turn on the radio, which burst into sound at high volume halfway through Lynyrd Skynyrd's 'Free Bird'.

'Ah, I *love* this song,' she said, running her fingers through her hair as if releasing it from a bun, and then put her foot down hard on the accelerator.

Sources

The details of studies cited in the book are as follows:

p. 30

'A passage from *Erotic Art of the East*, by art expert Philip Rawson': *Erotic Art of the East: The Sexual Theme in Oriental Painting and Sculpture*, Philip Rawson, Weidenfeld & Nicolson, London, p. 59

p. 92

'Roger Ballard, a British anthropologist and expert': 'Honour Killing? Or just plain homicide?', Roger Ballard in *Cultural Expertise and Litigation: Patterns, Conflicts, Narratives*, Livia Holden (ed.), Routledge, 2011, London, pp. 123–148

p. 142

'In 2012, a BBC survey about the honour system': BBC *Panorama* Honour Crime Survey, conducted by ComRes, March 2012

p. 143

'A global study by an American think-tank called the Middle East Forum': 'Worldwide Trends in Honour Killings', Phyllis Chesler, *Middle East Quarterly*, spring 2010

p. 251

'A 2010 American study of child gender': 'Child Gender and Parental Investments in India: Are Boys and Girls Treated Differently?',

Silvia Helena Barcellos, Leandro Carvalho and Adriana Lleras-Muney, dissertation, Princeton University, July 2010

p. 269
'In Britain the rate of mixed marriages': 'Who Intermarries in Britain: Explaining Ethnic Diversity in Intermarriage Pattern', Raya Muttarak and Anthony Heath, *British Journal of Sociology* 61(2), 2010

p. 269
'In America, mixed marriages': 'The Rise of Intermarriage – Rates, Characteristics Vary by Race and Gender', Wendy Wang, Pew Research Center, February 2012

p. 269
'And in Australia, less than': 'Intermarriage in Australia: Patterns by Birthplace, Ancestry, Religion and Indigenous Status – a report using data from the 2006 Census', Genevieve Heard, Siew-Ean Khoo and Bob Birrell, Centre for Population and Urban Research, Monash University for the Australian Bureau of Statistics Australian Census Analytic Program

Acknowledgments

I would like to thank everyone at Random House, especially Nikki Christer for believing in me and for her enthusiastic support from beginning to end. Thanks also to Catherine Hill, as judicious an editor as any writer could hope for, who rescued me from myself many times.

I am grateful to the following people for helping in so many different ways: Sanjeev Bhaskar, Simon Clews, Clare Forster, John Hobson, Eugene Hyland, Frank Maiorana, Nic 'the punk' Moore, Elliot Perlman, Bob Taylor and Tony Wood. I reserve a very special thank you for Chris Feik.

I have spent nearly all my life infuriating everyone in my family, and, inexplicably, they have always put up with me. They once again demonstrated the depth of their patience during the writing of this book. I thank them all, particularly my dad and mum for taking all the blows, for reliving painful memories so I could write this book, and for never abandoning me. And thank you also to Vin and Praveen for providing invaluable feedback.

I am indebted to Tom Hyland, my most brutal and honest editor, who kept me on the straight and narrow with his sharp eye and big heart. Finally, I would like to thank my remarkably patient six-year-old daughter, Lotus, who no longer needs to come home from school and ask, 'Did you make any progress today, Mum?'